WE EACH GET A
TURN

WE EACH GET A TURN

Charles Cross

To. Kassie

Success is someone saying, "I am a better person for having you in my life." I know many will say that about you in the years to come!

Dreams = Opportunities

Charles Cross

Writers Club Press
San Jose New York Lincoln Shanghai

WE EACH GET A TURN

Writers Club Press
an imprint of iUniverse, Inc.

For information address:
iUniverse, Inc.
5220 S. 16th St., Suite 200
Lincoln, NE 68512
www.iuniverse.com

ISBN: 0-595-25036-X

Printed in the United States of America

Contents

Part III

Part IV

PROLOGUE

Everything is in order for tomorrow morning's service. The wooden pews and piano keys are cool to the touch as I walk around the silent sanctuary in anticipation. Standing behind the lectern, surveying the empty pews where hundreds of people will be listening to my first official sermon in just a few hours, I ask myself, "How did I come to be here in this Mississippi church? But most of all-how have I managed to stay alive?"

Five years ago I would have called you a liar if you had said I would be preaching in a Baptist church today. People who knew me then would have said you were crazy to believe that, of all places in the world, I would be standing in the pulpit. Even I am surprised and sometimes bewildered that my life has taken this turn, that I could change so dramatically and become the man I am now at thirty. But it is more amazing that I have survived so many sweeps with death.

Perhaps it's not completely strange that I have become a minister. I was brought up in a strict, conservative home where dancing, make-up, card playing and all such sins were prohibited. I went to church three, four, sometimes five times a week for years and began singing in church at six. Life was simpler then, before the wild impulses and frenzy of adolescence, before I lost control of my life. Perhaps buried deep in my bones there is a sense of duty, a kind of cellular code put there by all the exposure I had to certain moral beliefs when I was a child. One day I would rediscover what it meant to make sensible, ethical decisions in a selfless way-but for years I drifted through life knowing there was another side of me, a side almost possessed, as if something besides my own reason was in control and I was at its mercy. My world was a playground with rules meant to be defied, and I broke them all.

My world was also a place of constant danger and threat, alcohol and violence, where somehow, by fate or divine providence, I was allowed to escape death over and over again.

PART I

1

When I turned sixteen in August 1968, I was sure that I had crossed the threshold to manhood, and partly it was the strength of my determination that made me think so. Two years earlier, I had told my parents that on my sixteenth birthday I would have a car. Like most teenagers, I was obsessed with the prospect of having the ultimate freedom: wheels-and once I got them, the world would be mine. Of course, my parents didn't understand. They thought I was foolish, so they absentmindedly agreed, laughed and shrugged it off. A part of my psyche began to emerge at the point-a fierce, sometimes dangerous determination, and I didn't realize then how significant a part it would play in my life.

As I had predicted, on my sixteenth birthday, my dream materialized in the form of a red, high performance 1966 Ford Mustang, a beautiful car. A year earlier I started bagging groceries after school, saving money for the down payment. By then, not even my parents were able to control what I did, where I went and with whom.

I was getting a stubborn, tenacious streak and had a serious problem with authority. I was unruly and impulsive, bordering on reckless, and things began to happen. There was a girl from Peoria, Illinois, sixteen years old, visiting a neighbor of ours. Not only was she great looking, she seemed worldly, more so than I was, and when I asked her out and she said okay, I spent the entire week planning for Saturday night, bursting with excitement. The Mustang had to be washed and waxed and I had to prepare for what was to be the night of my life. Of course, at sixteen my hormones were running wild, and inside I was about to explode. All my friends were "very experienced" with women, as they described themselves. I thought I was the only virgin in the world. I didn't realize then that half of them were probably lying.

Finally I was ready. All the details were carefully worked out in advance-where we were going and at what time, how I would act, what I would and wouldn't try to do with her. My car was vacuumed, clean and sparkling. I was dressed out in new blue jeans and shirt and had taken a long shower. Only one key element was missing: alcohol. The night wouldn't be complete without it, and even at sixteen there were several places I could buy beer or liquor, depending on who was working. This night as on many others I found a buyer, a man waiting for his wife at the local grocery store. At forty-five to fifty cents a quart, I got my four quarts of Pabst Blue Ribbon, chilled it in the back seat like expensive wine, then was off to pick her up.

On the way to her house, my imagination ran wild. After all this time, I would learn what all the other guys already knew about women, and step across the mysterious line that divided adolescence and manhood. When I got there, she met me at the door with a smile, even more beautiful than I realized, dressed in the flowered top and bell-bottomed blue jeans of the 1960s, and full of life. My hormones were like an avalanche. We hopped in the Mustang and took off for the movie to eat popcorn and drink. Although I was the perfect gentleman and kept my hands to myself during the movie that seemed to last forever, I was restless. I had a carefully laid plan—a night ride to a deserted beach, where I could have my way with her. I figured if I got her drunk enough I wouldn't be a virgin after that night, and though I didn't know for sure, I already suspected she wasn't. I remember nothing of the movie since my mind was focused only on this young, tanned creature sitting next to me and all the pleasure that lay ahead.

During the movie I was tempted more than once to turn and kiss her, to find out what she tasted like and learn about her body. She sat across from me-not all the way against the shotgun door-but close enough that I could smell her scent, close enough to provoke and make me suffer with expectation.

After what seemed hours, we set off for the beach, twenty miles away. The Mustang purred like a kitten all the way, and she sat quietly beside me, as if she knew the plan. She hadn't said no, so I figured she knew we would end up in the back seat. All I remember was her perfume, her skin glowing in the dashboard lights, and the pounding of my own heart like the racing engine. The highway rolled out like a ribbon before us, and the air from the open windows was summer sweet, blowing her hair. We each had polished off a quart of beer already and I felt good and figured she would out drink me. After all, she was experienced and more than that, she was from Peoria, Illinois where they brew Pabst! When her speech began to slur after the second quart, I saw it as a good sign—but there was a limit. I didn't want her to pass out, and already she began to sway and laugh out loud when we took a fast right turn down a narrow dirt road.

We were out in the remote woods miles from town, and the road, protected by heavy forest and a moonless sky, made for an even darker place. For at least a mile, we traveled fast down a rough, empty back road, my foot heavy on the accelerator, and my senses at their peak. I wanted to park before she got too drunk. I looked over and she was getting drowsy, so I stepped on the gas again, this time with a punch, and suddenly there was a curve. I grabbed for control, but the tail was already coming around, and at sixty miles an hour on this road, there was nothing I could do but ride it out. The Mustang careened into a pile of rocks, skidded off the road into the ditch, and sat up to the bumper in mud. It happened so fast that I was a moment or two recovering my sense of time and place, and when I did, I looked over to see if she was okay. She was asleep!

I felt at my feet for the beer that had spilled in the floorboard and in my lap. As I took the last swig, I reached over and touched her shoulder just above her breast, and she didn't budge. I could put her in the back seat and do whatever I wanted, I thought to myself, and she'd never know it, but then I said, no, that's rape. Besides, I wanted more than a limp dishrag for my first sexual partner; I needed her awake because I wasn't sure what to do. I needed somebody who could show me how to do it right! I tried to wake her up, but she was passed out, her hair messed, falling across her eyes.

The car was still running and in gear, so, still in a daze, I put it in first and gunned the engine. The wheel spun with a whir and I watched smoke rise in the rearview mirror. The car wouldn't budge. The woods were deep on both sides and there was no sign of human life-no sound now but the crickets and night birds. I was picturing the circumstances. I'm sitting behind the wheel of my car that's in a ditch in a desolate place, it's 12:25 a.m., there's a drunk girl beside me who's passed out. I'm drunk, too. I smell like a brewery. We're going to be late getting home, and her parents are expecting us in thirty minutes. I couldn't believe I was thinking so clearly.

Then I looked through the windshield. Four dark figures were walking toward the car.

My first thought was that we were being rescued, then as they got closer, I realized they were four men about eighteen years old, much bigger then I was, and black. Growing up, I didn't associate with black people because our neighborhood schools were segregated and we had little exposure to other races. I would have been scared to death if they were white, but this made it worse. I thought to myself—we're going to die. They are going to cut me up in small pieces and throw me in the swamp. No one will ever find me. And I knew they were going to rape her.

I got out of the car and moved slightly towards them. Their silhouettes were menacing in the dark, and there was no sound but the rustling of feet and one murmuring to the others. They hadn't seen her yet because she was slumped down and they were too far away. They walked toward me, now just four car lengths away. Here I was: a half-drunk, skinny, redheaded sixteen-year-old, scared to death, walking toward them in the inky blackness on this nowhere back road, and no clear way of escape.

"Hey man, what's happening?" I said out loud. There was no response. A few more steps and I spoke a little louder.

"Hey man, what's happening?" Again, I got no response. My heart was in my throat, the pounding so loud I could hardly hear my voice. I couldn't run because she was in the car. Panicked thoughts crowded my mind: what are our parents going to say, what's going to happen to her? To me? If I just had a gun or club-I said again, louder this time, "What's happening, man?"

One of them broke the silence, "I don't know, what's happening?" I could breathe. Praise the Lord, at least they speak, I thought. Finally, we came face to face.

I told them I had run off the road and asked if they could help me out. One said, "Yeah, let's see what we can do." All four walked back to the car, and in my drunken state, my mind raced with terrible possibilities. They could get my car out, then kill me, and take her *and* my car. Then they saw her slumped down in the seat passed out and didn't say a word, but one looked at the others with a wry smile. I knew they had something planned, especially the shorter one who smiled. He looked dangerous and had nothing to say while they rocked the car, even picked it up once with a grunt.

With all the rocking and commotion, the girl woke out of her stupor, rolled out of the car, and started talking non-stop. "What happened? What are you doing? I'm going to be late!" All of her words were slurred and overloud. I kept telling her to be quiet, grabbing her by the arm trying to lead her back to the car, but she was angry, drunk and full of endless questions and insisted on making the situation even harder than it was. "Who are these people?" she screamed. "What are they doing?" Finally they gave up. "I'm sorry but we can't get you out," one said. They offered to take us to their house up the road and around the next corner. "Maybe we can get a truck and pull you out," another offered. I asked about using their phone to call a wrecker, but if I did that I'd have to call the police and I knew I didn't want the law involved.

We walked back to their house in the silent darkness, the short one following behind me too close. I felt his eyes on her as she kept talking, and I waited for something to break out. Maybe he would take the first step and hit me from behind. My blood pressure was high as we approached one of four dimly lit shanties next to each other along the road. It was about 1 a.m. now and inside their whole family was awake. The mother, grandparents and some kids were watching television. My date wouldn't stop talking to everybody about everything and was having a wonderful time. I stood nervously by the door near the older woman, the grandmother, I figured. After a few minutes she looked at me and said, "Have a seat."

"No, thank you, I'll just stand by the door," I said. She gave me one of those if-you-don't-sit-down-I'm-going-to-cut-your-head-off looks. I sat. If I hadn't been drunk, I would have died of a heart attack during all this.

Finally, the father came and we all piled into a pickup truck and drove back to the car. On the way there was nothing said, and still my drunken thoughts raced with fear that it wasn't over yet. My car was still in the ditch, we were at their mercy and in their truck, and they could end it all right here. They hooked the car up, the girl got behind the wheel and I pushed. When the car rose slowly out of the ditch, I was relieved, but still paranoid. I thanked them like crazy, and she never stopped talking. The moment we hit the main road it was amazing how sober I really was.

She slept all the way home until I woke her and took her to the front door. We said nothing except a curt good-bye without a kiss or touch. I knew I'd never see her again. My chance was gone.

When I got home, I laid in bed in disbelief. In spite of all my careful planning, I was still a virgin. Of all the things that happened that night the one thing on my mind was that I was still a virgin, that I was still naive about sex.

That night and during the months that followed, I began to slowly realize that trouble and danger were always there in my life like a swift current, an undertow always ready to pull me under. Some of the trouble was because of my own ignorance, but much of it was because I had a bull's eye on my back to attract everything negative and dangerous. I didn't have to seek them out. Danger and trouble found *me*, and what I didn't know fully then was that this was just the beginning.

2

The 1960s were full of social unrest-civil rights, Vietnam, drugs and the new world order. America was changing, and inside, I was mirroring the times, experiencing my own private upheaval. Cars, drinking, fighting and dealing with the police became an addiction in the summer of 1969, and I relished every opportunity to stir up trouble. The world was all mine, and everyone who crossed me got a taste of my anger, craziness or violence, most of it due to my heavy drinking and disregard for the law. I wouldn't dare admit any wrongdoing because I was in control, despite the daily reminders that I was heading down the wrong path. Even my girlfriend at the time knew I was going to end up in the trash heap or jail.

Her name was Debbie Hardy. Her blonde hair reached her waist and her blue eyes were deep and lovely. She had a great sense of humor balanced by a stubborn streak to match my own, so the one thing she refused to do was ride with me when I was drinking. One time she was in the car when my lead-weighted foot took the speedometer to over a hundred on roads that begged for caution, when I could only see partially through a drunken fog, and after that she would get out of the car immediately if she smelled the slightest trace of liquor on my breath.

Training for a respectable profession, she was going to beautician's school in town. One night I had a date with her, and I was to pick her up at ten. But first I had other important things to do. Usually I functioned with at least some alcohol in my blood, so I picked up coke and a fifth of Bacardi's Rum-the dark stuff with the smooth draft-and started driving down Route 13 along the George Washington canal to North Carolina. Nothing waited for me there; it was more the need to be on the road-any road-in the summertime with the Mustang's engine humming, the breeze ripping through open windows, the speed, the liquor running in my veins like neon lights. It was like a song by the Dylan-ramblin' the open road in a fast car. There was nothing else like it in the world.

It took hours to get there, and then I simply turned around and headed back. Coming home, I finished the fifth straight from the bottle, and surprisingly, I could drive when I was drunk, or at least I thought so. It's easy to feel in control when every nerve is numb and everything has an intense glow.

When I got back early with nothing to do and nowhere in particular to go, I parked in the lot outside the school to sleep and wait for Debbie. It wasn't long before she walked out of the building, all slim and beautiful in her white beautician's uniform-but she wasn't alone. Three guys came out with her. Adrenaline flooded my body. I had had an explosive temper for as long as I could remember, but at that moment I was losing control; my mind was racing with every conceivable scenario. Here was my sweet, beautiful girlfriend whom I hadn't touched sexually climbing in a car with three young studs right before my eyes. I knew they were heading down to the lake to park. My drunken thought patterns were following every extreme and I went off like a cannon.

I got out of the car screaming, "Hey, man, get out of that car!" They were dumbfounded, especially Debbie who looked at me with big, saucer eyes. She was out of the car in an instant and so was the driver.

"Charles, what are you doing here?" she said. The driver was asking me who I was.

"I'm her boyfriend! Who the hell are you?"

"I'm the guy who's driving her home."

"I don't think so!" I laughed.

In a split second Debbie had sized up the situation and me. "Charles, you're drunk. I'm not going to talk to you when you're drunk." She turned on her heel, arms folded across her chest, shaking her head in disbelief.

I kept telling her to get in the car and she kept screaming that she wouldn't. I challenged her, "Either you get in the car or I'm going to whip his butt."

This took the confrontation in a new direction. The two other guys in the back seat started opening the car doors.

My mind was running a hundred miles an hour, and my body was a coiled spring, numb and immune to pain. Nothing could stop me now, not even the threat of three guys jumping me, all of them bigger than I was.

"Who do you think you are?" the driver asked.

"Shut up or I'm going to hurt you!" I screamed in his face. "And if you two guys get out of the car I'm going to hurt you! Don't get out of the car, I'm telling you!"

They were still climbing out of the car in slow motion, so I moved backwards to my car, opened the trunk and pulled out the tire iron to even the odds.

"All right-all three of you come on!" I yelled. Once I brandished the lug wrench, their expressions changed and they backed away.

"Don't let this bother you," I said. "Come on!" I was standing there swinging the tire iron like I was going to tear up the lot of them and I hit and dented the hood of my Mustang. That maddened me even more. I was close to foaming at the mouth, rocking and swaying on my feet.

"Come on chickens, let's get to it."

"No, we're not going to fight. You're crazy drunk!"

In my irrational mode I reconsidered the lug wrench, and slung it as far as I could across the parking lot, and the expressions on their faces instantly changed. They glanced at each other, nodded their heads, then moved towards me like three linebackers.

My body was ready, my mind empty of fear. They hit me but I felt nothing, like every muscle was totally relaxed. The guy on the right got in the first punch; his fist sounded like a muffled thud in my ears when it connected with my forehead, and then the next guy hit me from the left with a swift right hand. I didn't go down but leaped at the third-the biggest one of all-and knocked him down with a wild swing. I stomped all over him while I turned to face the other two. Then we all started wrestling and grabbing. They tried to hold my arms so they could pound me good, and I was grasping their shirts, hair or whatever I could get hold of, trying desperately to stay on my feet. We got in some punches but most of it was amateur wrestling, a lot of scuffling, cursing and missed swings.

I felt like I was doing pretty well at first, but it wasn't more than a minute and I knew I was going to get hurt. Out of the corner of my eye I saw my friend Mike's black Chevy pull up. His six-foot-three frame peeled out of the car and opened the trunk. Out he came with an aluminum pool cue. Swinging it like a bat, he clubbed these guys with the heavy end. There were screams of pain all around when he connected soundly with some heads and backs. They retreated quickly to their car, along with Debbie, who'd been crying and screaming through the whole fight.

All of this happened in five minutes of hazy time but it was long enough for the people at the school to call the police. They had witnessed the whole affair from inside. When I heard the siren and looked up, there were about ten of them staring through the window with horrified looks on their faces. People around the parking lot were watching, frozen in fear like statues. The three guys and Debbie had taken off, and Mike was back in his car, and after I finally got my mind back, I climbed in the Mustang and started the engine. Cars had stopped, the people pointing at me. A siren was wailing no more than a mile away, so I drove off, this time definitely more sober than when I arrived.

Still red-faced angry and feeling betrayed, I headed down Virginia Beach Boulevard, not towards home to lick my wounds, but towards Debbie's house to finish what was still unfinished, to pick a fight again with the three guys if they were there-and I hoped they were-to get things straightened out with Debbie. The anger was surging inside of me like a huge wave, and I was focused on having it out with whoever happened to get in my way.

Next thing I knew the police surrounded me. The first cop car raced up from behind with his lights flashing and siren screaming, which I pretended not to hear because I had my radio blaring. Suddenly another drove up beside me in the right-hand lane and motioned for me to pull over. Not more than a second later the third, a canine truck, was blocking me from the front. I had no choice but to stop, and just a block from my parents' house. When they all got out, all six of them, I knew this was it: I was going to jail. They had been given a description of my car and me, and according to the facts I gathered later, had been told I was dangerous and that all the witnesses thought I was so violent they were in fear for their lives. My yelling and screaming, and the threats I hurled at the three guys were enough to make them think I was going to storm the building and kill everybody.

One cop opened my door while I was rolling down my window. "Get out!" he said loud over the tunes on the radio.

"Why didn't you stop?" I turned off the engine but left the radio blaring.

"I didn't hear you."

"Son, have you been drinking?" I thought to myself, is this guy blind or what? "A little sir…about two beers," I said.

He told me he had a report that I was fighting and threatening people in the parking lot over at the school and that I was acting like a madman, swinging a tire iron at everybody.

In my most sober voice I explained that I was there to pick up my girlfriend to go out on a date, but when she came out of the building with three other guys, I lost it.

"Wouldn't that tick you off, sir?" Taking full advantage of the slightest sympathy from the officer, I told him I had gotten really angry, had a fight with them, then left.

"And where are you headed now?" he asked.

"Home-just a few blocks down here," I pointed.

"Okay, get in your car and I'll escort you home."

"I'd appreciate it very much, sir."

Astonished, I started the engine, put the Mustang in gear, turned down the next street, and cruised like a law-abiding citizen into my parents' driveway. I turned off the engine and got out and watched the cop car continue on. The officer waved, smiling as he passed. As I watched his tail lights grow dim in the evening light I considered the absurdity of the past half hour. I was still drunk, I had threatened and attacked three guys in a public place, busted more than one car, including my own, caused a public disturbance, gotten stopped by three police cars after ignoring a siren, and not only that—the police man waved to me as they passed by.

Once he was out of sight I was back in the car and on my way to Debbie's house, expecting another fight. I was also ready to let her have a piece of my mind about the whole situation. Near midnight, I pulled up in her driveway. The house was dark so apparently the guys were gone. I rang the doorbell, and Debbie opened the door and came out on the front porch. Having passed from drunkenness to a modicum of sobriety, I had planned to launch into accusation after accusation about her behavior, call her a whore, a slut and every other vile name in the book, and let her know what a despicable person she was for deceiving me.

"Who do you think you are?" I told her, "Going out behind my back when you knew I was supposed to pick you up at ten. I drive up and there you are getting in the car with three other guys."

She stood there, arms akimbo, staring me down, in total control, then launched into this long explanation about how she got off work early, which she couldn't help, how she wasn't going to wait in the dark for me for an hour, so she asked this guy who's a friend of her brother if he and his friends would give her a ride home. And they went to get in the car, and I came up like a drunken fool and attacked them! She said she had told me not to drink and drive and had warned me that she would break up with me if I did.

"I tried to call you, but you're not at home. You were out getting drunk! And who were you with? I don't know!" she screamed.

What I planned to say and do had fallen to pieces.

"So you weren't going out with these guys?"

That was it. "Get away from me!" She stormed in the house and slammed the door.

◆   ◆   ◆

This was the beginning of another pattern in my life: confrontations with the police. Over and over again, I found myself looking at a badge or a flashing light in my rearview mirror, trying to concoct a story, transfer the blame, or slip away secretly to get out of trouble-and I usually succeeded. Repeatedly, they let me off, and in the most obvious situations. Perhaps it was my naive, boyish appearance or perhaps they felt sympathy or pity for me. This was a dangerous pattern, not only because I could get locked up, but because it taught me a false lesson-that I wouldn't have to pay the consequences.

My relationship with Debbie was in ruins. My bones ached. On the way home I found the dried blood on my nose and a bruise on my cheekbone, and a childhood memory flooded back like it happened yesterday.

When I was walking home by myself, two boys taunted and picked on me. For a ten-year-old, I was small, and they took advantage and roughed me up, so I ran like a rabbit. They pursued, but I was too fast. I remember sprinting home as fast as I could to where my father was working in the garage. Out of breath, tired, crying uncontrollably and afraid, I ran to the place I could find certain refuge. When Dad asked what was wrong, I confessed that two boys had beaten me up and I had run. I wanted him to hold me. After all, he was my father—big, strong—and I knew he would defend me. Instead, he looked down at me with surprise and disappointment.

"Boy, don't you ever come running to me crying, running from a fight you say you lost! Next time you come running to me like this I'm going to whip you myself and give you something to cry about." Shaking his head, he turned from me and continued his work.

I was crushed. I left the garage and walked to the shady side of the house and crawled into the flowerbed behind an azalea bush and cried. Devastated by what I felt was utter rejection by my own father, I stayed hidden there for a long time, trying to understand his motives, whether it was to keep me strong or because he had had a difficult day. Sitting there in the shadows, I vowed I would never lose another fight, not because I wanted to prove to him that I could stand up against the odds, but because I knew I had no one to turn to if I lost. No one would be there to protect me, so the best option was never to lose-regardless of the cost. Hiding in the shadows, I felt utterly alone.

I would never lose a fight again.

3

Although Debbie and I finally mended the rift between us after that night, we drifted apart. I began seeing other girls, one of them Brenda Duncan, whom I had known since we were ten years old. She moved in behind us, and we became close, but my relationship with Brenda was compromised in another way, as it seemed most of my relationships with girls were during my teenage years. Though the parents of the girls I dated always liked me for unexplainable reasons, and Brenda's parents were no exception, something always happened to dismantle my relationships-usually my own immature behavior.

I had a softer side that emerged oddly at times-when I would do things for other people, try to protect them and help them out if I could. With Brenda, I stepped in to help her in a way that seemed inappropriate then, and even now seems foolish.

In the navy town where we lived at the time, there was the pecking order common among people in military communities. The arrogance of higher-ranking officers was part of the lifestyle. John Farrington's nose was usually in the clouds because his father was an officer. We all went to school together, and Farrington started showing an interest in Brenda. It wasn't that Brenda and I were serious; we were more like friends than romantically involved, but nevertheless I found myself feeling a certain envy when John became a regular visitor at her house.

One summer evening, I asked Brenda if she wanted to see a movie.

"I would Charles, but John has asked me to go out," she said innocently. Her mother piped up, "Brenda, you're not going anywhere until you clean up the kitchen." Brenda protested until I interrupted.

"Mrs. Duncan, I don't mind washing the dishes for her. Let me do it."

After arguing, Mrs. Duncan decided to allow me, and I spent the next hour washing dishes. Brenda went out with John. What started that night became a habit over the next several months. If I went to Brenda's, there was a good chance I'd end up washing dishes while she went out on a date. Mrs. Duncan thought it was foolish of me, but I was determined.

It was as if I had to express another side of who I was, the more benevolent side of my personality that knew sympathy, kindness and wanted to protect and defend others. This side of me emerged in a number of situations when I was younger; it was in complete opposition to the other crazed and violent aspect of my character. I didn't understand then the relationship between the two sides. A part of me thought I was intrinsically flawed at the core. I was sure to end up a statistic, either in an automobile accident or jailed for criminal behavior. The other side felt powerful, sensitive emotions.

When I was fifteen and working as a bag boy in the local grocery, a child in the store was crying uncontrollably and the mother suddenly turned in a rage and slapped the child across the face. I was so upset, livid, crying with anger, amazed that an adult would hurt a child like that. There was one thing I couldn't tolerate, and that was seeing a child cry. Without thinking for more than an instant, I walked up to the woman.

"I don't care if that is your child, don't you ever do that again!" I screamed at her, then turned on my heel and stomped away.

While I sulked and fumed, she went to the manager and told him what had happened and it wasn't long before he confronted me. "Who do you think you are?! You can't talk to customers that way! That's her child!" he yelled, threatening to let me go.

I couldn't help reacting this way, and it happened several times. Seeing a child cry struck me deep inside, and my protective nature exploded uncontrollably. Teenagers are often thoughtless about such things, content to sail along, mindful only of what's happening at this moment. Perhaps this was evidence I possessed a purer more benevolent character deep inside.

But I was too busy thinking about other amusements during these early years, lured by alcohol and women, but especially by the open road heading south towards North Carolina. I often found myself on the road late in the night, typically with a six-pack or more of beer in the back seat and a bottle between my legs. The George Washington Canal ran slowly along the east, with open fields down the west side of Route 13, a narrow, treacherous road that I always took at an unrealistic speed, regardless of my condition.

In my usual drunken state, I was driving about sixty one night, the engine and sound of the highway humming. The curve was there unexpectedly, coming up too fast to negotiate and I missed it completely. The right front wheel came off the road a foot or two and in a split second, the car was airborne. It went up and over a ten-foot-wide embankment, across a ditch, and into a muddy field where it landed with a violent thud in soggy turf. For a moment I sat there in the dark. Besides the ringing in my ears and my labored breathing, the hissing radiator and the settling wheels were the only sounds.

When I got out of the car a few minutes later, I remember first noticing a flat tire. Opening the trunk for the spare and jack, I trudged towards the front of the car. I tried unsuccessfully to jack up the front end. With each crank, the jack, along with my feet, sank deeper in the mud. I soon realized the driver's side rear tire was flat as well.

When you're drunk you feel nothing in your muscles and bones but a pleasant numbness. Your mind has a blank sensation of power and control; you believe that you can do anything and accomplish superhuman tasks. Somehow I figured I could still get the car out by fixing one tire, but then I discovered on the other side that I had two more flats. Curious, I looked under the car and realized I had entirely ripped out the ball joints on the front end and torn the tires partially off the rims. How had I lived through this? Pulling out the ball joints rarely happens except in wrecks where there is an violent force powerful enough to rip out the underside of a car. I must have been traveling at a hellish speed when I crossed the embankment, and by some stroke of drunken luck, had survived the impact when the joints were torn away.

At this point even I knew that driving out of the field on the rims the way I came in was impossible, so I crawled in the back seat and fell asleep in a stupor, expecting, I suppose, that some savior would arrive to transport me out. At five in the morning a man knocked on my window and asked if I was okay. He was on his way to work at the shipyard and dropped me off in downtown Norfolk. From there, I hitchhiked to Virginia Beach.

◆   ◆   ◆

Route 13 was one of my regular haunts during my adolescent years. Something about the highway was like a magnet. It was a perilous course, full of blind turns and soft shoulders like most country roads-perfect for a highway gambler like me. I had another near miss later that same year.

Drunk around dusk, I blew into a country store to buy more beer; my entrance was more dramatic than that of most customers. Traveling at sixty or near it, I had to jam my brakes entering the parking lot to avoid running another car down that was just pulling out. Full of adolescent insolence and power, I felt I was above everyone else, that no one could tell me what to do or control me in any way. Arrogance was evident in my speech and manner, especially when I was drunk. Every move I made was a billboard saying, 'Stay out of my way.' This particular evening, I was in full form.

I turned off the engine, opened the door, set my beer on the ground, and got out in that way drunks move when they try to overcompensate for the lack of coordination. In spite of my condition, I was confident that I was in control. The man whose car I almost crashed into confronted me immediately.

"What do you think you're doing?" He stood with his hands on his hips, his brow furrowed and eyes fixed on me.

"I don't think that's any of your business" I ignored him, and walked around him towards the store. He stood there in blue jeans with a flannel shirt, boots and a ball cap. His face was full of consternation.

"Did you know you almost ran me down?" he said. "Is that your beer?"

"I don't think that's any of your business, either." It was one of those moments when the alcohol had swept me up and carried me high, as if I rode on a giant bird above everyone else. I heard him, but didn't fully take it in. My mind was already miles ahead, cruising down Route 13, unencumbered and free. The only task at the moment was to get more beer to maintain the buzz.

"Excuse me, I have something to do," I said.

"I don't think you're going anywhere," he said, producing a badge.

I was stunned, caught again. I'm sure my face showed it, the "oh-no-not-again" look. My heart raced for a second. As if my blood suddenly cleared of alcohol, I began to think more rationally. I almost ran a cop down. I'm underage and drunk. I've probably just chalked up two or three more violations including reckless driving, speeding and driving under the influence.

But in an instant I knew at some level that I would get away with it. This was happening over and over. I always escaped, always got off in spite of being caught with the goods. There it was in his eyes-a kind of quiet sympathy or understanding that I was just a kid having fun. I was guilty, there was no doubt, but he would let me go. I knew it unconsciously before he said a word.

"You pick up that can, get in your car, and drive back to the Virginia state line, and don't stop until you get there. I'm going to call ahead, and if you stop before you get to that line, I'm going to throw you in jail."

I called up the other side of who I was, the benevolent, humble gentleman. I picked up my beer, got in the car, and drove away, knowing somehow that I would be left alone even if I didn't cross the Virginia line. I went back anyway, found another beer stop along the way and kept a can between my legs until I got back to Virginia Beach.

The world was there for the using, and I used every advantage or situation, regardless of who I might offend in the process. This was only the start and somehow I knew in my gut that there would be no stopping me in the coming years-that I would move through a labyrinth of trouble of various kinds, and come away from them unscathed, even more confident in my ability to get away.

◆   ◆   ◆

My antics were fairly well known in the back area of Sandbridge. Late one night I managed to sink my car in a massive ditch along an obscure road with no clear idea how I'd gotten there. With ground level halfway up the car window on my side, I snaked out the other side and stumbled to a nearby house a half-mile away. The dark house stood on a knoll in the middle of a field; there were groves of trees here and there in the moonlit landscape. I felt totally lost, and knew I had to find a way to get back home.

Sobered somewhat by the accident and the cool autumn temperature, I vaguely knew what I needed to do, and this was the only house for as far as I could see. I walked towards the light as if it were a beacon and finally approached the front porch. I had only one thing in my head and that was *get home*, however I needed to do it.

I knocked. A light came on and soon there was a man's voice behind the door. "Who is this?"

"I've been in an accident. My car's in a ditch, and I need to call the wrecker or someone to come help me."

"I'm sorry, it's late. Go away," he said.

I knocked again, this time harder. "Listen I need to use your telephone!" I was determined to get inside.

"I'm telling you to go away," he shouted.

That was when I kicked the door open and walked in like I owned the place. "Where's your phone?" I demanded.

The man stood there, his mouth agape. His wife came in wearing her robe. Obviously they had been asleep. "You get out of this house!" the man screamed.

"Look, why don't you try to throw me out if you can." Defiant, I was determined to see this through, regardless of the consequences. "I'm going to use your phone to call a wrecker. I've had an accident. Sit down and shut up!"

The man was in his fifties wearing a robe; his hands and body were shaking. I was oblivious to any wrongdoing and furthermore, I didn't care. Getting the wrecker there and the car out of the ditch were my main concerns at that moment, and what this couple had to say about it or what they were feeling was unimportant.

Looking back now, I know they were shocked and terrified. Stinking of alcohol and with a deranged look on my face, I had invaded their house in the middle of the night, demanding to use their phone. They must've been stricken dumb with fear. At the time, I didn't think about how foolish it was and how easily I could have been shot. The man would have been absolved by the law for shooting an intruder who kicked his door open.

Once I discovered the police had to respond to calls of this kind, I called my brother-in-law to prepare my bail, since it was inevitable I was headed for the county jail. After a courteous farewell to the dumbfounded couple, I left the house and walked to my car to wait for the wrecker.

The wrecker arrived along with the police who locked me up. Around 3:00 a.m. my brother-in-law bailed me out, and I went to sleep at their house. The next day I went to pick up the car and was amazed to find that there wasn't a scratch on it. Each week or month I stepped a little further out of control, a little farther down the path that was changing me and bringing an unconscious force to bear on my life Most teenagers are swept along by the forces of parents and friends. I seemed to be driven by my own foolish motivations and desires. But somehow, whenever I faced threat or danger, I was protected by luck, or perhaps by something which at the time I didn't consider-a kind of divine intervention.

4

Addicted to making a fool of myself in an attempt to help others, I continued to wash dishes for Brenda Duncan while she and John Farrington went out on dates. He was growing more and more smug about it, and spending evenings in her kitchen was beginning to grow stale for me, although I still thought a lot of Brenda and was willing to continue. My parents even pointed out how demeaning it was to keep playing this role. At some level, I wanted to change my life, but didn't quite know how.

As adults, it's difficult and sometimes frightening to make dramatic changes in our lives, but even more so for adolescents who have little knowledge of the paths open to them. They flounder-as I did. Looking back, a combination of fear, anxiety, hopelessness, and disenchantment were all forming a knot in the center of my chest, and I felt my life was beginning to fall apart. Still, I kept moving in the wrong direction, almost as if a momentum towards disaster was so strong that there was nothing I could do to stop it. I knew there had to be a shift, but first I had to teach John Farrington a lesson, preserve my personal honor, and release all the anger that was gnawing inside.

John and I had a modicum of friendship-at least we spoke when we saw each other. His arrogance was creeping under my skin, however, and I had to prove he was on a lower peg than he thought. He was walking near Brenda's one afternoon and I drove up and got out of the car. I had made a conscious decision to set him straight.

"John, I know you're my friend, but I've decided you shouldn't see Brenda anymore." I was matter-of-fact.

"Why do you say that? We're going steady," he replied, obviously taken by complete surprise. I told him he wasn't going steady because I was going steady with her. "Did you ever ask her?" he said. I ignored the question.

Words rolled off my tongue with little hesitation, and after a minute or so, the situation escalated. I told him I was going to kick his ass right there, and he said I wasn't big enough to do it. That of course sprang the hair trigger in my head, and I exploded and began to beat him severely. He scratched me and ripped my shirt, but ultimately left the loser. Blood dripped from his nose, and one eye was starting to turn black. His shirt was covered with blood and his ears, neck and face were red. I had done exactly what I intended to do, and he walked away saying nothing, his arms hanging limp with humiliation.

Later when I talked to Brenda, I found out she would have accepted my invitation to go steady if I had only asked her, but I hadn't, so she had chosen John.

"Break up with him and go with me," I wasn't pleading but I was firm.

"It's too late," she said.

"Well, don't expect me to wash any more dishes," I responded.

I was angry with myself for not acting on this earlier, but finally accepted what I couldn't change. I decided to give her something for Easter that year anyway, almost as a peace offering since I had beaten up her boyfriend, but also because it was my nature to want to please and keep a friendship. Because I had spent most of my money getting drunk at a beach party, I was only able to give her this fancy chocolate Easter egg, but it was an honorable gift and I went to deliver it. She thanked me then showed the gift John had given her, an elaborate five-foot-tall Easter basket spilling over with a real bunny, ribbons, bows and stuffed animals. I stood there in the living room with Brenda, her parents and John, feeling small and embarrassed. After a few terribly uncomfortable minutes of silence, I made an exit.

That was the last time I saw John Farrington. I didn't see Brenda for several years. I've always remembered the discomfort I felt that day. It was almost a symbolic event. Because of my own foolishness and lack of responsibility, I had spent all my money on booze, with nothing left for an Easter gift for a girl I liked. This was clear evidence that my priorities were askew, and that I had a lot of growing up to do. I can't say that at the time I consciously knew this, but I intuitively knew that something was terribly wrong and that my life had taken a bad turn.

During this period around 1968 it was easy to be lured by the endless prospect of having a good time at the beach. For a fifteen- or sixteen-year-old, it was a magical time. Staying focused on school, my work at the grocery store or other responsibilities was nearly impossible. The sun, surf and beautiful women were constant temptations. I usually caved in, taking advantage of the visiting tourists, girls from New York, New Jersey or Pennsylvania who were fascinated by local beach boys and our antics. We thumbed rides with our surfboards and rarely waited long, cruised around the local haunts, built night fires on the beach, fished and crabbed, and found plenty of opportunities to test the law.

It wasn't long before I met a new girl-whose name I can't even remember now-and not long before I had another encounter with the law because of irresponsible driving. Near Virginia Beach Courthouse on a two-lane road, returning from Sandbridge, I was drinking, talking with her, and traveling ninety in a fifty-five. At this speed, a slight shift in the front wheel to the grassy shoulder was all it took, and I made the mistake of pulling too hard in the opposite direction to bring the wheel back on the road. Suddenly, the car was out of my control and there was nothing I could do. The Mustang went into a spin, dropped into the wide ditch on the right side, traveled about a hundred feet or so, and accelerated to the ditch on the other side. For an eternity that lasted just a split second, the car went from one side of the highway to the other, two times barely missing a telephone pole and ending right side up in the ditch on the other side. Although the car didn't roll, we were thrown around like dish rags from the front seat to the back. My elbow busted through the driver's side window, and miraculously, I had avoided being cut in two. When the hood speared through the front windshield and into the front seat, shoulder high, I was spared because I was hurled to the back seat. Having a seat belt on would have meant my life. Instead, my elbow was banged up and bleeding pretty bad and I was sore. Other than that, I was unhurt and amazed that I survived a wreck at ninety miles an hour. The girl had broken her wrist and was shaken up pretty badly. Later, when I went to see her father, he knew the circumstances of the accident and gave me a stern look along with a piece of his mind, asking questions that of course needed asking. After all, I had almost killed his daughter.

The car was towed to my backyard. Both axles were broken, the hood, front windshield and seats were destroyed, and the bumpers were bent. My father refused to repair the car anymore. By this time, he expected me to report a new accident or arrest every time I walked through the door. He had reached his saturation point. The car would sit untouched until I could afford to fix it myself, and at $1.70 an hour, it would be months before I drove again.

In spite of the inherent contradiction between the way I was leading my life and the structure and discipline required in the military, the army was calling me. Like many adolescent boys, I was lured by the romance of foreign countries, the macho power of the uniform, and the possibility of dramatic change in my life. I was hooked by the idea, not by the reality of the military. For me it was an adventure-traveling, earning some respect and feeling good about myself for a change. It was 1969 and the Vietnam era, and I anticipated hearing from the draft once I finished high school, especially if I didn't go to college right away.

There was a certain inevitability that I would make this choice. Running a film clip through my mind of recent months projected a clear picture of failure. The mess of my life-the endless drinking, the string of accidents, the Mustang sitting like a corpse in my backyard, the fiasco of my relationship with Brenda, the other girl's broken wrist-symbolized a life which had come to nothing, and it had to go somewhere else from here. The military was the classic solution to a life gone wrong.

PART II

5

The U.S. Army recruiter certainly knew how to talk to a seventeen-year-old eager for independence and change. He told me that if I signed up for three years, I could do whatever I wanted to do in the army. When he asked what I wanted to do, I told him that I loved to drive and that I would drive anything the army had. I didn't mention that I loved to drive drunk.

"If it's got wheels, I can drive it," I informed him. The recruiter told me that I could be in transportation. We filled out all the forms and he gave them to me for my parents' signatures. This was the first of October in 1969 and I had just turned seventeen at the end of August, so I needed my parents' permission to join.

I went to my mother and explained to her what I wanted to do. She cried a little, but eventually signed the papers. Next I went to the market where my father had become a manager after he retired from the navy. I rang the bell at the meat shop and he came out. He was not very happy with me at this time and we both just looked at each other without saying a word. I handed him the papers, he looked at them, pulled out his pen and signed. He handed them back to me and walked away. I knew my father was ashamed of me and embarrassed by me. I was glad I had come to the decision to join the military. I wasn't what he expected in a son, but perhaps I could change my life and change his perception of me.

I took the papers back to the recruiting office and they asked me when I wanted to leave. A popular option was the 110 day delayed enlistment plan, where you sign up and then in 110 days, you leave, which I suppose gives you time to prepare. I told them I wanted to go right away and asked how soon I could leave. They told me that I could go the next day at noon and I agreed.

I had been seeing Debbie Hardy again and the next morning I called her. "Debbie, I have something to tell you. I won't be seeing you for a while."

"Why not?" she asked.

"Well, I've joined the army." All of a sudden I heard this huge peal of laughter.

"Yeah, right! Really, where are you going?"

I repeated to her that I had joined the army and she got upset.

"Charles, why didn't you talk to me about it? Why didn't you tell me? When are you leaving?"

"In about two hours." She started crying and then got angry because I was deserting her. We hung up and I packed my bags. I didn't speak to Debbie again for a number of years.

My parents took me to the bus station in Norfolk. My mother was trying to hold back the tears and so was I. Yet, I was excited. I had joined the army! I was going to have stripes on my arm. I was going to be saluting and shooting things and learning karate. I was going to be driving trucks. I was going to see the world. It was going to be marvelous! At the same time, I was sad because I was leaving the security of my home, my girlfriend and even my crumpled car in the backyard. I was leaving everything behind and I was overwhelmed with fear, guilt, excitement and joy all at once.

When it was time for me to get on the bus, my mother began to cry and hug me and told me to write, to telephone-all the kinds of things a mother would tell you to do. As I sat on the bus, I looked out at my father and he smiled at me and gave me the thumbs up. I hadn't seen him smile at me in a long time. At that moment, I was happy because I had finally made him proud of me and was actually doing something worthy of his approval. He had joined the navy when he was only seventeen. It had made a man out of him and I guess he thought that the army would do the same for me.

I rode the bus to Richmond where I boarded a train with dozens of guys from all over the East Coast. We were heading to Ft. Benning,

Georgia where our lives would begin again. There were people from all different backgrounds and of all different physical types-short, fat, tall, skinny, black, white, bullies, sissies, and we were all going to a new world.

Of course, the first thing we did on the train was have a party. We all bought bottles of liquor and took them on the train. We played cards and drank all night. I had never before been on a train or been away from home and my natural response was to get drunk.

At 5 a.m., we pulled into Ft. Benning. I hadn't slept, was half-drunk and had a headache. I got off the train and stood in line with all the other idiots who were feeling about as horrible as I was and a sergeant started hollering and screaming at us. I was thinking, what is wrong with this guy? What I need is an aspirin, some breakfast and a hotel room. I didn't get any of these things, but I did get a rude awakening. Ft. Benning seemed a strange place to me. I thought, well, here I am: I'll train and become a man and I'll be in the army for the rest of my life. I'll be a good soldier. But as fortune would have it, trouble followed me, even to the army.

6

In the nine weeks that I spent in basic training, I had two opportunities to leave the base. The first time we went to Columbus, Georgia, not far from Ft. Benning. The second time we headed for the big city of Atlanta.

I had become friends with another guy from Virginia and he and I spent a lot of time together. We didn't know what we were going to do or where we were going to go in Atlanta, but we did know that we wanted to have a good time. We shared a taxi for the 100-mile trip with two other soldiers. After we had dropped them off, the driver asked us where we wanted to go. We told him that we didn't really know and he asked us if we were looking for a party or some action. Of course, that was exactly what we wanted. He asked if we were looking for women. Yes to that, too! The driver took us to a place called the Sans Souci Club and pulled over. The two of us sat there with our tongues practically hanging out of our mouths as I watched the most gorgeous women I had ever seen entering the club. They were wearing mini skirts and it looked like their legs went all the way up to their necks. The problem was that this seemed like a high-class place and neither one of us had much money. We told the driver that and he offered to take us somewhere else. We assumed that he meant to another club.

We drove to another part of town that looked like a residential neighborhood. He pulled up to a two-story wooden house and said, "How about this one? I know the people at this house and I know there's a party going on there tonight." It looked like a place we could afford, so we got out of the cab and he drove away.

We went up to the house and knocked on the door. A man answered and we told him that we had heard there was a party there. "Yeah, man," he said. "Partying all the time. Come on in."

I couldn't believe how nice the people in Atlanta were. We didn't even know this guy and he just invited us into his house. We walked in and went into the living room where a woman, his wife, sat on the couch in her underwear.

"Hello, boys. Come on in," she said. There was no one else there.

My friend and I looked at each other. "Is there a party here? We thought we were coming to a party."

"Sure," she said, "we'll have a party."

"No, I don't think so," I said. "Sorry, he must have dropped us off at the wrong house." We turned around and left. Yes, there were definitely friendly people in Atlanta.

We started walking down the road, not knowing where we were. We had heard about the Commodore Hotel, a rather nice and inexpensive place where a lot of soldiers had stayed. It was downtown. In the meantime we thought we'd just walk around and see the sights.

As we were walking, a guy drove up in a black 383 Plymouth Roadrunner, my dream car, aside from my Mustang of course. He asked if we needed a ride and we told him that we didn't, but we knew there was one thing missing: alcohol. We asked if he knew where we could get something to drink. He told us that there was a liquor store not far from there and that he would drive us. Another friendly Atlanta citizen!

We talked cars all the way to the liquor store. When we pulled into the parking lot we told him that we were actually underage and asked if he thought we'd have any problems buying stuff there. He found out what we wanted and went in and bought it for us. He wouldn't let us give him any money. I was marveling at the southern hospitality in this city-not only did the guy give us a ride to the store, but he was buying our liquor for us too! Both of us were naive enough not to think that anything was wrong with this picture.

When he came back to the car, he asked if we wanted to ride around. Riding in that car was heaven to me, so of course I said yes. We rode around for a while, sipping our pints. I had Canadian Mist and my friend had vodka. We were talking and having a great time when he said, "I'll tell you what, why don't you come over to my place and I'll call up some guys and some chicks and we'll have a party. This is the weekend!"

His house was a really nice place in a nice part of town. He got some mixers for our liquor and we sat around talking. I was beginning to feel pretty good.

I said, "Okay, so you said you were going to call some women and some guys and we're gonna have a party, right?"

"Oh yeah, yeah, let me do that." He got up and made a call and hung up.

"You know, I'm running out of mixer. If we're going to get this party going, we're going to need some ice and some 7-Up and some Coke to go along with this stuff. There's a store about a mile down the road. Charles, how about running down there for me?" He tossed me the keys to the Roadrunner.

"You want me to drive?"

"Yeah, it's just down the road." He gave me directions and some money to get the mixers and chips and whatever else I wanted. He said that he would make the phone calls while I was gone and the women would come over and we'd have a big party. He asked my friend to stay there and help him get the place straightened up.

I was going to get to drive the Roadrunner! I couldn't believe it. I was ecstatic. I zipped down the road with my pint and got stuff at the grocery store and piled the bags in the back seat. That didn't take very long, so I thought I'd just drive around a bit. After all, how many opportunities would I get to drive a car like this one? I drove around for twenty or twenty-five minutes and then decided that I'd better go back before he thought something had happened to me or his car.

I'd been gone for at least forty-five minutes. When I got back to the house and went inside with the groceries, my friend was sitting on the couch looking like he'd been crying. "What's wrong?" I asked.

"That guy."

"What happened?"

"When you left he said he was going to take a bath to get ready for the party. He went into the bedroom and was in there for a few minutes and then he called me. I went in and he was lying on the bed naked."

"What are you trying to say?"

"What do you mean what am I trying to say?"

"Oh, he was just going to take a shower and he called you in there and he happened to be naked. Don't blow things out of proportion. I think your imagination is running away with you here. Where is he now?"

"He's in the bathroom taking a bath."

"See? It was all innocent."

"He wanted me to take a bath with him."

"Did he say that?"

"Yes, he told me that he wanted me to take a bath with him."

About that time, I heard him calling, "Is that you Charles? Are you back? Why don't you come on in here?"

I put the keys down. "Let's get the hell out of here!"

We ran out the door, not forgetting our pints of course. We must have run two miles before we stopped. I turned to my friend and said, "You know what, I bet he wasn't going to call any women."

"Well, yeah," he replied. "He wanted us."

What I was beginning to realize was that I had to stop taking people at face value. Coming from such a protective environment, I assumed that everyone was like me.

7

In November of 1969, it was cold in Georgia, especially at night. Coal-burning furnaces heated the barracks, which housed about one hundred people. There were three-hour shifts of shoveling coal to keep the fires burning. We were exhausted from working, running and exercising and it was very difficult to stay awake in the toasty furnace room. Often, guys fell asleep and the coals would burn down and the fire would go out. When it got cold in the barracks all those one hundred people would come looking for you.

There was also K.P. (Kitchen Police) and guard duty. If you had K.P., you had to get up at 3 a.m. instead of the usual 5 a.m. The cook would send someone who had been on night K.P. to wake the people with morning K.P. duty. If you were on K.P., you tied a towel around the end of your bed so that the person knew who to wake up.

One morning, the lights came on at 5 a.m. and the sergeants came in hollering, screaming, knocking on our beds, and banging on the lockers to wake us up. The sergeant came to my bed and saw the towel tied around the end, as I was supposed to be on K.P. that day.

"Trainee, what are you doing here sleeping? You're on K.P.!"

"Yes sir," I said, still sleepy and trying to make sense of his words.

"Well, why aren't you down there?"

"Well, I guess no one woke me up."

"No one woke you up?"

"No sir," I said, "not that I know of. No one woke me up. I'm still here."

He told me to come with him and we went to the kitchen and he got the cook and found the man who was supposed to come through the barracks and wake people up. It was a friend of mine, another seventeen-year-old kid from Virginia. We had become friends at Ft. Benning and we hung around together a lot.

They asked him, "Did you wake this man up?"

"Yes."

They looked at me and I said, "No. He didn't wake me up."

They looked back at him and repeated the question. He repeated that he had woken me up.

"No," I said, "If you had, I would have gotten up. I don't remember you being there. I don't remember you waking me up."

We got into an argument and it was my word against his. They made him go outside and do push-ups. After about fifty push-ups, they called him back in.

"Now, did you wake this man up?"

"Yes."

They sent him back out to do gorilla stomps. To do a gorilla stomp, you jump up in the air as high as you can, beat your chest with your fists, yell like a gorilla, kick behind you so that your heels hit your rear end, come back down into a squat and spring back up. It's a very difficult move to do. They had him do fifty of them and then called him back in. They went through the same questioning and he continued to insist that he woke me up. I maintained that he hadn't. I don't know why they didn't make me go out there with him. I ate breakfast while he was outside doing more push-ups and gorilla stomps. He had been up all night working in the kitchen and was supposed to be in bed right now. He was exhausted, crying and angry. Finally, they asked him again and with tears streaming down his face he said, "No, I didn't wake him up." They sent him back to the barracks and me to K.P. to do the pots and pans.

The next day we went out on maneuvers. We used rifles and bayonets. Everything that we used in the army was assigned a number and we checked it out so that if anything was lost and someone found it, he knew where it belonged. At the end of the day we turned in our rifles, bayonets and any other weapon that had been issued that day. They checked to make sure that every weapon was accounted for, and no one was allowed to leave formation until this was done. On this particular day, the sergeant told us that there was a bayonet missing. He gave its number, but it wasn't one that was issued to a trainee. It had been an extra one. For the next two hours, we looked under every rock, under every building, under every bush, everywhere, trying to find the missing weapon. No one found it and no one had any information about it. Finally, they dismissed us and we went to the barracks, took showers and went to bed.

I laid in my top bunk, thinking about the events of the day. My former friend had missed breakfast and they had worn him out until he confessed. The thought went through my mind that there was a bayonet missing and maybe this guy had stolen it and was planning to use it to get revenge on me. I don't know why that thought occurred to me. It wasn't like me to think like that and it seemed a remote possibility. Even so, I couldn't shake the feeling, so I got up, opened my locker and pulled out an entrenching tool, a little field shovel that's about 2 1/2 feet long when it's closed, got back into bed, pulled the blanket over me, the entrenching tool in my hand by my side. I laid there listening in the darkness, probably for at least two hours. I could hear people snoring. I began to doze off when I felt something pushing down on my mattress. Normally, I would have thought that it was the guy below me turning over and shaking the bed, but the bed underneath me was empty that night. The only way that my bed could have moved was if someone had touched it. I didn't move and didn't open my eyes. I held my breath and my heart was pounding. I was terrified that the guy was there with the bayonet and was going to run it through me. The more rational part of me told me that it was my imagination. Then I felt the bed shake just a little bit and I knew that there was someone at my bed on my left side. I had the entrenching tool in my right hand, my eyes closed, holding my breath for what seemed like an eternity. I thought that if I felt something one more time, I would come up swinging. Sure enough, I felt someone push down on my mattress and I threw off my blanket with my left hand and just swung with my right. I didn't open my eyes. I just swung as hard as I could and hit the man square in the side of the head. It knocked him down and he hit one of the lockers, knocking it over. Lights came on and people were jumping up to see what the noise was. The sergeant came out of his room to find my former friend lying on top of a fallen locker, screaming, holding his head, blood everywhere. I was sitting up in bed. The bayonet was on the floor beside him. Not much was said. The sergeant took the guy out and most of the people just went back to bed. I tried to go to sleep and I eventually did, but I laid there for a long time thinking how close I had come to death.

I was able to go to sleep after that, not only because I was exhausted physically, but also because I was drained emotionally, or maybe numb would be a better way to describe what I was feeling. The next day, I felt guilt as I began to retrace the events from the night before. Would a person actually try to murder someone if he was really guilty of the offense? Maybe he did wake me up and I didn't remember it. Eventually, for my own peace of mind, I convinced myself he had not tried to wake me up.

As I was trying to relax and get to sleep, I thought about the other experiences where I had nearly died. The first time was when I was about four years old. I was underneath the kitchen table playing with the pots and pans and had unscrewed one of the black tops that come on the metal pans to lift the lids off. I had a propensity for putting objects in my mouth and that is exactly where the top ended up. It got stuck in my throat and I couldn't breathe. My mother couldn't hear me gasping for air over the sounds of Patsy Cline on the radio. I crawled out from under the table and over to where she was singing and cooking. Not only couldn't I breathe, but I was also in pain from having the top lodged in my throat. I wanted my mother to help me, but she panicked and all she could do was grab me and run out of the house. This was about a year after my parents had built their home; the roads were dirt, and there were only three houses and woods around.

My mother ran frantically down the dirt road with me, towards Virginia Beach Boulevard. I was on the verge of choking to death, but I was saved by the fact that she had picked me up upside-down and as she was running down the road, the top fell out of my mouth. If she had run out of the house with me in an upright position, I would have probably been dead by the time she reached the boulevard. Years later, as I looked back on this event, I wondered if it was just by chance that she happened to pick me up in such a way as to save my life. Was it luck? Was it fate? Or was it divinely ordained that my life would be spared?

Another incident that was in my mind as I laid there in my bunk took place about ten years later. I was down at the beach in Rudy Inlet on the jetty out on the rocks. The tide was coming in and the water was rough, and I had walked on the wooden planks to the rocks out through the jetty. A bunch of us had been out there playing around for several hours, and we couldn't walk back because the tide was in. The waves were coming up strong, and if you got knocked over in the inlet itself, a whirlpool would pull you down. Everybody started going back. We had to go one at a time across the planks holding onto pillars of wood about twenty feet apart along the way. Each person raced from one pillar to the next before the next wave came along with the potential to knock him into the inlet. Everybody made it. It took about thirty minutes. I was the last one to go. The boards were slick and slimy and there were hundreds of little jellyfish. I made it to the first pole and grabbed it and held on for dear life. A wave splashed up and hit my back. I made it to the second one, grabbed on and the next big wave came crashing up against me. I made it to within about an arm's length of the third pillar, which would have put me a little more than halfway to shore. A wave caught me just as I reached the pole, knocking me into the inlet. The undertow caught me and I could feel myself being pulled down. My life actually flashed before my eyes in an instant, scene after scene. It was amazing. I was fighting for all I was worth, trying to claw my way back to the surface, but I wasn't getting there. Finally, tired and out of breath, I just thought to myself that this was it. I knew that I was dead and I quit. I couldn't struggle anymore. The next thing I knew I popped to the surface. I was shocked that I hadn't drowned. The undertow had dragged me about two hundred feet out into the water. I was beyond the jetty out in the open ocean. Once I was at the top, it was easy to swim as long as I didn't go underneath very deep and get into that undertow current. I found the strength to swim back in. Once again, I had escaped what could have been my death. I still don't know how I managed to come to the surface of the water.

For some reason, this near-death experience didn't frighten me enough to keep me away from the beach the very next weekend and many weekends to come. I certainly would not want to go through something like that again, but as I look back on it, it was an exciting experience and it was also exciting to relate this experience to others. Was I learning at this early age to defy death or was I beginning to believe that I was invincible? As it turned out, both would be true.

It seems the more that people go through experiences, good or bad, the more they become immune to their severity and these experiences become a way of life.

8

Not surprisingly, boot camp and I were not suited to each other. For a person like me who had such a problem with authority, constantly being ordered around was not a pleasant experience. I became depressed and wanted out. I remember one night sitting on my top bunk in my underwear eating homemade peanut butter fudge that my mother had sent. It was pouring rain and on my little radio came the song "Rainy Night in Georgia." I started thinking about ways to get out of this place and get home. I wanted to just pack my bags and go, but of course, I knew that they would come after me and throw me in jail for being Absent Without Leave (AWOL). I felt like I was in prison, even though there were no physical bars. I was away from home for the first time, living with strangers, doing strange stuff and had been almost murdered. Even today, whenever I hear that song, I flash back to that night sitting on my bunk and can feel the same desperation and depression that I was experiencing then.

Besides the homesickness and chafing at authority, I had other reasons to feel that the army was not going to turn out the way I had envisioned it. Shortly before the end of basic training, I received my orders and they said that I was going to be a medic. Remember that I had signed up for three years instead of two because they told me that if I did, I could do anything that I wanted to in the army. What I wanted to do was drive trucks. I brought that to the army's attention, but the guy just laughed and said, "Who told you that, your recruiting sergeant? They'll tell you anything to get you in." Apparently when I had taken an aptitude test, it was revealed that I was not mechanically inclined. I didn't want to fix trucks, I wanted to drive them, but it turns out that you have to know a little bit about fixing them in order to be assigned to drive them. The three areas that I had qualified for were clerk, data processing and the medical field. I didn't want any of those, but I didn't have any other choices. I knew that I didn't want to be inside working in an office, so clerk was out. I didn't know what data processing was. They told me that in the medical field I could be a hospital corpsman or a combat medic. Combat medic sounded exciting, so that's what I signed up for.

Finally, boot camp came to an end. It was Christmas and that meant graduation. Though I still had advanced individual training ahead of me, I would now get my first stripe, my first ribbon, and actually become part of the U.S. Army. Up to this point, I was not allowed to call myself a soldier. I was referred to as a "trainee." They impressed upon me and the other trainees that we were lower than pond scum. I thought that now the real army life would begin and it would be great. I would have stripes up and down my arms. I had survived boot camp and now I was going to get what I had come for-excitement, adventure, travel and a great life.

On the day of graduation, I stood in the barracks putting on my dress greens, getting ready for the ceremony. This was a big deal. There was to be a big parade and parents and girlfriends were supposed to come and watch as we graduates celebrated having made it through the training. My parents weren't going to be there for the graduation. I never asked them why and I was very disappointed, but I was excited to be graduating just the same. The sergeant came into the barracks and asked to see the hands of everybody who had someone coming to see them at graduation. Almost everybody did.

The sergeant called out the names of those of us who hadn't raised our hands and told us to get out of our dress uniforms, into fatigues and report for K.P.

"Excuse me," I said, "I'm graduating."

"Yes, you're graduating," he replied, "but you won't be there. You're doing K.P. Somebody has to wash those dishes. You don't have anyone coming to see you, no one cares. So get out of those dress greens, get into fatigues and get to the kitchen now!"

I was devastated. I couldn't believe it. My own graduation, and I wasn't even going to be allowed to be there. Everyone else was graduating, having a good time and three or four other guys and I were stuck in the kitchen. I got the worst job that you could have at K.P.-washing the big old iron pots and pans. We stayed in that kitchen all day, but I reasoned with myself that it would be okay. I had still graduated and now the good stuff would begin.

A lot of people were going to be leaving the next day to go home for a week or two before being assigned to their next station. The sergeants warned us to be careful of thieves that night. Many of us had tickets for the plane, bus or train, as well as money for the trip. They told us to be sure to put our money and tickets somewhere safe. I tried to think of the safest place to put my wallet. People had broken into the footlockers and the big metal lockers, so that wasn't secure. I had forty dollars-just enough to buy a bus ticket back to Virginia. Suddenly, I had an idea and I hopped up onto my top bunk, got in bed, took my wallet and put it in my underwear, right in front. Just let someone try to steal it from there! I went to sleep thinking that this was the last night I'd have to spend in this place and then I'd be free! I slept like a baby.

First thing the next morning, I checked to see if my wallet was still there. It was gone! Somebody must have seen me hide the wallet and had taken it during the night while I was sleeping so soundly. I panicked. I went to the sergeant and explained to him what had happened. When I told him where I had hidden my wallet and that it had still been stolen, he thought that was the funniest thing. I asked him what I was going to do and he said, "Well, I guess you'll have to stay here." That was not what I wanted to hear. I called my parents and they wired me money to get home. It was not computerized like it is today and so it took several days for me to get the money. So I spent several more cold days at Ft. Benning, filling sand bags for eight to ten hours a day, thinking about the injustice of the whole situation.

After some time at home, in January I was off to Texas for my medical training. I had never been to Texas and I assumed that it was always warm there, so I packed all summer clothes and took off for Ft. Sam Houston. When I stepped off the plane, I discovered that it was just as cold in Texas in January as it was in Virginia. I hadn't even worn a coat on the plane, anticipating the warm Texas sunshine! Instead, everyone was wrapped up in coats, scarves, hats and gloves!

My training in Texas went well. I realized that the things I was being trained to do could help people and possibly even save someone's life, and I took my responsibility for learning very seriously.

Another positive thing about this part of my army life was that we had a little more freedom. In basic training, we had been allowed to leave the base only twice in eight weeks. In Texas we worked from Monday through Friday, a half a day on Saturday and had Sunday off. We actually had a day and a half of freedom each week! I usually went out and got drunk on Saturday nights, as did everyone else. There wasn't much else to do. On Sunday, we would sleep it off, take it easy and get ready to go back to work on Monday. It also seemed to me that everyone else was going out and finding women during their time off. Some guys went to prostitutes and others said that they met nice girls, though now I realize that those "nice girls" were probably prostitutes as well. I couldn't figure out what was wrong with me. On the last weekend before graduation, I went out with a bunch of guys and got drunk with them, as usual. I thought to myself that this was a ridiculous situation. I was nearly eighteen years old now. All my training was almost over and I was going to be part of the "real" army. I was a man now and still a virgin. I kept hearing guys talk about the women they met and what they did with them and I wanted to be a part of that too. I didn't want to go to a prostitute, but I thought that at least she would know what she was doing and after all, everyone else was doing it.

I was drunk enough to just say the hell with it and I went out to find myself a woman to make a real man out of me. I went to a street in downtown San Antonio where a lot of guys had hung out and found "nice girls." From listening to their stories, I knew that I should go to a certain hotel and a man there would bring a woman to my room. I sat in the room, nervous, but excited. I waited and drank. After a couple of hours, I was beginning to think that the guy had forgotten about me. I was wasted and I had run out of beer and so I lay down and dozed off. I awoke to a knock at the door and I opened it. The girl came in and asked me what I wanted. I said that I wanted to sleep with her and she replied that it would be thirty dollars. I agreed to the price and she told me to get into bed. I was weaving and the room was spinning, partly from the beer and partly, I'm sure, from the excitement of the situation. We both took off all of our clothes, except for underwear, and got into bed. I asked her why she was in this business. She was a lovely girl and I didn't understand why she did this for a living.

The next thing that I remember was waking up with a terrible hangover. It was daylight and I was the only one in the bed, with my underwear still on. I was still about half drunk and it dawned on me that this was graduation day.

9

After one week of leave, I flew on to my first real assignment. When I signed up for three years in the army, as a bonus, I was supposed to be able to choose anywhere that I wanted to be stationed and I believed that. I had chosen Germany. I had a friend who had joined about six months before I had and that's where he was and I thought it would be great to go there. There were 466 men in my company and 460 of them got orders to go to Vietnam. Five got orders to Germany. When I opened my orders, I found that I was being sent to Hawaii. I didn't get sent to Vietnam because I was too young. It would have been very bad to be in Vietnam as a medical corpsman because I found out later that the North Vietnamese were offering special monetary rewards for medic bags, which meant that they killed the medic in order to get his aid bag. At first I was disappointed that I wasn't going to Germany, but I began to like the idea of Hawaii more and more.

In March of 1970, I flew from Virginia to California to Hawaii. When we got off the plane, there was Hawaiian music playing and girls in grass skirts put leis on us and kissed us on the cheeks. This was paradise! I was on Oahu and I was going to be stationed at Trippler Army Medical Center. We were taken to our barracks, a pink building up on a mountain. Beside the barracks was the club and beside that was the hospital. All three buildings were bright pink. The breeze was blowing and it was eighty degrees. The clouds and sky were beautiful, and there were palm trees everywhere. I had never seen palm trees before! I thought that maybe my luck was changing for the better. The flowers and the ocean and the breeze felt like heaven.

The barracks were like a hotel. There were two people assigned to each room, with two floors. I was on the second floor. Another guy and I climbed the stairs and walked along the balcony to find our room.

On the balcony were about fifteen guys sitting around, all smoking. I didn't think anything of it at first, but then I realized that the smoke smelled different and the cigarettes looked different. What they were smoking was marijuana, not cigarettes. As we turned to go into the barracks, one of them stopped us and asked if we were new medical personnel. We said that we were and they told us their names and offered us a hit off their joint. I had never even seen marijuana before and at first I said no. They insisted, however, and I wanted to be cool so I took a drag off of it like I was smoking a Marlboro. My friend and I went on inside and I told him that I didn't see what the big deal about marijuana was-it didn't do a thing for me.

On my first full day in Hawaii, I did what any surfer boy from Virginia Beach would do-I went to Waikiki, rented a surfboard and spent eight hours in the waves. I am a person with red hair and a very fair complexion and I usually wore a T-shirt when I went to the beach. I was referred to as "turn and burn" and I never got tan. As a child, I sometimes got blisters on my shoulders and back as big as silver dollars. I didn't have to be in the sun very long for that to happen. At Waikiki, I was so excited that I didn't even think about a shirt. So I spent eight hours in the sun and by the time I got back to the barracks, I looked like a lobster. Not only that, but the bottoms of my feet had little razor blade cuts all over them from the coral. I was supposed to go to work for the first time the next morning, but I knew that there was no way that I was going to be able to wear the white, heavily starched uniform, with a long shirt that buttoned up the side to my neck. I called the hospital and told them who I was and what I had done. They informed me that I could be court-martialed for doing something stupid like that. If you did something that was in your control, like stay out in the sun for eight hours and get a terrible sunburn that prevented you from working, it was actually a serious offense. I hadn't realized that and fortunately, they didn't press the issue. I didn't leave the building for three days. Finally, on the fourth day, the blisters were gone and I was able to put my uniform on. It still hurt, but I went to work.

Working in a hospital was not something that I had anticipated. I was, after all, a combat medic, but being too young for combat, I ended up working in a hospital. It was interesting work, though not always pleasant. If I worked the morning shift, I would make all fifty-five beds and then take fifty-five TPRs (temperature, pulse, respiration) and blood pressures. I learned a lot and felt like I grew up a lot working there.

I worked with a Filipino civilian nurse by the name of Furacowa. She was a short lady of about fifty-five who loved to gamble in Las Vegas. She would fly to Vegas six or seven times a year and said she always won a lot of money. She was apparently connected with some underground shady characters, for lack of a better term, the Hawaiian "mob." One night when we were both working the 11 p.m. to 7 a.m. shift, she was going to go down to the cafeteria and asked if I wanted anything. I said no and she went to get her billfold out of her purse and discovered that it was missing. She asked if I knew anything about it and I told her that I didn't. I had been alone at the desk for fifteen or twenty minutes and obviously she thought that I had stolen her billfold. I asked her if she was sure she had it with her tonight, but she became rather angry and insisted that I must have taken it. The fact that there were fifty-five patients who could have come to the desk while no one was there didn't seem to impress her. In her eyes, I was guilty. She told me that she was going down to the cafeteria and that when she returned, her wallet had better be back in her purse. She said that if it wasn't, for fifty dollars she could have me killed and that's exactly what she would do! I had no doubt that she could do just that. While she was gone, I looked all over for the billfold, but never found it. When she returned, she said, "All right, I warned you." I tried to tell her again that I had no idea what had happened to her wallet, but she still didn't believe me. We didn't speak to each other for the rest of the night and when we left the next morning at seven, she gave me a look that said she would carry through with her threat.

We never worked together again and never talked to each other again. Obviously, she didn't go through with having me killed, but she had me scared. For a long time, I looked over my shoulder everywhere I went. I was scared to death that somebody was going to step out of the bushes and knife me, or that a sniper would shoot me from a hotel window. This very real fear gave me an excuse to hide out in the bar more and more. I never told my superiors about her threats. I thought that would just make her madder and then she would actually follow through with the threat.

One afternoon after getting off from work, I stopped into the club to get drunk. There were pool tables there and if you wanted to play, you put your quarter on the table next to the coin slot behind anyone else's quarters already there. Of course, if you have guys drinking and there are six or seven quarters lined up there, you don't always remember whose quarter is whose. I had put my quarter down and thought I was next. I put the quarter in the slot and started playing. Two guys with a reputation for being bullies came up and said that I was playing their game. I said that I wasn't and a big ruckus ensued. I wouldn't back down. From that moment on, these two guys decided that I was their target. I was rather small-my mother used to call me wiry. I may have been tall for my age, but always very thin. I just looked like someone bullies could pick on and it had happened all of my life. I never really fought anyone unless I got mad, and when I say mad, I mean an uncontrollable rage where all I could see was red. I wouldn't fight back unless I got to that point and then I would go berserk. I always felt that no one could defeat me when I was like that and no one ever did. I hated being that way. After an angry outburst, I would be a quivering mass, shaking all over. Presumably, without my conscious awareness of it, the discipline and structure of army training had taught me some self-control, which would have greatly pleased my father.

So these two bullies, one from New Jersey and one from Mexico, did their best to harass me. No matter where I was-the barracks, the bar, the shower-if they saw me, they made it a point to threaten to beat me up and to try to intimidate me. The tension was building up inside me. Not only did I have these two idiots after me all the time, I had Furacowa's threat to worry about. "The Rock," as we called Hawaii, didn't seem like a paradise anymore. We were 3,000 miles from the mainland on an island only twenty miles wide and forty miles long. Psychologically, it felt very isolating, very far from home. I was always looking over my shoulder, afraid to go out, afraid someone was going to kill me, afraid someone was going to beat me up. These two guys knew they could pick on me and I wouldn't do anything. They just hadn't made me mad enough. Hawaii lost much of its beauty for me during that time.

One night I had gotten drunk at the club and was on my way to the barracks when I met up with the two guys, also going to the barracks. They split up and the one from New Jersey kept trying to pick a fight, even pushing me down on the ground a couple of times, but I wouldn't fight back. I walked up the stairs to the balcony and he was right behind me. I got up to the balcony and he walked by me and shoved me and said something to me. I don't even know what he said, but I had taken all I could take. I called his mother something and he got furious. I started cursing him out and he came back toward me. I said, "Please don't come back here," but he kept coming. We got into a fight and at the end, he was lying there on the concrete on the balcony. I went into my room and there was a heavy metal extension lamp that was bolted to the wall over the bed and I ripped it out of the wall, went back out and proceeded to beat him with it. When I finished, I picked him up and was going to throw him off the balcony, but something snapped inside me and I didn't. I think if I had, he would have died. Instead, I left him there and went into my room and went to bed. He sustained no permanent injury and after that, the two bullies stayed out of my way. Perhaps I should have done it sooner, but I couldn't bring myself to fight someone until I was in such a rage that there was no going back. In that state, I didn't see much and I didn't feel much.

10

It was very difficult to do anything that cost money in Hawaii. After all, I was a Private First Class and didn't make much, so about the only thing I could afford to do was see the sights. Some friends and I got together and went down to what is called Hotel Street where the prostitutes, transvestites and drug addicts hung out. The transvestites, some of the most beautiful women I'd ever seen, waited around behind the buildings to look for "dates." Unless they spoke or actually showed you what was underneath their dresses (which some of them did), you would never know they were men. We started to drive around the block and make fun of them and call them names, the sort of stupidity that young men often find so hilarious. They started throwing beer bottles at us and then came after us and so we didn't do that anymore.

At about 2 a.m. we parked the car and made a dumb decision to walk around. We were four guys, ages seventeen to nineteen, far away from home. We put the car in a parking garage and started walking down Hotel Street, a wide two-lane street lined with hotels and businesses. Prostitutes stood in the doorways asking if we wanted a date and trying to get us to come into bars. I looked across the street and saw a neon sign that read "Massage" and underneath it said "Open." I stopped and stared in amazement. The rest of the guys had walked on ahead of me and then they realized that I was still standing there and came back.

"Charles, what are you looking at?" one of them asked.

I said, "2 a.m. and a massage place is open. Why would anybody want a massage at 2 a.m.?"

They just looked and me and kind of laughed and started to walk away. I said, "What, what are you laughing about? Who would want a massage at 2 a.m.?" It didn't dawn on me until about a year or so later when I was a little more worldly, exactly what the "massage" consisted of. I was pretty naive and innocent about a lot of things at that point.

I ran to catch up with the guys and a prostitute standing in a doorway called to me, "Hey big boy, would you like a date?"

"Sure," I said, just joking and kept on walking. I thought that she would know that if I were serious I would have stopped and worked out a deal with her. A few minutes later, the woman pulled up to the curb in a slow-moving taxi. She rolled down her window and asked if I had a room. I told her that I didn't and asked why. She said that she was going to go around the block and when she returned, she wanted me to get in. The taxi took off.

The guys asked me what was going on and I explained to them what had happened, but that I had just been joking about wanting a date. The taxi came back and she told me to get in. I refused and she went around the block again, came back and asked if I was getting in. I told her that I wasn't. At this point, she was mad. I had gotten her off of her stoop and into a taxi, she had apparently gotten a room at one of the sleazy hotels and now I was wasting her time. At the other end of the street, we saw her get out of the taxi and talk to four really big guys. We stopped walking because this did not look like a good situation. The other soldiers were pretty irritated that I had gotten us into this. The four guys started walking towards us and we had to decide what to do. We turned around and started walking in the opposite direction. We walked faster and looked behind us to see that they were walking faster too. We started running and so did they. We turned down an alley, a really stupid thing to do since we had no idea where we were going except that we were heading in the general direction of the parking garage. At the end of the alley was a fence. We managed to get over the fence and get away from them. I'm very sure that if they had caught us, we would have disappeared or been severely harmed.

◆   ◆   ◆

At the hospital, I was transferred from the Orthopedic Ward to the Recovery Room. I didn't think that I was ready or qualified for that position, but apparently someone did and it turned out that I was. Back then, a medical corpsman in the army did almost what a registered nurse did in the outside world. In fact, when you got out of the army, you were already qualified to be a licensed practical nurse.

One of the saddest things that I remember happened to me during this time. There was a two-day-old baby in the hospital. When she was born, her heart wasn't right and her lungs were underdeveloped. The medical team, consisting of two doctors and several nurses, was working on her. They had taken her out of the incubator and put her on a table to treat her. For some reason, they needed for her to be held and they called me over to hold her. I knew that the baby was in very bad shape. The doctors were looking at her x-rays and began to argue with each other about what they should do for her. I stood there with the baby in my arms getting more and more angry with them. I wanted them to do something for her, not argue about who was right. Suddenly I realized that the baby was no longer moving and I looked down and I knew that she was dead.

"Hey!" I said, but they didn't hear me. "Hey, something is wrong!"

They took the baby, laid her on the table and pronounced her dead. Then she was placed in a rollaway crib and taken away. They put the x-rays down and went on about their business. I just stood there, simply angry with them, because I thought that if they had just stopped arguing and worked on the baby, maybe they could have saved her. Having that two-day-old baby die in my arms devastated me. After just a couple of months in the recovery room, I asked to be transferred back to orthopedics. I couldn't stand being in the recovery room any longer.

◆   ◆   ◆

One day we learned that General Westmoreland, the supreme commander of the army, was coming to Trippler to give out medals to the wounded. Everything had to be perfect. We always had great food because there were always a lot of dignitaries and high-ranking people at the hospital, but it had to be extra-special for Westmoreland. Everyone was rushing around trying to getting everything just right for the visit. Quite frankly, I couldn't have cared less. I was anti-authority, anti-establishment, anti-everything. I was totally ticked off at the world. The army was not what I expected or wanted and I certainly didn't care about a visit from the head of the whole organization.

The day of his arrival, I had to take some blood samples down to the lab. I got into the elevator and headed downstairs. The elevator doors opened and I got off with my tray of specimens, turned right to walk down the hallway and literally ran into General Westmoreland. He was much taller than I was, if I remember correctly. I stood there looking up at a four-star general and he said, "Good afternoon, soldier." I didn't say anything. I noticed that a colonel was carrying his hat and a major was carrying his briefcase and there were a few other officers following him around. I went on about my business. Everyone was in an uproar about this man's visit, but it meant nothing to me. Many of the soldiers who were to receive medals from him actually turned them down. There was a lot of anti-Vietnam sentiment among the vets. Most of them didn't want to go and weren't happy when they came back, especially if they had been wounded. So despite all the pomp and circumstance surrounding him, General Westmoreland wasn't a welcome visitor to all.

11

There were good times and bad times in Hawaii. One of the nicest things that I remember was going out on Waikiki beach with a blanket and spending the night there. Probably as many people were on the beach at night as there were in the daytime. It was 1970 and it felt safe. Police officers patrolled the area. I felt safe there because I didn't have to worry about someone shooting me from a hotel window. Having grown up on the beach, it was comforting to lie there and listen to the waves. It made me feel a little closer to home. Unfortunately, too many times I took a case of beer or a fifth of liquor out there with me. I had reached a point in Hawaii where I really couldn't function anymore. I could do my job, but when I wasn't working, all I would do was hide and drink. The fear of someone killing me, or beating me up, the isolation, the emotions associated with the baby dying in my arms, the homesickness-all of these things added to my obsession with getting drunk in order to numb the feelings. I was psychologically drained. And even though it had happened months before, the fact that my parents didn't come to my boot camp graduation really stuck with me. I felt like they didn't care. I called them once in a while, but it didn't seem that they were really there for me. I had just turned eighteen and felt like I didn't have a future. I was supposed to spend three years in Hawaii, but I knew that I couldn't live there for two more years. I had to get out. I was in paradise and I couldn't stand it.

I did the only thing that I could think of to get me off "The Rock:" I volunteered to go to Vietnam.

Volunteering for Vietnam must have sent a red flag up to someone, because the next thing I knew, they were calling me into the psychiatrist's office, trying to figure out what was wrong with me. I was based in Hawaii for three years, then I could get out, go home and that would be the end of my service career if I wanted it to be. I had it made. Why had I volunteered to go to Vietnam? I had a long talk with the psychiatrist and I tried to explain it to him the best that I could. He thought that I needed some tranquilizers, so I got the tranquilizers and they mellowed me out all right. They also gave me the munchies. It seemed like I couldn't get enough to eat. I remember once eating six hot dogs, an order of french fries and two drinks in one sitting, and I still could have eaten more. That's when it dawned on me that something was not right. I was eating four full meals every day. In the cafeteria, they served a full meal after 11 p.m. for the shift that was just getting off work. I never missed it. I ate breakfast, lunch, dinner and second dinner every day. In no time at all, I had gained thirty pounds.

I went back to the psychiatrist and told him that this wasn't working and that I had to get out of there. So they gave me a physical and the doctor said to me, "Your liver is hanging to your knees." I asked him what that meant and he said it meant that I was drinking too much. I was drinking more than my liver could get rid of and the sugar was building up around my liver. If I kept drinking, my liver would keep getting bigger and the membrane that encases it would eventually burst. That's cirrhosis of the liver and he told me that I would be dead in ten years.

He said, "My suggestion to you is to quit drinking."

"Forever?" I asked.

"At least until your liver returns to its normal state, but don't drink like you are drinking now. How much are you drinking?"

"Well, not that much," I said.

"How much are you drinking a day?"

"A day, oh, I don't know, I probably average about twenty-two to twenty-four Budweisers a day."

He said, "That's a case. You're drinking a case of beer a day."

"Well, not every day."

"How many days?"

"About five or six a week."

That was the truth. I was drinking close to a case of beer just about every day. Sometimes I would start as early as 11 a.m. I would drink for about fifteen hours without stopping. I probably drank more than a case of beer on some days.

About a month later, I was sent to the psychiatric ward at Walter Reed, not for further evaluation, but to wait for my next assignment. I was so glad to go somewhere else! I had grown a lot in Hawaii out of necessity. I had seen a lot that I wish I hadn't seen. But I still had a lot of growing to do. I was only there for thirty days and then I got orders for Ft. Benning. I had thirty days leave coming to me, so I took it and went home.

12

When I got home, neither of my parents asked me what had happened in Hawaii. I took this to mean that they were ashamed of me or maybe that they just didn't care. My father's silence in particular screamed disappointment. My father, the navy man, had always thought that people should pull themselves up by their bootstraps and take what they had been dealt. I felt that in his eyes, I wasn't a man. To this day, I am not sure if my perception of my father's attitude toward me was correct, but I was profoundly affected by it. I couldn't express my anger toward my father, so it remained bottled up and came out at inappropriate times.

During my thirty days leave, I did manage to get my car fixed. I had it painted metallic blue and it was back in shape again. I thought that once I got settled in Georgia, I would come back for my car. That would make everything better and my last year and a half in the army would be great.

In December of 1970, I reported to Ft. Benning. I wasn't happy about having orders to go back to Ft. Benning, where I started. It seemed like taking a step backwards. Even worse, I was a medic and my orders were for Light Infantry Brigade, which meant a lot of marching. The army and I had not seen eye to eye up to this point, and it only got worse.

I was even more anti-establishment. I was listening to Joan Baez, Crosby, Stills, Nash and Young, lots of anti-war music. I wanted to protest and grow my hair long. I was determined that in this battle of wills with the army, I was going to emerge the winner. I was going to follow my own course and if it took fighting the whole government and the U.S. Army, so be it.

When I arrived at Ft. Benning, I reported to the Replacement Company and told them that my orders were wrong. They sent me to see a captain who told me that the orders looked perfectly fine to him. I explained to him that I was a medic and had been assigned to an Infantry Unit.

"It says that that your MOS is combat medic," he said.

"Well, yes it is, but I've never been in combat. I've always worked in hospitals."

"You're in the Infantry now."

"No, I'm not. I'm not going into the Infantry." In the Infantry, when they aren't in a real war, they play army a lot. They spit shine everything. They have all kinds of inspections and parades and they march and march. In the medical field, there were civilian doctors and nurses as well as military and I had been used to a much more lenient atmosphere. If I couldn't get along in that environment, how was I going to function in a real army environment? The captain said that he would see what he could do and I was assigned a bunk in a huge warehouse called the Replacement Center.

The Replacement Center had hundreds of beds and everyday people came and went. People came in from all over the world for reassignment and left everyday for all parts of the world. Every morning, there were big signs up with cities and countries on them. If you were leaving that day, you would stand in line behind the sign that corresponded to your orders. You couldn't really get to know anyone because most people weren't there more than two or three weeks at the most. Day after day I waited for my new orders. One day ran into another and soon a week had passed. After ten days, I thought that maybe they had forgotten me and I would just spend the rest of my one and a half years there, and no one would ever know. Since there wasn't anything else to do, I did a lot of thinking. I realized more and more that joining the army had been a mistake. I thought about how much I hated the military and how much I wanted out and how ridiculous the whole organization was. Nothing had turned out the way I envisioned it. I was now nearly eighteen and a half and my life wasn't going the way that I wanted it to.

I spent two weeks in the Replacement Center and then got orders reassigning me to Martin Army Hospital. I really didn't want to work in another hospital, but at least I knew what I was doing there and it was familiar. I was pretty good at what I did. Also, in being reassigned, I felt like I had just won my first victory against the army.

At the barracks, I had a roommate from Fondulac, Wisconsin. I went into the room and we introduced ourselves. I was trying to be a hippie in the army, like just about everybody else, and he was a bit of a geek. I listened to Jimi Hendrix, Bob Dylan and folk music-anything that was anti-government, and he listened to and was crazy about Dean Martin. Despite our different tastes in music and the fact that he was from the North and I was from the South, we grew very close and cared a lot for each other.

After about three months in CMS, just as I was learning most of the equipment, I was transferred to an ambulance company. I was happy because now I would finally get to do what I had wanted to do all along-drive. At first it was a boring job because we had to do duty at the airport. We worked twenty-four hours on and twenty-four hours off. I would go to the airport, park the ambulance and go inside where the civilian firemen were and they would have nothing to do with army guys like me. They had a nice kitchen and cooked wonderful food every night, but they never invited me to eat with them. I would eat a cold box of C-rations-some of them still left over from the Korean War! Sometimes, when everyone was sleeping, I would sneak into the kitchen to see if there was some chicken or steak left over and I would help myself.

It was a boring job because not much happened during a twenty-four hour shift. Maybe two planes would come in. When a plane did come in, a siren went off and everybody got into their vehicles. I drove the ambulance all the way down to the end of the runway. As long as the plane was there, I had to sit there in the ambulance. It could be three or four hours sitting out there in the hot sun before the plane moved off the runway. My ambulance didn't have air conditioning. Sometimes I had to sit out there for two hours just waiting for a plane to come in. Usually, I would drive the ambulance out there, then get in the back where I would either read or sleep.

One day, the airport was the busiest I had ever seen it. A helicopter was flying low coming in. Another one was taking off laterally. Somehow, as one was flying up, the other flew over and they crashed into each other. Just about everybody on board was killed. Other ambulances were called in, and I was there. The helicopters caught on fire and one of them exploded. Of the eight people on board, six of them burned. I'll never forget as I drove my ambulance up there, it felt like slow motion. I was numb. People were screaming and the fire was blazing and you could hardly go near anything. There were pieces of bodies lying out on the pavement burning. I was horrified and I was trying to think what I was supposed to do. Something in me took over and I grabbed my aid bag and I remember thinking that it wasn't going to do much good. I tried to put out the body parts that were in flames. My ambulance was chosen to transport the burned body parts and the dead to the morgue. I'll never forget the smell in the vehicle. Nothing smells quite like burned flesh. When I got to the hospital, I was like a robot just going through the motions. I backed the ambulance up and others unloaded it and that was the end of my involvement. I took the ambulance back to the motor pool and we had to clean it out. The next day, it still smelled and they cleaned it out again. They gave me another ambulance. Several days later, I went back to get my ambulance, Number 28, and it still smelled. They just could not get the smell out of it. Finally, they took it to the main base motor pool and parked it in a corner by itself and that's where it stayed for as long as I can remember.

Up to this point, my army life was mostly boring, consisting of hospital runs, sitting at dispensaries or at the airport. This event didn't call for any of the skills in which I had been trained as a medical corpsman. There were no wounds to bind or people to rescue. I was eager for a chance to prove to my father and to myself that I could do more than cause trouble, but this incident did not provide such an opportunity.

13

Besides having duty at the airport, I also pulled assignments at the dispensaries where soldiers would come for sick call. If anyone needed to be taken for x-rays, I would take them to the hospital and bring them back. I would take blood samples, lab reports, things of that nature. I was essentially a taxicab, a courier between the hospital and the dispensary. It was a very boring time, but I thought that I had it made. I would sit around and eat in the air-conditioning. I could go inside and watch all the sick people and those who were faking being sick to get out of duty that day. At about that time, I made Specialist 4, or E-4. No longer was I a PFC, but I was the equivalent of a corporal. I was very proud of this and rushed down to get my new patch sewn on all of my uniforms and clothing. I also got a little more money each month, which helped.

At the barracks, when we got up in the mornings, we were supposed to go to formation. Everybody would line up in front of the barracks and the First Sergeant and the captain of the company would come out. The captain would say a few words and give us a little pep talk and any problems like thefts or fighting would be addressed. If anything was going on in town, they would fill us in on that. Afterwards, they would dismiss us and everyone went to breakfast. I never really cared much for that sort of thing, so I decided that I wouldn't go to formations. What were they but a waste of time? If I didn't go, I could get to the mess hall and get in line first. I simply decided that I wasn't going to go. I adopted the same attitude towards the mandatory guard duty-I simply decided that I wouldn't do it.

Things that the army thrived on, like formations and guard duty, really bothered me. One day, I remember coming in from my afternoon duty and I was walking down the hallway and the first sergeant came over and told me to go out and cut the grass. The grass had just been cut the day before and I told him that.

"I know that," he said.

"Then why do you want me to cut it again?"

He said, "The general is over at the company headquarters (which was right down the street from the barracks). In case he comes over here or looks over here, I want him to see that everybody is doing something."

"Top, I just got off duty. If you want me to do something worthwhile, I'll do it, but I'm not going out there to cut grass that was just cut yesterday."

"I'm not arguing with you, Cross. Go get the lawnmower and cut the grass! Don't make me tell you again."

So I did. I got the lawnmower, filled it up with gas and took it out in front where I started walking up and down a long patch of grass. It was hot and I was going over this grass and not a blade was being cut. The general was across the street and one of the officers over there looked out the window and saw me mowing. He called Top at the barracks. Top came out and yelled for me. I cut the lawnmower off and went in. He took me into his office and started chewing me out about regulations, about being out of uniform. When he finished, I said, "What are you talking about? Out of what uniform?"

He said, "Your sleeves. They are not rolled up properly."

You see, sleeves had to be rolled up in a certain way to a certain length. Mine were below the elbow, but regulations said that they either had to be above the elbow or all the way down and buttoned. Stupid meaningless things like that really rubbed me the wrong way and increased my disdain for the army.

Army food was another problem. Once when I had K.P., I saw the cook putting a case of thirty dozen eggs in the trunk of his car. I just assumed that he was transferring them from one barracks to another. The next morning at breakfast, I heard someone complaining about having to eat powdered eggs and wondering aloud why we couldn't ever get fresh eggs. Then it dawned on me why we were having pow-dered eggs. The cook was stealing the fresh ones! Thirty dozen eggs at a time! This kind of thing apparently went on all the time. We always knew when there was a congressman or a senator or a general visiting because when they came, we always had the same meal-T-bone steak, french fries, and salad. It was good! They always fixed too much. Very seldom did they run out of anything. They always had more than they needed. I actually saw a fifty-five-gallon barrel filled up with rolls and T-bone steaks dumped into the garbage because they were leftover. I was thinking of all the people who could have used that food, but no one cared. It was army money, taxpayer's money, and it seemed that it was in endless supply.

There was a mess hall in our barracks and when you ate there, you had to sign in. The mess hall would turn in the sheets with everyone's signatures and that's what determined the amount of food that they got. The food was so bad that most of us went down the road a block to the bowling alley, which had a restaurant, where we ate french fries, hot dogs, hamburgers, chili, pizzas and had soft drinks. Fewer and fewer people were eating in the mess hall; that meant that they were going to get less and less food. If the number of people eating there regularly fell below a certain point, the army would close the mess hall and soldiers would have to go to another barracks to eat. The company commander decided that everyone should eat in the mess hall, but most people didn't listen. His next idea was for each person who did eat there to sign in three times. They would sign their own name and then something like Donald Duck and Mr. Magoo. It worked. They turned the sheets in and got their ration of food. The mess hall stayed open and all was right with the army world.

The waste of money and time in the army was amazing to me. The sergeants who were E-6s and E-7s were essentially just biding their time to get their twenty years and retire. Most of them already had twelve to seventeen years. After formation in the morning, they got their work assignments and then spent most of the day sitting around in the bowling alley drinking coffee, or going home and coming back at the end of the day in time for formation again before they officially went home. They were just mooching off the government. Seeing this waste really turned my attitude even more against the army.

14

Racial disharmony in the army was festering. The base was about 65% African-American. Most of the Caucasians were very afraid and intimidated. There had been several incidents of white soldiers being beaten up by African-Americans. We were told not to go out at night and if we did, to make sure that we went in pairs. One guy in my barracks had been beaten up and threatened. This guy hated the army, probably even more than I did, but he was so scared for his life that he re-upped for five years just to get out of Ft. Benning. His situation brought back memories for me of Hawaii and the fear for my life that I had felt there.

Some guys began to carry weapons-knives, baseball bats, things like that. Since I worked in the hospital, I got myself a heart needle. A heart needle is used when someone is having a heart attack and the doctors need to go directly into the chest and into the heart. It is about five inches long and a pretty good size gauge. If anyone messed with me, I had no qualms about using it. My friend from Wisconsin and I buddied up a lot in order to go out. One night we had been at the bowling alley and he left a little bit before me to go back to the barracks. When he got there, he heard a commotion and went to find out what was going on. There was a group of four black guys beating the life out of a white man. When they saw him, they knew that they had been caught and they threatened to kill him if he told anyone. When I got to the barracks, it was all over with, but he told me what happened and he said that in formation the next morning he was going to tell the captain what had happened. I begged him not to do that and told him that they would follow through on their threat. He said that he had no choice. He had seen a boy get beaten up for no reason whatsoever and he thought it was time that someone did something about it.

Even though I didn't usually go to formation, I went the next morning. I kept thinking, "Please don't let him open his mouth." He was a pretty big guy, about six-foot two, but I was still afraid for him. He raised his hand and said that he had information in regard to the boy who was beaten up last night. He pointed out the four guys who had done it and after they dismissed everyone, they took those four to another building and talked to them. We went back to our room and a little while later, the guys came in.

"We warned you," they said, "Don't let us catch you outside, we're going to get you."

They were talking to both of us, so I said, "What did I do?"

"You're in the same room with him. You're going to get it as well."

At that point in time, something snapped. I've said that I only fought when I was severely provoked and saw red. Usually it took a great deal for that to happen, but I guess that everything that I had pent up inside me just exploded and I lost it. I had the heart needle, but my friend had a baseball bat over by his bed. I jumped up off my bed, grabbed the bat and I told him, "Look, if you dare touch him or me, I'm going to kill every single one of you! If you want to do it, do it right now! I'm ready!" I was screaming and cursing and they must have thought that I'd lost my mind. I started banging on the locker with the bat and hollering and screaming.

"Come on! Let's do it now! Don't be waiting until some night! Don't be waiting until one of us comes around the corner and you jump us!"

I was using every four-letter word in the book. They turned around and took off and that showed me something. If you stood up to someone and they found out they couldn't bully you, there was a good chance they would leave you alone. They never did touch either one of us. I'm sure they thought I was crazy, banging on lockers, screaming. I think that I could have whipped all four of them, with or without a baseball bat. I decided that I wasn't going to put up with this anymore.

I blamed the army for letting this kind of thing happen. There were plenty of guys who got knifed and beaten and people who were walking around scared to death and the army wouldn't do anything about it. I was bound and determined that I was going to do things my way.

15

Sometimes I did manage to relax. I would go to the bowling alley and bowl and drink. On some nights I could bowl from 6 p.m. to 6 a.m. for two dollars and sometimes we'd get a bunch of guys together and do that. A pitcher of beer was a dollar fifty-and it was a big pitcher. On the army base, everything was sold at cost and it was cheap. We would eat hamburgers and drink beer and bowl. Sometimes we'd skip the bowling and just drink.

At Martin, there were drugs everywhere, so every so often, they would bring marijuana-sniffing dogs through the barracks. If someone was standing outside and saw the dogs, he would yell, "The dogs are coming!" and windows would start opening up and drugs would fly out of almost every window-bags of marijuana, pills, hashish. It was amazing to see all of this stuff raining down onto the ground. People burned incense to hide the smell of marijuana, but of course they weren't really hiding anything because if you smelled incense, you knew why it was burning.

I got into smoking pot at Ft. Benning. It was very easy to come by. I knew which guys in the barracks sold it. I never bought any, but I would smoke when it was offered to me. Getting high was another way of coping-another way of forgetting fear and forgetting the where I was. It was a way of forgetting homesickness and loneliness.

I didn't always have money to buy beer or liquor and there wasn't always someone there offering pot, but since I worked in the hospital and dispensary, I was around a lot of drugs. There was a large pill called Molot, a muscle relaxer. It was purple and about three times the size of an aspirin. There was also Darvon, a pain reliever, a big drug in the army. They gave it out for everything. If a soldier went to the dispensary and said that he had a pain in his leg, they gave him a bottle of

Darvon. Headache? Take some Darvon. Leg blown off? Here, have some Darvon. The pills were little capsules, half pink and half gray. If a man was out of money and needed to get high, there were always drugs available at the dispensary. We used to take the powder out of the Darvon capsules, take half the tobacco out of a cigarette, insert the powder, put the tobacco back, and smoke it. We could walk around smoking this cigarette and no one would know that we were also smoking a painkiller.

Killing or numbing pain seemed to occupy a lot of time in the army. Medics were the second line of defense after alcohol. Every medic has an aid bag and in the bag are tons of pills to get high. One night, a guy turned me on to Molot, the giant muscle relaxer. He told me to start off by taking four or five pills, so I did. I waited and waited, but nothing happened. A few nights later, some guys were drinking beer and taking Molots and I told them that I had taken five of them, but they didn't do me any good. They told me that I needed to take more. I took the bottle to the water fountain with me and took ten pills. A couple of hours later, I was feeling pretty good, very relaxed and calm. It started to wear off and I wasn't feeling quite as mellow as I had been, so I went to the water fountain and took five more. People were lying around, drinking, smoking marijuana, listening to Jimi Hendrix and Deep Purple-we were having a wonderful time. I kept thinking that I really wasn't high enough, so took ten more pills. I had now taken a total of twenty-five muscle relaxers. When I went back into the room, I felt like I was walking four feet off the ground, numb and spaced out. I went outside and looked up at the moon and the stars on that beautiful clear night and thought how cool it all was. I sat down on the steps of the barracks and the next thing I knew, I was lying down on the steps looking up at the stars. I don't know how long I laid there, but it must have been a long time. The sergeant who was on duty came outside and told me that it was late and I should get up and get to bed. He thought I was drunk. I told him I'd get up in a minute and he barked at me to get up right then and he went back inside. I laid there for a little while longer, thinking how groovy and far out it was to be looking up at the stars and then I decided that I'd better go upstairs and go to bed. It dawned on me that I wasn't moving. In my mind, I was saying, "1, 2, 3 stand up," but nothing was happening. I had lost all control of my body. I couldn't move. My mind was telling my arms and legs to move, but they weren't responding. The only thing that kept me from panicking was the fact that I was so mellow. I just decided to stay there for a while longer. I assume I was there for quite some time and then I decided to try again. Amazingly, this time it worked and I got up and walked inside. I walked up the stairs, but it felt as if I wasn't touching them. I laid down on my bed, but couldn't feel the bed. I remember thinking to myself that I must have overdosed on Molot, but it didn't concern me. I surprised myself by waking up the next morning. I had the mother of all headaches. I realized then how fortunate I was to be alive and to have nothing wrong with me except for a giant hangover. I took the couple of bottles of Molots that were still in my aid bag and threw them in the trash. I never messed with any kind of pills after that because the feeling of losing control again scared me deeply. Sometime in my earlier years, I realized that if I didn't control my life, someone or something else would. Losing control to a drug would be the same thing as losing control of my life to the army or to authority in general. It was probably a good thing that I had that experience because otherwise I probably would have started taking something more serious like LSD. I decided to stick with drinking since I felt that I still had control when I was drunk.

16

My friend from Wisconsin got transferred to Alabama, which was rather devastating to me because we had been a source of strength for each other. After he was gone, I really didn't have any friends. The only good thing was that now I had the room to myself. One of the benefits of being an E-5 was having a private room. I still refused to go to formation, to guard duty and to K.P. The company commander just put up with it and didn't bother me. He left and we got a new company commander, a black man named Joshua J. Mosley, Jr. Before too long, he realized what I was doing and called me into his office. He told me that from then on I was to do the things that I was supposed to be doing. I looked right at him and said, "No, I won't pull guard duty, I won't pull K.P. and I'm not going to formation." That's the sort of thing that you just don't do in the service, and it became a challenge for us to see who was going to win this battle. Captain Mosley was a young officer fresh out of college. His expertise was in administration, not in the medical field. The Fort Benning post was his first command. When I told him that I was not going to fulfill the required duties, he was speechless. After a few seconds of contemplation, he came back with what I perceived as a challenge. He stood up from behind his desk, looked me in the eye and proceeded to tell me in a raised voice what I was and was not going to do. What he did not realize was that this was the worst way he could have responded. I didn't say a word; I just left his office with a "we shall see" attitude. He took me off ambulance duty at the dispensary, a really cushy job, and sent me out into the field.

Ft. Benning is a great training ground. They train Airborne, Rangers and Green Berets-the Special Forces. I was assigned to Airborne. One of my duties was to follow them out on their runs in my ambulance and pick up those who passed out. Another job was to go along when they made their first jumps out of a plane. Some of them would land in a creek and I had a little boat and a rubber raft to pick them up. Sometimes they would land on their knees, arms, backs or heads. Broken bones weren't a rarity. That job was rather exciting.

Mosley wasn't satisfied with that assignment so he put me with the Rangers. They would go out for three weeks at a time in the Georgia wilderness, then come back and be off for a week or ten days before going back out. Most of the rangers, the leaders anyway, had been to Vietnam at least once and they knew how important a medic was. They called me Doc and took really good care of me. Once they built me a little shack to live in where I set up my aid camp. I don't know where they got it, but every night they would bring me a watermelon. They respected me because I knew what I was doing and they took care of me because they knew that in a war there might come a time when I would have to take care of them.

Once, I was supposed to be at Hill 351 at 8 or 9 p.m. I had my map and I was driving on dirt roads trying to find the place, but I was lost. Finally, off in the distance, I saw lights and knew that's where they were. I could see the glow, but I couldn't figure out how to get there. I went down a little logging path in the woods until I had gone as far as I could in the ambulance, then walked to the camp. I could come back and get the ambulance in the daylight after I found out how to get there. I walked over several hills and finally came to a really big one and the lights were brighter just on the other side. I got to the top and below I could see jeeps and trucks and soldiers. I started down the hill and all of a sudden things started popping up all around me. They popped up and then down, to the right, left and in front of me. I realized that they were pop-up firing targets-silhouettes of human beings from the waist up. I was standing in the dark in the middle of a firing range! I didn't know what to do. The targets popped up and I heard "Fire!" M-16s started going off and I hit the dirt. I was scared to death. I couldn't get up and I couldn't go back. Finally, there was a lull in the action and I thought that my only chance at survival was to let them know I was there. I jumped up and started running down the hill screaming, "Don't shoot, don't shoot! It's me, the medic!" They put a spotlight up on the hill and saw me running and screaming down the hill. I got to the bottom and I couldn't even stand up because I was so scared. A major and two captains came over and asked me what in the hell I was doing. I explained that I had been trying to find them. They wanted to know where I had come from and how I had gotten to the top of the hill. I told them who I was and they asked where the ambulance was. I replied, "Where do you think it is? It's on the other side of the hill that you were firing at." They weren't angry at me, just relieved that I hadn't been shot. They were concerned not so much for my safety as for their careers because they were not supposed to start any type of maneuvers without medical personnel present. Had I been shot, they would have been court-martialed.

Another time, I was out with the Rangers at night when it had been raining for several days and the logging trails were nothing but mud. I pulled off to the side of the road, facing downhill. I had the ambulance in gear and the emergency brake on and I decided to settle in for the night. I had just drifted off when I thought I felt the vehicle move. I rolled over and listened to the rain and was just about asleep when I felt it again. The ambulance started sliding forward. I jumped up, got in the front seat and jammed my foot onto the brake. The vehicle stopped. I estimated that I had slid about five feet. When I took my foot off, it started sliding again, so I hit the brake again. Apparently, the emergency brake wasn't working at all. I didn't know what to do, but finally decided that I would stay in the driver's seat with my foot on the brake and just try to rest. I kept switching feet and the ambulance didn't seem to be moving anywhere. I decided that if I went to sleep in the front seat and it started to slide, I could just jam my foot on the brake again. I don't know how long I slept, but I felt it move again and I hit the brake. I turned on my lights, but couldn't see anything in the pitch black and pouring rain. This time I stayed awake with my foot on the pedal until the break of dawn when I did doze off a bit. When I woke up, the rain had stopped. I got out of the ambulance as the sun was beginning to rise and the fog was lifting. I walked a few feet to the front of my ambulance and almost passed out. I had slid quite a bit farther than I thought. I had slid down the mountain a total of forty feet and was about ten feet from going over the edge of a cliff, a two hundred-foot drop. There was nothing at all in front of the vehicle that would have kept it from falling. We got a wrecker to get the ambulance back up because there was no way I was going to get back in that vehicle.

◆   ◆   ◆

Once in a while, I really got to do something that I was trained to do. Out in the boonies, I treated people for snake and ant bites, blisters on the feet and hands, sunstroke, food poisoning and things of that nature. During one trip, near the end, I got a call on my radio that there had been an accident, but they didn't say what kind. They gave me the coordinates and I hopped in my ambulance and took off. I drove for about ten miles and then saw the accident. A jeep had flipped over, trying to make a curve too fast. One of the guys was okay, but the other had gone through the windshield and was lying on the side of the road bleeding profusely from the back of his head. I tried to stop the bleeding, but I couldn't, even with a big bandage and a lot of pressure. We were forty miles from the hospital and I knew that he had to get somewhere quickly. The lieutenant said to put him in the ambulance and drive him to the hospital, but I knew that he wouldn't survive the trip and I said so. He ordered me to put him in the ambulance. The wonderful thing about being a medic in the field is that no one can override your medical advice or opinion, no matter what their rank. I refused to follow his order. I told him that there must be a helicopter in the area and that was what we needed. I told him to radio and get it here. He protested that there was no place for it to land, but I insisted and told him that it could land on the highway. I told him to do it right then because this man was going to bleed to death. He did it, the helicopter came and we flew to the hospital. I was able to slow the bleeding quite a bit on the way. We dropped him off at the hospital and they flew me back out to the field. Being able to use my skills made me proud and happy, and being able to contradict an order from a higher-ranking officer was even better.

17

After that particular outing, I put in for leave. My plans were to go home for a week and get my 1966 Mustang, and drive it back to Georgia. I thought that if I could get my car there, I'd have some freedom because I wouldn't have to catch the bus or rely on someone else. I could leave the base when I wanted. So I did just that-went home and got my car. When I left to drive back to Georgia, I had just enough money to pay for the gas. It's usually about a twelve-hour drive, but I'd been known to make it in nine and a half hours. I thought that I'd eat before I left and then just drive straight through and wouldn't need to stop on the way.

I found it very hard to leave home. I thought about calling the army and saying that they really didn't need me. I wasn't a good soldier. If they would just forget I was ever there, I'd stay away. I seriously thought about going AWOL. I wondered if they would really come looking for me. I rejected those ideas, however, and started my trip back to Ft. Benning. I began to feel better about it because with my car there, I'd have freedom. I thought about all the things I could do and the places I could go.

The next couple of months were relatively uneventful. I had my car and my freedom and everything was pretty good. I had some leave time saved up so I decided to go home again, but after the trouble with the car the last time, I decided to fly.

After a few days at home, I got on the plane in Norfolk to fly back to Georgia. There was a stopover in Fayetteville, North Carolina. The flight from Norfolk was fine. We were coming into Fayetteville and as soon as the airplane touched down on the runway, the landing gear broke and the plane crashed into the runway and started sliding on its belly. The plane was rattling and shaking so violently that the inside paneling was falling off. The oxygen masks fell down. People were screaming. Kids were crying. I was next to the window and the plane was shaking so much that I couldn't see out. My head was shaking and every bone in my body was jolted. We hit the end of the runway and slid off. The doors came open, the chutes came down and people slid and jumped out. Fortunately, there were no major injuries, just bumps and bruises, though some people were taken to the hospital. We were escorted to the terminal. When we got inside, I looked out and saw our airplane sitting cock-eyed, one wing touching the ground in the dirt. Seeing it that way was almost more frightening than the event itself. I had been in a plane crash! It was nerve-racking. People could have died. We were informed that there wouldn't be another plane for twenty-four hours. I had to wait in the terminal, contemplating getting on another plane and flying back to the base. The twenty-four hours that I spent in the Fayetteville Airport gave me time to think about some of the things that had almost happened to me. Each event individually didn't seem to amount to much, but looking at them as a whole was a bit frightening. At this time, I didn't think of fate or destiny or luck or a higher power watching over me. I didn't think in terms of near misses, but in terms of near hits. My life seemed to fit the title of an old country and western song I used to hear on the radio as a child—"Live Fast, Love Hard, Die Young"-and I was sure that that's exactly what I would do.

I was supposed to have been back at Ft. Benning by midnight the day before, the last day of my leave. I didn't know if anyone would have noticed my absence and I decided that I'd just tell them what happened if anyone mentioned it. I got back to the base and went up to my room. The next morning, I was in the orderly room and they asked me where I had been. They told me that I was AWOL. I explained all about the plane crash, told them all of the details and even told them to call the Fayetteville airport to check it out. They wouldn't believe me, so it went on my record that I was AWOL. At the time, I just let it go and thought it was no big deal, just another example of the army out to get Charles Cross, but this incident would come back to haunt me later.

18

One afternoon when I was off duty, I went to one of my favorite bars. I went to this particular bar not so much to drink, although I did do that, but because it had one of the best pinball machines around. I had played pinball since the age of thirteen and I was somewhat of a pinball wizard. I could sometimes play for six straight hours on one quarter. That particular afternoon, I met a girl there-Glenda-who was about my age and we began to talk and became friends. We played pinball and shot pool. I found out that she and I knew some of the same people in the service. A few days later, she called me up and asked if I could take her to see her parents, who lived about an hour away in Manchester. I thought it would be a good chance to get out and drive, and maybe her mom would feed me and tell me what a nice young soldier I was. I certainly didn't anticipate anything out of the ordinary happening, but I guess I should have, given that trouble was always following me everywhere.

We were driving along country roads and I stopped at a little country store to get a six-pack of beer. I had drunk about half a beer and we were coming to an intersection. At about the time we reached the intersection, she told me to turn left. I hit the brakes and started to turn left and then she said that she meant right. I swerved in the intersection and jammed on the brakes a bit and went right. There wasn't anyone around. We were surrounded by fields. We had gone maybe a hundred yards down the road when I saw a Manchester police car behind me. I pulled over and tried to hide my can of beer. The six-pack was on the seat, but I wasn't too worried about that. The officer looked at my license and told me to get out of the car. He saw my opened beer on the floor and asked if I had been drinking. I told him that the beer on the floor was my first one and that I hadn't even had half of it yet. He told me that he was going to have me blow up a balloon.

"Look," I said, "I told you why we were swerving. I'm taking her to her parents' house and I was coming to the turn and she said turn left, no turn right and I made that kind of U-turn and squealed my tires and went on down the road. There was no one around. It didn't hurt anything."

He said, "All I know is that you were swerving in the road and obviously you have been drinking."

"Look, you can see the six pack and no empty cans and this one is half full."

"That's fine. Just blow up the balloon."

So I blew up the balloon. I wasn't worried about it. I was standing by the car waiting for the results and thinking that the worst thing that could happen would be that he would give me a ticket for reckless driving. The officer came back to the car with a capsule that was about an inch or an inch and a half long and had granules in it. He showed me that the granules had changed colors that indicated that I was legally drunk. I tried to argue with him and tell him that there was no way that I was drunk. It didn't do any good and he told me that he was going to have to arrest me and impound my car. He ended up letting Glenda drive the car to the station instead of calling a wrecker and he put me in the back of the police car.

We drove into Manchester, a tiny town with one blinking traffic light. We pulled into the parking area for a building that had the courthouse upstairs and the fire station downstairs. The police station was in the back and the jail was in the basement. He took me downstairs and locked me up. He said that they were going to impound my car and ignored my requests to make a phone call. He came back a while later and told me that Glenda had said that she would go get help. Another officer came downstairs and the two of them started talking, but low so that I couldn't hear them. The first guy came back and told me that they wouldn't impound the car if I would let them release it to the girl. I thought this was a great idea. I told Glenda to take my car, go back to the base and get a friend of mine to come bail me out. I asked how much it was going to cost, but he couldn't tell me that until the next morning when the judge came in. So she left with my car and I sat there the rest of the afternoon and all night. There was one little window in the cell and it was half underground. The cell was dirty, cold and dark, and no one but Glenda knew where I was.

First thing in the morning, they brought me breakfast, then they opened the cell and took me out. I asked again about making a phone call, but they didn't answer me. They took me to see the judge. We had to walk through the fire station, between the fire trucks. We went up a narrow staircase into a small, dimly-lit room. The only furniture in the room was a table and chair. The man sitting behind the table wearing a flannel shirt said he was the judge. The policeman and I each told our sides of the story. The judge told me that it would be a hundred and twenty dollars or a hundred and twenty days. I couldn't believe what I was hearing. I told him that I didn't have $120 and asked how I was supposed to get it if I was in jail. He told me that was my problem and that I shouldn't have been driving drunk. I tried to tell him again that I wasn't drunk, but he just told the officer to take me away. He put me back in the cell, where I sat for the rest of the day. I was beginning to get really scared. What if Glenda had taken off with my car? I didn't really know her all that well. She should have had plenty of time to get to the base and back by now. I could sit here for the whole 120 days and nobody would know where I was.

I didn't get much sleep that night. The next morning, they brought me breakfast again, a pretty good breakfast of eggs and toast, but still no word from Glenda. I was pretty depressed. At lunchtime, the policeman came down, unlocked my cell and told me that my commanding officer was here. I was relieved that I was going to be getting out of there, but the next thought was that she had told my commanding officer and I was going to be in big trouble. I almost decided to stay in the cell, but I went upstairs. There stood Glenda and the captain.

The captain jumped all over me and I stood there and took it. He turned to the police officer and said, "Well, I'll see that this man is punished and we'll take him now."

"Whoa, wait a minute," said the policeman, "There is the matter of the $120 fine that he owes."

"I'll see to it that he pays you," the captain replied, "Payday is just a couple of days away and I'll make sure that he gets back up here and pays you."

The police officer agreed and had the captain sign a form saying that he was responsible for me. He wrote down the date and gave me a week to come back with the money. We walked out of the police station and there was my beloved car. We all got in the car and started driving down the road. I looked at the captain and smiled, because he wasn't a captain at all. He was a friend of mine that Glenda had talked to and he had gotten a captain's uniform. He had come into the police station and claimed to be my commanding officer. No one questioned his identity. Impersonating an officer would have landed him in jail, but we laughed about it all the way back to the base.

It was true that payday was a couple of days away. I only got paid once a month and I knew how much money I would need to get through until the next payday. I planned to go back and pay the police in Manchester the $120. The next weekend, I got into a poker game in the barracks and won $300. I thought that maybe Lady Luck was finally shining on me. I escaped spending a hundred and twenty days in a cell in the middle of nowhere and I won money to boot. I was going to Manchester on Monday to pay my debt to society. Saturday night I was in another poker game and by the next morning I had lost not only the $300 that I had won, but also most of the $120 I had earmarked to pay the fine. I still had some money, but if I had taken the $120 out of that, I wouldn't have had enough to live on until payday. I thought that perhaps I could pay them at least a part of the money. Fear was a motivation here because when I left Manchester they had told me that if I didn't return within a week, they would call the Provost Marshall and I would be arrested and have to finish serving the hundred and twenty days. I certainly believed that and so I went back to the town by myself. I went up to the courtroom and stood before the judge.

"Your honor, I don't have the money. I have tried everything I know to get it. They messed up my paycheck and all I got was a check for $7." This had actually happened to me earlier, but not this month. "I tried my best. I went and hocked my stereo to try to get some money. I have the receipts right here in my back pocket to show you that I pawned all the stuff I had and got some of the money together." I reached back and was fumbling in my pocket when he said, "Never mind, never mind. You be back here with that money or send that money in the mail by the third of next month. No more excuses."

"Yes sir," I said, "I'll have it. Thank you very much."

I left. I didn't have one single pawn ticket in my pocket. I didn't hock anything. I suppose that if he'd actually wanted to see the receipts, I would have thought of something else. I knew that I could make it through the rest of the month on the money that I had and then I would pay them after my next paycheck.

During that month, I told lots of people what had happened to me. I was in the bar drinking and playing pool and telling my story to this guy and he said that the same thing had happened to him in Manchester. He had the same choice, a hundred and twenty days or a hundred and twenty dollars. He signed a paper promising to come back and pay the money. That had been at least a year ago and he hadn't heard anything from them.

I thought that I would take the same risk. I never went back. I never paid them and I never heard from them again.

19

There was a big table tennis tournament between the different companies. The champion of each barracks would play for the company championship and the champions of the various companies would go on to battalion. I used to be a very good Ping-Pong player. I ended up in the finals for our barracks. Captain Mosley, the new commanding officer, was also in the finals. He was a college graduate and he was made C.O. because of his administrative ability. He was a by-the-rules kind of guy. He may have taken a dislike to me from the beginning, but he really got upset when I beat him in the tournament and he was very vocal about it. Up until that point, everything had been going along fine, by which I mean that I still wasn't going to formations or K.P. or guard duty. He hadn't pushed the issue, but shortly after the tournament, he called me into his office.

"Cross," he said, "why did you not pull guard duty?"

I said, "I don't pull guard duty."

"I had you put on guard duty and you didn't show up."

"I didn't know I was on guard duty," I replied.

"Well, you should have checked the roster on the bulletin board."

"No. I don't need to check the roster because I never pull guard duty. If you wanted me to pull guard duty, you should have told me you were going to put me on guard duty. I never check it because I don't pull it. I am never on it."

He said, "You were on K.P. and didn't pull it."

"Same thing. No one told me."

"No one is supposed to tell you. You're supposed to check the roster."

"I don't have to check the roster because it's a waste of time because I never pull it. I'm never on there."

That was all he said. A week or two later, I was in the orderly room. I had duty as the back-up driver. My job was to stay in the barracks all day in case there was an emergency and they needed an extra ambulance. It was a boring job because I was very seldom called. I was sitting behind the desk and thinking about the holidays. It was November and I was going to take leave to go home for Christmas.

In walked Captain Mosley and two M.P.s. One of them said, "Specialist Cross?"

"Yes sir?"

"Let's go. You're going to the stockade."

I was flabbergasted. "Why? What did I do?"

"You're AWOL."

"How can I be AWOL? I'm right here. I've never been AWOL."

He began to read off the charges that he had filed against me. Not going to K.P. Not going to guard duty. He read a list of all these different days. There must have been thirty of them. AWOL in the army is serious business. It means you're gone and they can't find you. It's like taking a vacation without telling the boss that you're going. Every date that he was reading off was a day that there had been formation and I didn't go. On paper, it looked like that over a sixty-day period, I had disappeared and come back about thirty times. In reality, I was working. I was on duty or out with the Green Berets or the Rangers. He knew where I was, so these were really trumped-up charges, but I knew that there was no point in arguing. They put me in a jeep, took me to the stockade and locked me up.

I was in a wing of the stockade where there were probably fifty or sixty beds, double bunk beds, in one long room. They were going to assign a lawyer to me, kind of like a public defender. Everyone in the stockade also had a job. There were three choices. One of them was to go out on the garbage truck and pick up garbage cans. I thought that wouldn't be too bad because at least I would be able to get out of the stockade and ride around the base. Then I thought about having to pick up other people's garbage and decided that one wasn't for me.

Another choice was digging graves, cutting grass and taking care of the cemeteries. I didn't want to do that. The last choice was working in the kitchen preparing food. I thought that was definitely the best choice. It would be warm and there would be food. It was rare that there was an opening for the kitchen, but I lucked out and that's where I was assigned.

I worked ten to twelve hours a day in the kitchen washing pots and pans, cleaning the stove, mopping the floor, cleaning the grills and preparing the food. I got to eat all I wanted and before anyone else. It was actually a pretty nice job. One morning, my job was to make the toast. Of course, hundreds of guys ate every day, so we needed hundreds and hundreds of slices of toast. I dropped bread into the top of a big machine and it ran through a rack and fell out of the bottom, toasted. I had three racks of loaves of bread on one side of the machine and I put the toast on the other side when it came out. I had done probably about two-hundred pieces of toast when I noticed that under the machine there was something dried that was kind of a dark red color. I turned the machine off and looked up underneath it and saw blood running down from inside. I called the sergeant over and showed him what I had seen. He took the top off of the machine and inside there was a rat. It had obviously gotten in there and when I turned on the machine, it heated up and the racks were going around and it killed him. Not only did that make me sick, but now I was going to have do to all of the toast over again.

The sergeant said, "Look, we'll clean the machine. You get the toast out there. Shut up. Keep your mouth shut and put the toast on the serving line."

He was talking about the toast I had made when the rat was in the machine. Normally, I ate breakfast before everyone else, but because we had to clean the machine, we were running behind and I ate with the rest of the guys. I sat down at the table and was thinking how terrible this was. I nudged the guy beside me and said, "Don't eat the toast." Of course, other guys around heard me and I told them the same thing. I didn't tell them why. Nobody at my table ate toast. I looked around the mess hall and saw other guys putting butter and jelly on their toast and swallowing it down and I couldn't eat. I had to get out of there. I guess I should be glad that they at least cleaned out the machine before making any more toast that day.

Days went by. They seemed really long and I was glad to be able to work all day. I got to go outside in the yard and get some fresh air, the best time of the day. I really had to spend very little time in my cell. It was just like a barracks where there were maybe a hundred men on a floor. Obviously, the lack of freedom and being locked in scared me, but at least I felt that I was doing something worthwhile by working in the kitchen. The nights were the worst part. This was pretrial confinement and the time didn't count. I was waiting for some word about when and if I was ever going to have a trial. I remember looking out the window one day and watching the cars go by freely, the people laughing and walking down the street and I began to wonder if I was ever going to be able to do that again. Then I happened to look over into the fenced area of one of the motor pools. Sitting all alone in the corner by itself was ambulance #28. That was the one that had carried the dead bodies from the helicopter crash. They had never been able to get the smell out of it and it sat alone, destined to be destroyed. I really identified with it. There were lots of other people and vehicles inside the enclosed area, yet they had separated that ambulance and through no fault of its own, it was destined to be alone and destroyed. Everyday, I would walk by the window and look out at it and it became like an old friend. I felt like I knew what it was going through. It seems kind of strange, I know, but it helped me to understand a little bit better the situation that I was in.

November rolled into December and I thought that surely I'd be out by Christmas. I couldn't spend Christmas in the stockade. One evening during the first week of December, I was in my cell lying on my bunk when guards and a couple of officers came in, got me out of bed and took me downstairs into the basement. There was a guard on each side of me and they put me in handcuffs. All this time I was asking what was going on, but no one would answer me and I was scared to death. They were handling me rather roughly. Finally, one of the officers got about two inches from my face and started yelling at me, wanting to know why I did it. He wanted to know where I got the stuff. I had no idea what he was talking about and told him so. This made him even madder. As he continued to talk, I managed to piece together what had happened. Someone had tried to burn the building down. It had been on my floor and another inmate had identified me to the authorities as the one who had set the fire. I was nearly speechless. Nothing I said would have made a difference to them anyway. They brought in the guy who identified me and I was relieved, thinking that he would realize that he'd made a mistake. They asked him, "Is this the man who tried to burn the place down?" He looked right at me and said, "Yes, it is." I didn't know why this guy was doing this, but he was just out and out lying. I started talking to these guys a mile a minute. I didn't know what was going to happen next, but I did know that if I was convicted for this, I'd never get out. In fact, they would probably send me to Ft. Leavenworth, Kansas. I continued to deny any involvement and they put me in isolation.

I was in a dark little room with a slit in the door where they shove in the food, a damp and scary place where there was no noise and almost complete darkness, except for the little bit of light streaming through the crack in the door. I sat there for four days. No one talked to me. Whenever they brought me food, I would ask what was going on, but no one would say anything. After four days, they opened the door and pulled me out and asked me again why I had done what I did. I actually began to cry and begged them to believe me. I didn't do anything. He got in my face and started screaming and cursing at me again. That just made me cry harder. I was trembling. They put me back in isolation and I knew that there wouldn't be many more times, if any, that they would come back and ask me to confess again.

The next day, the door opened and I was shocked. They removed my handcuffs and unchained my legs and brought me out and sat me down. The same officer who had been screaming at me the day before looked at me and said that they had interviewed the man who had identified me and he finally said that they guy he saw had blond hair.

"I don't have blond hair, it's red," I said immediately.

"We know that," he replied. He never apologized for what they had put me through. In further interviewing the witness, they believed that they had found the man responsible for the arson. They took me back up to my room and that was the end of it. It was as if nothing had happened. I was so relieved that I couldn't even be angry at the guy for falsely identifying me. I just wanted to put it out of my mind and never think about it again.

Over the next couple of weeks, as Christmas drew closer, I couldn't believe that no lawyer had come to see me. No trial date had been set that I knew of. I was in limbo. I had a lot of time to think. At the age of nineteen, I didn't have a lot in the past to think about, but I thought about the present and the future. My anger and hostility towards authority in general and the army in particular continued to grow.

Christmas came. I remember lying on my bunk, looking through the bars unable to believe that I was spending Christmas in jail. Certainly my family must have written or called and they didn't know where I was. I could have written to them, but what would I have said? Hello, Merry Christmas, your son's in jail. I didn't want anybody to know that. I thought I was there unjustly, though technically the CO was within his rights to do what he did. It was the way he did it, with no warning, that made me angriest. I felt that, in a sense, I had unwritten permission not to go to formation. I saw myself as the completely innocent victim. I know now that I wasn't totally innocent, but I didn't deserve what I got. Everyone knew that I had not fulfilled my duties for months and no one seemed to care. I felt that I was in prison for winning a pingpong tournament against Captain Mosley. I did learn that sometimes it might be better to work within the system, if for no other reason than to make things easier for myself. My actions in this one area of my army life caused more than one negative consequence, much like a domino effect. Pulling guard duty or K.P. would not have harmed me, but from that defiant action, I was imprisoned, demoted, fined, and my car was stolen while I was locked up.

Christmas came and went and I figured that everyone was home with their families and I wouldn't be getting a trial anytime soon. New Year' Day, 1972, rolled around and I was still there. A couple of days after that, my lawyer came to see me for the second time in two months. He told me that the trial date was set for that week. He interviewed me again and explained some things to me and we went to court. I had no idea what was going to happen, but I was glad finally to be able to go to court. Even if they found me guilty and sentenced me, at least I could start serving my time. But I wasn't really thinking about serving time. I planned to get out of there.

The courtroom was about forty by sixty feet with a bench for the judge, a table for my lawyer and me, and a table for the prosecuting attorney. Both attorneys were lieutenants in the Judge Advocate General's (JAG) office. This meant that they were young and that the army had helped put them through law school and in return, they had to serve a certain amount of time as lawyers. I was anxious and excited. I had a feeling that I was getting out of there. Then the prosecuting attorney stood up and said, "Your honor, we request the maximum penalty for the charges brought against Specialist 5 Charles Cross." Then he said what the maximum penalty was—five to ten years in Ft. Leavenworth. I was totally shocked and devastated. How could they do this to me? What had I done? I was taking this personally. I was thinking, what have I done to this man? I was looking at him. He couldn't have been more than twenty-five years old. I wanted to yell out, "What have I done to you? Why are you doing this to me? I don't even know you!"

In the meantime, the judge was talking to the two lawyers. The only thing that my lawyer said that I could make out was that the maximum penalty was too severe. Their voices sounded muffled because I was so engrossed in my own thoughts. I wasn't even paying attention. They went on for another thirty minutes or so and another date was set for the next week. The judge and the prosecutor left and I was sitting there with my attorney. I asked him what was going on. He said that we had presented our case and they had presented their case and he would get in touch with me before the next week. He left and they took me back and locked me up.

All week I thought about Leavenworth. That was a prison, the big time. That's where they put rapists and murderers. In the army, Leavenworth is Attica, it's Sing Sing, it's Alcatraz. I imagined some big guy coming up to me and asking what I was in for. Well, I didn't go to formation, I didn't go to guard duty and I didn't go to K.P., so they gave me ten years. I wanted to die.

The next week, we went back to the same place. Before we went into the courtroom, my lawyer came to me and told me that we had made a plea agreement. For my plea of guilty on all charges, they had agreed to demote me from E-5 to E-1, that I would forfeit all my pay from the time that I had been in the stockade, spend sixty more days there, pay a fine of $250 and get a general discharge from the service. I asked what he thought I should do.

"That's a pretty good deal," he said, "The man asked for the maximum, which is ten years in Leavenworth. If you don't take this, it could go either way."

I said, "But I don't deserve that."

"What you think is not really relevant."

"Well, let's see, sixty days and I'm out of here, right? Free?"

"Yes. I'll talk to them and maybe we can get them to drop the discharge."

"Okay," I said, "but sixty days guaranteed and I'm out of here or possibly up to ten years in Leavenworth?"

"That's your choice."

I only had a few minutes to think about it. He asked me for my decision and I said, "I'm sorry, but I don't plan on spending another day in this place. I'm not going to plead to another sixty days. I've been in here sixty days and I'm not going to spend another sixty in here."

He said, "Do you understand what you're saying?" He pulled out a piece of paper. "You sign this showing that you waive your right to the plea agreement and that you waive the guaranteed sixty days. I'm pretty sure I can get the discharge dropped and you'll go back to the army and you'll pick up where you left off as an E-1 or an E-2, but at least you'll be free. I can't guarantee what's going to happen to you here."

"I'll take my chances. I'm not going to settle for sixty more days." I don't consider myself to be a gambler, but I seemed to be faced with an all or nothing situation. I felt that I was in the right. I was in jail without a real reason.

We went into the courtroom and the proceedings began. My lawyer didn't say very much. He told them that I had already spent sixty days in the stockade and I was remorseful. He tried to throw me on the mercy of the court by emphasizing my youth. I looked at the judge and he didn't seem to be very sympathetic. The prosecutor got up and began to read all the charges. There were dozens of them, every day that I hadn't been at formation. "On such and such a date, Specialist Cross was AWOL." He went through all of the dates and said "AWOL" after each one. It sounded like I had never been in the army.

The judge dropped a couple of the dates because it was plain that I was there and on duty, but there were so many of them. I could sense that it wasn't going well. I figured they were backing the Leavenworth bus up to the door to take me away. The judge asked my lawyer if he had anything else to say. He brought me a piece of paper with my name and information like my social security number and asked if it was correct and if it was spelled right. I said that it was and he told the judge that he had nothing further. The judge looked at me and asked if

I had anything to say. The first thing that came to my mind was that if I didn't say anything, I was definitely going to be sent away.

"Yes, your honor, I do," I stood before him and said, "Your honor, I just turned nineteen years old and I've been away from home for a long time. This is the first time I've been away from home." I explained to him again why I hadn't gone to formations and I realized that he was probably looking at it as not a good reason. I told him about the unwritten rule with the other commander that it was okay not to go and that no one ever said anything about it, even though it was against regulations. I started thinking that maybe the judge was looking a little more sympathetic, but I could still see myself sitting on that bus headed for Kansas. So I pulled out the big guns and said, "I have a drinking problem. I just can't quit drinking and I drink up all of my money. That is one of my major problems. I drink a case of beer a day and I just can't seem to stop. I have had a physical and the doctor told me to stop and I can't."

"How old are you again?" the judge asked.

"I just turned nineteen years old. I drink constantly. If I'm not working, I'm drunk. Two weeks into every month, I've already drunk up all my money. One reason that I can't get up and get into formation is because I'm drunk and hung over." I was laying it on thick.

The judge said, "Well, son, have you ever tried to do anything about this?"

"Yes sir. I am attending AA meetings."

"You are? When did you do that?"

"I started when I was in here. You know, your honor, I've been here two months already. I've had a lot of time to reflect and I haven't been able to drink anything in sixty days. I feel much better. I started going to AA meetings and they have really helped me quite a bit. I'm sorry for what I've done and I won't do it again." That was the truth. I had gone to one AA meeting because I thought it would get me out of working in the kitchen for an hour. In fact, the meeting took place during free time in the evening and so I never went to another one.

I believe that was the turning point for the judge. I think that if it hadn't been for that one meeting, I would have ended up in Leavenworth. As I was telling the judge my story, I put on my saddest face. He asked if I had anything else to say and I said that I didn't. I looked at my lawyer and he had a bewildered look on his face, as if he didn't know where all this had come from. I was feeling rather smug because after all, he was the one who went to law school and I was the one who had to save myself. The judge took a few minutes and then looked at me and handed down his verdict.

"Charles Cross, I am going to demote you from E-5 to E-1 and you will forfeit your salary while you were confined here. I'm going to fine you $250. I figure that if I take your money from you, you won't be able to buy beer. I think it is a sad thing indeed for a nineteen-year-old to drink as much as you do, but I commend you for going to the AA meetings and I certainly trust that you will continue those."

"Yes sir, I will." That was it. I was waiting to see how many years at Leavenworth I was going to get because he was looking down at his papers. He looked back up at me and said, "You have spent sixty days in pretrial confinement?"

"Yes sir, I have."

"I will sentence you to sixty more days and I will suspend those sixty and the term will be completed with the sixty days that you have already spent in pretrial confinement."

There was silence. I still wasn't sure that I was free. Then it finally sank in. Court was adjourned and the judge got up and left. I got a little cocky at that point and gave the prosecutor a dirty look and kind of laughed at him. Forty-eight hours later, I was set free.

20

Not all of my troubles were over when I left the stockade. About two weeks before the trial, word came to me that my beautiful 1966 Mustang had been stolen. It had been in the barracks parking lot and when I got there I found out that it was true-the car was gone. I reported this to the first sergeant and he confirmed that he knew that it had been stolen. He believed that one of the guys in my barracks by the name of Dallas had taken it and gone AWOL. I asked if anything had been done about it, but he replied that since Dallas had gone off the base, they had no authority to look for it. He told me to go to the civil authorities.

I went downtown to Columbus to the police station and told them what had happened. They told me that there wasn't much they could do. If he had gone AWOL, he certainly wasn't around there and they were, after all, just the city police. Plus, since it had been stolen on base, they couldn't do anything anyway. This made no sense to me.

I called my insurance company to tell them that my car had been stolen, and they weren't particularly sympathetic. I decided that if the army and the city police and the insurance company wouldn't help me, the next step was the FBI. So I called the FBI. Since it was interstate theft, they said they would look for it. About a week later, I found out that someone had forged and cashed one of my paychecks. I had gotten paid right before I went to the stockade and I had put the check underneath the floor mat in my car. So not only did I not have my car, but I had no money either.

A few days later, the FBI called and said that they had located my car. I was joyful-my wonderful car, my good friend. They told me not to get too excited. They had found the car in Minnesota-where Dallas was from. He had wrecked it going eighty miles and hour on the interstate. It was totaled.

I thought that at least I'd get the insurance money for the car. In 1968 I had paid $1,500 for it. It was now January of 1972 and the insurance company only gave me five hundred. I had put thousands of dollars into that car. And in 1972, you couldn't get much of a car for five hundred dollars. I thought that things really couldn't get much worse.

Putting the events of the last year behind me, I tried to concentrate on staying out of trouble. While I was in the stockade we had gotten a new commanding officer Mosley had been discharged because the army didn't need him anymore. They didn't kick him out, exactly, but they wouldn't let him re-enlist. I had gone looking for him when I first got out of jail because I had so much anger and hostility towards him for what he had done to me, and now I couldn't do anything with those feelings.

The new commander knew everything that had gone on. I was put back on the duty roster and resumed going out into the field. I was glad to get away from all the people at the base. When I came back in at the end of three weeks, I was tired and cold. All of the events of the past few months were, of course, still fresh in my mind. I was still very angry. I had never told my parents where I had been. They asked me why I hadn't written, but I just told them I had been really busy and I made excuses. In fact, I never did tell them what happened to me. My money had been greatly reduced. I was now an E-1, a private, again and that really hurt. I came back in from the field and I had my stuff with me and I was tired and dragging it upstairs. I got to the door of my room and heard noise coming from inside. I thought that someone had broken into my room and was trying to steal something. I put my stuff down and was getting ready to rush into the room and beat someone up. I finally had a target for my pent-up anger and hostility. I opened the door and there was a guy standing there. There was a locker on each side of the room. There was a bed on each side of the room. I had had my stereo and records and lamp on the desk in between the beds and all that stuff was now on my bed.

"Excuse me," I said, "Who the hell are you?"

"This is my new room," he answered.

"No, you have the wrong room. This is my room."

"No," he said, "I have been assigned this room as well."

I was fed up. "This is a private room. This is my stuff. You take your stuff, you get it off and you put my stuff back up there. Put your stuff in your duffel bag because you're not staying."

He looked at me as if I was crazy. I went downstairs to the first sergeant and told him that I couldn't believe that I had come in from the field to find this guy unpacking his things in my room, my private room. He told me that they needed the room and there wasn't anyplace else to put him. He said that there was nothing I could do about it. As an E-1, I was no longer entitled to a private room. I told him that there certainly was something I could do about it and I went back upstairs. I told the guy to pack his stuff and get out of my room. He packed and left. I had a single room again. They did find another place for him. I had made up my mind that I wasn't going to put up with it anymore.

I still didn't go to formations or K.P. or guard duty. Everything was back where it was before Mosley showed up. Everyone seemed to have tacitly agreed to leave me alone. I went out in the field and did my thing and no one bothered me. The fact that nothing really changed made my incarceration and trial even more ridiculous. All of it had been for nothing.

♦   ♦   ♦

I started my short-timers calendar. When you have a year or less to go, you make a calendar and check off the days until you get out. You let everyone know it-one hundred days, ninety days, forty days. I'm on my way out.

The worst winter of my life had passed and spring was coming up with the sun shining and flowers blooming. I began to get more and more into music. I started to write more, in part to vent the anger and hatred inside. I was so eager to get out of that place. I thought that if I just stayed out of everyone's way, everything would be fine. But that was not to be the case.

I was beginning to turn even more inward and was becoming a real loner. The two months in the stockade had really affected me. I just wanted to be left alone and serve out my last few months. There was a shortage in the hospital and since I had worked in the hospital before, they assigned me there for a little while. I enjoyed being back and taking care of people. It made me feel like I was doing something worthwhile and accomplishing something.

I was assigned to a short, stocky marine in his late thirties who had developed a blockage in his bladder and couldn't urinate. I looked at the doctor's orders and thought, uh oh. I went to the nurse and told her that I didn't really want to do this procedure. She told me that I didn't get to pick and choose my assignments and to get on with it. I went into the supply room and got the proper pack. I returned to the marine's room and as I was opening up the pack, I was explaining the procedure to him.

"First, I will sterilize the area and then I take this catheter and I run it in your penis into your bladder and then I hook this syringe to the end of it and I push this fluid in, which blows up the balloon which keeps it in place so it doesn't accidentally come out of your bladder and you'll be able to relieve your bladder."

This man was in great pain. His stomach was swollen. I got the pack ready and poured out the antiseptic. I got the forceps and a cotton swab and told him to pull down his pants. The next thing I was supposed to do was to take his penis and sanitize the head before running the tube into his bladder. I was wondering what would happen if he got an erection when I touched his penis. He was looking at me. My face must have given away my uneasiness.

"Doc," he said, "Have you ever done this before?"

"Oh yeah," I replied, "it's simple."

"Have you ever done it?"

"Well, yeah, I've done it before."

"On a live person?"

"Well..."

"How many times?"

"Well, after today, it will be one."

About that time, the guy pulled up his pants, got out of bed in obvious pain and waddled down the hall. I followed him down the hall. He went into the bathroom and stood in front of the urinal. He took his fist and started beating on his bladder area as hard as he could. I thought he had lost his mind. I ran out to get the nurse. We got back there and he was urinating. His face was red and there was sweat rolling down his face, but he was smiling. He must have stayed in there ten minutes. Whatever kind of blockage he had was gone.

A couple of days after that, I had a man who needed to be prepped for surgery. Just like with the catheter, I technically knew how to do this, but I had never actually done it. His arm was being operated on and so I was supposed to shave the area. I opened up the surgical prep pack and looked for the razor. There was a razor there, all right, but it was a straight razor, and I had never used one of those before. I didn't want to go back to that same nurse to complain again like I had before. I had seen people in cowboy movies shave with straight razors, so I thought how hard could it be? I lathered his arm up from the shoulder down to the hand and started shaving. It wasn't until I was almost finished that I noticed little specks of blood. I washed it all off and it started stinging and there were hundreds of little dots of blood all over his shoulder, arm and hand. The man got upset and the nurse came in and she was not happy with me either. His surgery had to be postponed until his arm healed. I was thinking that this hospital assignment wasn't working out too well and I needed to get back to the field. I was actually a very good medic, but those particular instances didn't go too well. After I served my couple of weeks there, I did get to return to my company.

The scuttlebutt going around was that the army was letting people out six months early. They had too many people they didn't need. Vietnam was winding down. It was April of 1972 and I was scheduled to get out in October. I thought how great it would be to get out of this place early. At the end of April, I got orders that said I was going to be discharged on May 20. Three weeks! I was to start my processing to get out right then. I couldn't believe it. I was the happiest person on the face of the earth.

It takes about three full days to go through the discharge process, and that's if nothing goes wrong. There are stacks of papers to be signed and tons of places to go. I got a jeep and was zipping around everywhere, happy to do it. I was taken off duty because they knew I was leaving. It was exciting, but it was also a long and boring process.

I had my physical and I had called my family to tell them I was coming home. I was dreaming about what I was going to do when I got out and how long I was going to grow my hair. I was nineteen years old and I was still going to be a teenager when I got out. It was great!

The following week, I got orders in the mail that canceled my orders to get out on May 20. My new orders said June 16. I couldn't believe it! I was really upset, but I tried to take it in stride. My physical was good for thirty days, so I wouldn't have to get another one. I wouldn't have to do any more paperwork. It just meant that I'd have to hang around for another month. Fortunately, I went out into the field for a couple of weeks and when I got back, I knew that I'd only have a couple more weeks to go. No problem. I could handle that. When I got back to the barracks there were new orders for me. They said that I was no longer getting out on June 16. My new discharge date was July 28.

I thought they had to be messing with me. It was one thing after another for three years. I went to the company commander. I went to the first sergeant. No one could tell me why my orders had been changed. The orders came from Washington, D.C. and the local guys had nothing to do with them.

I had turned in all of my equipment and I had to get a lot of it back because I would need it. I had to get an ambulance again because I was going to be back on duty. I had to get another physical. I had to go back to personnel and finance.

In personnel, I asked why this had happened. They either would not or could not tell me. I told them, "Let me tell you what, come July, I'm out of here. When July 28 rolls around, I'm gone. I don't care. They can cancel my orders. I don't care what they do, I'm out of here."

The personnel guy said, "Now wait a minute. They probably won't do it again, but you don't want to do that because then you'll be AWOL and then they'll just come after you."

I said, "What are they going to do? Put me in the stockade?" That was kind of a private joke with myself. I was threatening. I told them I was going. I was going home. No one was going to stop me. On the 28th of July, I was going to be gone.

July came and sure enough, the second week I got more orders. My July 28 date had been canceled and my new date was August 25. Another month. This started as a six month early-out and every month they were chopping it. It meant I had to go through all the paperwork again. I was angry. I told personnel that I really meant it this time. If they canceled those orders I was leaving. The second week of August, I got new orders. As I was opening them, I was thinking that this couldn't be happening. It said "Your orders for discharge on August 25 have been rescinded. Your new discharge date…" Before I read further, I thought, I just don't care. I went upstairs to pack my bags because I was leaving. I looked at the orders again saw that the new discharge date was August 26, one day later than the last one. Aha, they were playing with my mind. All of that for one day. I went back to personnel and told them, "I'm leaving on the 25th. I don't care if the new orders are one day or one year later, on the 25th I won't be here."

The guy told me again that I'd be AWOL and the army would just come get me and bring me back. It was only one more day, after all. For me, it was the principle of the thing. They started this in May and it was now August. I should have been home for three months by now. I was mad and yelling. Finally, I calmed down enough to realize that it was only one more day. I was getting out. Instead of six months early, it would be six weeks early, but I was getting out.

The wonderful day finally arrived. Everybody gets money when they get out of the army. People got hundreds, even thousands of dollars. I knew that I was going to get some too. The last place I signed out was finance where they gave me a pay voucher. I started signing all the papers in finance and the guy told me that I was getting five hundred dollars, which I thought was great. Then he started taking it back. He said that I owed the army money because once when I was on leave in Virginia, I had gone to the navy to get paid. He called it a partial pay. I had gone through this all earlier. Once I was home on leave on payday. I was supposed to be able to go to any army installation to get paid, so I went to the one nearest my home, Ft. Story, but they wouldn't pay me. It was the beginning of the month and I needed my money. I got the bright idea of going to the navy. I showed them my leave papers and they wrote me a check right away. On my next payday, however, I got a check for $7. When I protested, they told me that the army's records showed that the navy had given me an advance on my pay-check and they took it out of that month's check. I couldn't get across to them that the money hadn't been an advance, it was my regular pay. The following month, my check was for $14. Same story. I never did get my two paychecks. And now they were trying to take the same money again! I raised cane, hollering and cursing. The guy offered to get me some forms and they would check on it, but I knew that meant that nothing would happen. So I just told him to give me whatever was left out of the five hundred that they owed me. He finished reading all of the money that I owed them and gave me a bill for $177.44. I owed the army money! But by law, the army had to give me enough money to get back to where I came from and so he gave me enough money to get the bus home and the bill for $177.44.

At least I was out. My military career was full of many highs and lows. When I was working in the medical field, it was wonderful. I learned a lot and grew up a great deal in those three years in the service. I had made it back up to an E-4 and now I was going home with an honorable discharge. No one was happier than I was to get out of the army.

PART III

21

I had no idea what I was going to do once I was out of the army. From the time that I was about nine years old, I had assumed that I would join the army and spend the rest of my career there, and I didn't give a whole lot of thought to what my life's work would be after the army. I could go to college under the GI bill and the service would pay for it all. I just had to decide what I wanted to do. I was very angry and bitter towards the service and the experience didn't help with my authority problem. I felt that I had wasted three of the best years of my life. I know now that the time wasn't wasted and as I got older I came to see the benefits that I gained and how much I learned. At that time, however, I thought that I might as well have been in a coma for those three years. I felt like I had lost a great deal of my youth and that I was three years behind in my life. When I got out on August 26, I had one more day to be a teenager. My twentieth birthday was the next day. All I could think about was making up for the years that were gone. It was unrealistic, but I really thought I could do that. I didn't know what I would have to do in order to make up the time. I had no plan, no direction, no thoughts on it at all.

Even the twenty-four hour bus ride from Georgia to Virginia didn't go smoothly. We had a flat tire that took hours and hours to repair. To me, all of that time was connected with the army. I spent the time not looking ahead to the future, but looking back at the past and the several times in about two and a half years that I nearly lost my life. I thought about being in Hawaii and not being able to enjoy the beauty of the place and about how wonderful it could have been. Hawaii seemed like a lifetime ago. It would have been better for me to spend some time contemplating my future on the bus ride instead of dwelling on the past. The good things were in my mind as well. I thought about the lives of three people that I had been able to save during my three years in the service and about all the things that I had learned to do as a medic. But in my mind, the positive did not come close to outweighing the negative.

I finally got home, back to my parents' house. I had no car, no job and no money. I borrowed some money from my dad and borrowed his car and went out to visit the places to do the things that I had done when I was fifteen and sixteen years old. Nothing had changed much. There was more traffic. The people had changed, though. Most of my friends were either in college or had gotten married. They had moved on. It was August 27 1972, my twentieth birthday. If I had known what was to transpire over the next eight years, I would have probably gone back into the army. My time in the service was easy compared to what lay ahead of me.

For the time being, I did what I was used to doing. I got some beer and got drunk. I met up with a young man named David who was two years younger than me. He was actually a friend of my brother. We rode around in my parents' car and I drove up to what we called "The Rec"-the Recreation Center at the elementary school where people could use the gym in the evenings. It was dark, but the lights were on at the basketball court. Two girls were standing on the court talking. Both had long straight hair and were wearing bell-bottom jeans. I asked David who they were and he told me that the one on the right was Melanie and the other was Darlene. He asked which one I wanted and I said I'd take the one on the left, Darlene. That meant that we were going to introduce ourselves and try to ask them out sometime. Even though I was twenty years old, I was still rather naive when it came to dating and relationships. We got out of the car and introduced ourselves and talked for a little while. Nothing much happened, so we got back in the car and left.

As the days went by, my father continued to ask me what it was that I wanted to do and I continued to tell him that I didn't know. I knew that I had to have some money and he definitely wanted me to have a job. He was the market manager for a local supermarket chain and told me that he would get me a job. It was against company policy for me to work with him, but he would get me a job learning how to cut meat. I didn't really think that I wanted to cut meat, but money was money.

I started the job a few days later. I went in at 7 a.m. and worked until 5 p.m. I found out that I was actually very good at cutting meat and I enjoyed it My father gave me a car, a 1961 powder blue Comet station wagon. It was eleven years old and I called it "The Heap." After work, I would go home, take a shower, get dressed and hit the streets. Of course, before I left the store, I always bought some beer. I spent the next several weeks riding around and meeting new people, since most of my friends weren't around anymore. Most of them were my brother's friends, so most were two or three years younger than I was. A few were my age and some were a year or two older. Everyone gathered at the Rec and that's where we decided what we were going to do. The Rec was a central meeting point. I had talked with Darlene several more times, but we hadn't gone out. I figured that she was about seventeen or eighteen years old. I knew that she was still in school, but I thought this must be her last year.

One night a group of us were standing around talking and I noticed another group of young men and women coming up in their cars and walking around like they owned the place. I had grown up in the neighborhood, but I didn't recognize any of these people. I asked Darlene who they were, particularly one guy I noticed.

"That's Tom," Darlene said, "He's the leader of a gang."

"They have a gang around here?" I asked, stunned.

"Yes, there's a gang and it's called the 'Wrecking Crew.'"

This was not the kind of neighborhood where you would expect to find a gang. We lived in a middle-class, very respectable neighborhood called Hollywood Homes. A lot of service people, policemen, and church people lived there. Most of the people in the gang weren't from that neighborhood. Some of them lived in better areas.

I thought this was interesting and I began to watch these guys, Tom in particular. He looked older and I found out later that he was twenty-four years old. Although I didn't realize it until later, a lot of the new friends that I had met were in his gang and he had actually heard of me. He had been in the service, been to Vietnam and had gotten out a few years earlier. He came over to me and asked who I was. I told him my name and he began to talk about how this was his neighborhood. He knew that I had been in the army and apparently he perceived me as a possible threat to his authority. I didn't even know him or that there was a gang. He made it pretty clear that he was in charge around there. It didn't bother me. I didn't care. At least I didn't care until the following week when my brother came home after getting beaten up by two of the gang members. He had been beaten up because of me. I was an unknown. They knew very little about me. Gang members had been talking about me, and my brother got involved. He got mad and they got mad and apparently they jumped him. Of course, since the whole thing was about me and because it involved my younger brother, I had to avenge it. There was honor at stake.

I went to the Rec and eventually a bunch of them showed up. I asked Tom who had hit my brother, but he refused to tell me. He said, "What are you going to do if you find the two who beat him up?"

"I am going to whip their ass." I said it was as plain and simple as that.

He said, "Do you think you can?"

"I'll take them both on at the same time. It doesn't make any difference to me. If anybody else interferes, they can line up and we'll go from there."

He still refused to tell me who they were. "Well, I tell you what, Tom," I said, "I don't know you that well, but you don't know me."

He was about the same size as I was. I was six feet tall and I was down to about a hundred and fifty pounds. His hair was longer than mine. My hair was just barely beginning to grow out and I was starting to grow a beard. He started to stick his chest out. He had all these guys behind him and he had to save face. We got into a verbal battle. I couldn't have gotten into a fight with him unless I was really angry and I wasn't angry. At the end, he actually backed down because he didn't have the confidence to test me.

From that moment on, something began to change. Over the course of the next few weeks, the guys in the gang began to hang around me more and more. I thought this was pretty cool. People were looking up to me. We rode around. We went out to the beach and got drunk. We didn't bother anybody. Just about all of us either worked or went to school and we would party at night or on the weekends. On the weekends, we partied pretty hard.

One night, all of us were having a good time, shooting the breeze and smoking marijuana at the Rec. Tom arrived with some of his gang and he was ready to challenge me. I didn't know what this man could do. I didn't know his background except that he had been to Vietnam. He came up to me and challenged me in front of everyone. He got right up in my face and said, "I hope you're not looking to move in on my turf. This is my neighborhood and these are my people. Find somewhere else to hang out."

He didn't even live in that neighborhood. I was raised there. Who was he to tell me that? When he finished, I said, "Tom, I'm going to say this one time and one time only-you are no longer the leader of the Wrecking Crew. That is my position and if you don't like it, we can have a discussion about it."

We looked at each other to see who was going to call whose bluff. As we stood face to face with everyone looking on, it was plain that we were in a poker game. If I was ever going to get rid of him, now was the time. I slowly started walking around the basketball court, mumbling to myself, taking off my jacket and dropping it to the ground as I walked. My voice got louder and louder. "I guess I have no choice. I'm going to have to stomp his ass right now. I hate to do it in front of everybody, but I guess I have to do it right now." I was talking and acting as if no one else was around. It must have worked, because I heard him tell some of the guys that I was crazy and they were crazy if they stayed with me. He got into his car and drove away.

Tom lost his authority and over the course of the next few weeks, and I actually became the leader of the Wrecking Crew. These people looked up to me. It probably went to my head a bit. My hair had gotten longer and I got a little wilder. We'd drive down to North Carolina and drink and smoke pot and party. We very seldom caused trouble for anyone else and never deliberately set out to hurt anyone. We weren't that kind of gang.

My reputation began to grow as tales of my exploits got out. One night I was driving down Virginia Beach Boulevard with Darlene in the front seat and two or three others in the back. A car with four guys pulled in front of me and cut me off. I was drinking and I didn't like that. I followed them to their house. Unfortunately, I was drinking liquor, which tended to make me more violent than if I was just drinking beer. They pulled into their driveway and I pulled in behind them, blocking them so they couldn't get out. I told everyone to sit tight and stay in the car. I got out and walked up to their car. The guy rolled down his window. I said, "What do you think you're doing? Who do you think you are? You cut me off." I went on and on. The guy starting arguing with me, so I told him to get out of the car. He did and we were ready to fight. The other three guys started to get out to help him. I turned around and told them in a very strong voice, "Don't get out of that car! If you do, I'm going to kick your ass! I'm going to hurt you! Don't get out of that car!"

The force in my voice must have made them believe me. We got into a fight in the guy's front yard and I beat him up and the other three sat there and watched it. I got back in my car and drove away.

The story that started circulating was that I had whipped four guys at one time. Stories do tend to get blown all out of proportion. Of course, I didn't say anything to dissuade or defuse any of it, but stories like that helped to build my reputation as a bad guy. Don't mess with Charles! The man is crazy! He'll whip up on you.

Of course, as with any such reputation, there are people who want to test it. Hardly a week went by when I wasn't confronted by somebody who wanted to topple the king of the mountain. No one was able to do it. My reputation grew each time. It didn't always involve getting into a fight. Sometimes it was just a matter of who would back down first. I actually believed that if I got mad, there was no one who could beat me. No one. I never lost.

22

One of the members in my gang sold a pound of marijuana to a guy in the Norview Aces, a tough motorcycle gang from the bad part of Norfolk that had been around for several decades. He got in trouble because he was accused of ripping this guy off. The Aces let us know that they wanted to set up a meeting time and place. That meant a fight, gang against gang, so we began to prepare. We picked the place, the Rec, and the time. Some of our guys had knives. I even brought knives from the butcher shop, nice big ten-inch ones. We had clubs, baseball bats, chains and homemade devices with nails in them. We had brass knuckles, shotguns, rifles and pistols. Guns were a new addition to our arsenal. Since we didn't have any of our own, we obtained them from our fathers, without their knowledge. We knew that we needed and edge over the Aces. Not knowing what they would bring, we wanted to be prepared.

They rode up on their motorcycles. Darlene was standing on the basketball court and their leader called out something to her. She didn't understand what he said, so she walked closer to him. He repeated, "Do you wanna be my motorcycle mama?"

"What?" she said.

"Hop on, you can be my mama."

"Suck off," she replied.

I walked over and said, "Oh man, you've done it now." We needed a spark to get things started and that did it. I said, "All right, let's rumble." So we did. People started fighting. We had a guy on the roof of the school with a rifle. He was our safety valve. If we were losing, he was going to open fire, not to shoot anyone, but to scare them, we hoped. Sticks were being pulled out and used to hit people, but no knives had been used yet. I had learned things from the Green Berets and the Rangers. I learned how to rip a person's throat out. I learned how to walk up behind someone and break his neck. I learned how to break a knee or an arm. I shared all this wonderful knowledge with my guys. The most important thing I had told them was that if you're not going to use a weapon, don't bluff because it will get taken away and used on you.

There were fist fights, sticks, clubs, bats and chains, but no knives or guns that I saw. One of the Aces spotted our guy on the roof and he went up there and actually threw him off the top of the school. Fortunately, it was only a one-story building. I shimmied up the drain pipe to the roof and came up behind the Aces guy who was watching the action below. He had our guy's rifle in his hand, an M-1. I was sneaking up behind him to throw him off and I got about five feet away from him when he heard me. He turned around and pointed the rifle at my chest, about two feet away and pulled the trigger. It didn't go off. We stood there frozen for what seemed like several minutes, but I'm sure it was just a couple of seconds. I was scared to death. Suddenly, I reacted and took the rifle from him and threw him off the roof. I pointed the gun up in the air and pulled the trigger and it fired.

All I can say is that God did not want me to die that night.

I slid back down the drain pipe. It broke and I fell about twenty feet. I heard sirens in the distance, getting closer. The Aces were hopping on their motorcycles and taking off. My guys were getting in their cars and I jumped into one of their cars and we sped away. Then I realized that my car was still there. I wasn't thinking. I just wanted to get away and I forgot about my car. I had no choice but to go back there. I knew that they would get the license plate number and find out whose car it was. There were some knives and a shotgun in my trunk. The gun wasn't mine, but I was storing it for someone else. We drove back to the Rec and police were everywhere. I walked through the parking lot to my car and started to unlock it. Of course, the police were right there and asked for some identification.

"Is this your car?" one officer asked.

"Yeah, what's going on?"

He began to tell me that there had been a gang war up here. I said, "No kidding. Goodness gracious. Wow, is my car hurt?" I started looking at my car, examining it for damage. He asked how long I had been here, how long my car had been there and where I had been. I made up a lie and told him that I had gone across the street to get something to eat at the Bermuda Inn, a bar and pool hall.

The officer shined his flashlight in the front seat. I knew that if he wanted to search the car, I was in trouble. He would find the shotgun in the trunk. He shined the light in the backseat and walked around to the trunk. I knew that he was going to stop at the trunk and ask me to open it. But he continued walking around the car and looked in the other side.

"Where do you live?" he asked.

"About five blocks that way."

"This is getting to be a rough place and if I were you, I wouldn't leave my car sitting around anywhere late at night."

"You're right, officer. I didn't know that."

"All right, you better get on out of here. Have a good evening."

I got in my car and went home. There were a lot of cuts and bruises among our guys and even a couple of broken bones, but fortunately, no one was shot or stabbed. I look back on that night now and realize that we all could have died. I had a rifle pointed right at me. The story of what had happened on the roof spread like wildfire. My legend began to grow even more.

Everybody in a gang has to have a nickname. Our gang didn't have names like Killer or Undertaker. My brother's nickname was Heehaw because he had big ears that stuck out. That would really strike fear into the hearts of rival gang members. Some of the nicknames were a bit manlier than that. After the rumble, one of the guys in my gang said that I reminded him of J.C. I said, "J.C.-what is that?" He said, "That's Jesus Christ." By then my hair was long and parted in the middle and I had a beard and I was thin. He said that I looked like the pictures of Jesus that you always see. From that time on, they called me J.C. I didn't think of it as blasphemous. It just added to my persona. I was getting swept up into my status and reputation.

23

Darlene and I had been dating and getting to know each other for a while, about six weeks. We were with a bunch of friends one night and the subject of school came up. I said, "You'll be graduating, right? This is your last year?"

"Oh no," she said, "I'm in the 10th grade."

"The 10th grade. How old are you?"

"Well, I turned fifteen in May."

Oh no, I thought. I had just assumed that she was a senior and seventeen or eighteen years old. I was on my way to twenty-one and she was fifteen. At that point, it didn't matter. There were six years between us, but we liked each other.

One night at the Rec, I saw a guy that I had known in junior high school, Eddie. We talked for a few minutes, talked a little about a fight we had gotten into back then. He had become a merchant marine and traveled all over the place. When he wasn't on board ship, he lived with his parents. After a while, he said that he had to go and he turned to Darlene and said, "I'll see you at home." She replied, "Okay."

I asked her what was going on and she told me that Eddie was her brother. Then it hit me. I remembered Darlene as a little girl of about four or five running around when I was over at Eddie's house. We had put her inside the oven one time just to see if she would fit. It seemed strange that I was now dating her.

◆　　　◆　　　◆

I was still in the meat business, working in a small downtown supermarket, learning all the tricks of the trade. When meat in the case reached its expiration date, we would pull it out, but we wouldn't throw it away like many places do today. Every morning, we'd check the dates of all the packages and look for anything that seemed like it had gone bad. We would take all the stuff into the back and open up the packages one at a time. For example, with a package of chicken, the first thing to do would be to open up the package and use the "smell test." If it didn't smell right, we went on to Phase Two. Only if it smelled really bad did it get thrown away. If it just smelled a little bit bad, we would put it in the sink with some salt water or some soda and water or vinegar and let it soak for a few minutes. Then we would wash it off, let it dry, wrap it up, reduce the price and put it back in the case for another two or three days.

With hamburger, you could always mix it with other things like blood or food coloring. There was also what we called "Jesus burger." When we pulled ground beef from the case that had turned dark, we didn't throw it away either, but mixed it with that morning's grindings then put it back in the case. Usually we had more old brown hamburger than we could put in one grinding so instead of throwing it out, we'd take it out of the package and put it in the lug. The lug was a container about ten inches deep, twenty-four inches long and fourteen inches wide. We would fill this up with outdated hamburger meat, pressing it down into the container. Then something heavy would be placed on top, something weighing about thirty pounds. This lug would be put inside another one so that the air couldn't get to it and the whole thing was placed in the cooler. We would let it sit there for three days. Over the course of three days, the gas in the meat would turn it red again. On the third day, we would bring it out, take the weight off and the meat would be just as red as fresh hamburger. This was Jesus burger, or resurrection burger, because it rose from the grave in three days, just like Jesus. We would put the meat out in the case and it would look really good for about four or five hours and then it would turn dark again. Usually about 25% of the Jesus burger that was bought would be returned, but overall we made money because most people either ate it or just threw it away.

The owner of the supermarket, a short guy about seventy years old, had a two-week ritual with one of the most well-established restaurants in the area. The restaurant had been in business for about thirty years. The meat at the market that was too bad-spare ribs, hot dogs, lunch meat, sausage-would be thrown into a box in the corner of the cooler. Every two weeks, the restaurant owner would come by and the super-market owner would come in and dump the contents of the box onto the meat block and they would haggle over the price. A box of about forty pounds of bad spare ribs and hot dogs, for example, would be sold for about ten dollars. Then the restaurant guy would put the box in his car and take it to his restaurant. I really didn't know what he did with the meat. I thought maybe he fed it to his dogs or something. One day I was making delivery to the restaurant the same day that he had picked up a box of bad meat. He had some of our spare ribs that were green and had a yellowish, thick slime on them. I watched a man in the kitchen scrubbing this stuff off the ribs with a brush. He was washing the hot dogs and cleaning the spare ribs and then it dawned on me that they were actually going to serve this stuff in the restaurant.

The first day that I was working at another store, the manager was getting ready to leave and told me to clean up. Every meat department is a little bit different in the way that they clean up. I asked the manager what he wanted me to do. Did he want me to pull out the meat blocks and clean behind them. He told me that he'd been there a year and hadn't ever done that, so I should just clean up the rest of the area. In those days, the meat blocks were wooden and this one was pushed up against the wall. Meat and blood gets down behind the block and I thought, well, if I'm going to clean up, then I'm going to clean behind the block. I thought it was disgusting that it hadn't been done in so long. I pulled the block away from the wall and the back of it was covered with maggots. It was gross. If I had eaten lunch, I would have lost it. I couldn't touch it. I pushed the block back against the wall, finished cleaning up and left. The next day, I told the manager about it and he said well, I'm going to have to do something about that. I was just fill-ing in at that store, so I don't know if he ever did anything or not.

I often volunteered to go to different stores to fill in when somebody was out. Lots of times they needed someone who was a self-starter because the person would be working alone. They needed someone who could just go in and stay until the job was done. I was good at what I did and I liked being in different places. One day I was going to a store where I hadn't been before and I got there a bit early. I didn't want to go in that early and I hadn't had breakfast yet, so I decided to find a McDonald's. It took me about fifteen minutes to eat breakfast and I returned to the store and parked far away, where the employees were supposed to park, locked my car and started walking towards the store. The closer I got, I realized that something wasn't right. It looked too empty. I got to the door and went in and all the employees-the manager, the produce guy, some cashiers and a couple of vendors-were handcuffed to each other. Just then, all hell broke loose. There were sirens and police cars and fire trucks started pouring into the parking lot. I was just standing there, not knowing what to do. In the time that I had left to go get something to eat, three men had come in with shot-guns, robbed the store and handcuffed everyone. Apparently, someone had been able to get to the alarm after the robbers left. About fifteen policemen came rushing through the door and then it dawned on me that I was the only one standing and not handcuffed and I had three big knives in my hand. They were wrapped in paper, but the ends were sticking out. From the policemen's perspective, I must be the robber. They grabbed me and threw me down on my stomach. I dropped the knives. They put their knees in my back, twisted my arms behind me and handcuffed me. The whole time I was screaming, "I work here! You've got the wrong guy!" Everyone was screaming. There was so much noise that the police weren't listening to me. Finally, after I was secured, they listened to the other people who were telling them that I worked there. They didn't know me because I was just filling in, but they realized who I was. I was lucky that I didn't just get blown away.

◆   ◆   ◆

Around the beginning of 1974, I bought Darlene a ring. I was twenty-two, she was almost seventeen and we had been going together for about a year and a half. I took her to the beach and we walked in the moonlight. It was a little cold, but it was a beautiful night. We sat on the beach and I asked Darlene to marry me. She got rather quiet and she seemed upset. She said no. I was stunned. It felt like I had offended her in some way. I thought we were in love with each other. After a few minutes, we got up and walked back to the car. We were driving home in silence and I said, "Well, what's wrong? What did I do? What did I say? I just asked you to marry me. I didn't know it would make you mad." She was silent. She didn't say anything until we pulled into the Rec center.

"If you ask me to marry you," she said, "then that means if I say yes, then we are engaged."

"Well, I think that's usually how it works. I've never done this before, but I think that's what they call it."

"That means I have to go to bed with you."

"What?"

"That means I have to sleep with you."

"Well, I would hope so. If you marry somebody, yeah, you sleep with that person."

"Oh no," she said, "I'm not talking about after we get married. I'm talking about now. An older guy I knew said that when a man asks a girl to marry him and she says yes, then it's understood that they are going to sleep together during the engagement."

"No," I said, "That doesn't mean that you have to sleep with me. That guy was lying to you. He was conning you or something. That's not true. Even if it was true, that doesn't mean we have to."

"Okay, well, yes."

"Yes what?"

"Yes, I'd love to marry you. Yes! As long as I don't have to sleep with you right now. I want to, but not until we are married."

And so Darlene had accepted my proposal. We began to spend more and more time alone together. Our friends began to notice and make comments because we were separating ourselves from the rest of the group and they didn't like it much. We would go driving around and to the beach a lot. Sometimes we'd build a fire and lie on the beach and talk. We'd go to the airport and watch the planes take off and land. We'd walk. It didn't matter if it was freezing or 100 degrees. We'd go out towards Sandbridge, park the car and walk down the back roads. We'd walk for miles in the middle of the night, in the pitch blackness. There wasn't anything out there except woods, swamp and a little country road. We had a wonderful time and got to know each other much more. We talked about our dreams. We planned for the future.

I bought her flowers and candy. Once, I bought her a stuffed St. Bernard that must have been four feet tall. She got to know another side of me that no one else ever saw, a side I didn't realize that I even had. I didn't feel right when we weren't together. She was my first real love and I was hers.

Her mother did everything she could to persuade Darlene not to see me. She told her that I was just out of the army and only after one thing. That really made me angry because it wasn't true. I did try things with Darlene, but she kept me in my place. She was gentle, but at the same time, very strong. I had never met a person like her. How could someone be so strong, yet have a heart as big and soft as hers. I found that amazing.

She never drank or smoked marijuana until I came along. She would have eventually with someone else, but, unfortunately, I was the one who started it. Even though she was the teenager and I was the grown man, I never thought of myself as being a grown-up. I wasn't a grown man in any real sense of the word. To me, a grown man was someone who took responsibility for his actions, worked a nine-to-five job and respected authority, none of which I did. I still thought of myself as a teenager, meaning that I was expected to push the boundaries and be rebellious. In my eyes a man would have matured beyond this. I was still making up for the three years that I thought I had wasted in the army.

I never thought I'd live past the age of thirty-three. At twenty-two, that sounds like a long way off, almost middle-aged. Perhaps that's one reason that I lived the way I did. There was something missing or something wrong. No matter what I did or tried, I always knew that it was temporary because it never was "it." I could never put my finger on what "it" was, except that I knew there was an empty spot in my soul, a hole. I tried to fill it with all sorts of things in my search for "it," but nothing worked. No matter what I did, the hole was still there.

Darlene was in her last year of high school and I gave her a ride whenever I could. One morning as I was dropping her off, I saw several guys that I knew and we started talking. They had several pints of liquor. There was one guy with them who lived in my neighborhood, but whom I didn't know. He was really trying to fit in with the group, with the gang.

It was about 9 a.m. and one of the others challenged this new guy on a dare to drink a pint of liquor as fast as he could. They were talking about who could drink the fastest, and he claimed that he could. They gave him a pint of Bacardi's Rum 151 proof. He broke the seal, took the top off and downed the whole thing probably within two minutes. I told them they were crazy and I got in my car and left. Probably about two hours later, the same guys rode by me and flagged me down. The boy who had drunk the pint was passed out and they wanted to know what to do with him. They had tried for an hour to wake him up. They knew that I'd been a medic and thought I might have some ideas. I told them that he'd probably be passed out all day long. They were scared and wanted me to come look at him, so I agreed.

He was in the back of a pick-up truck near the school. He was clammy. I still thought that he was just passed out and would eventually wake up, but I didn't think that we should take any chances. I told them that we should take him to a doctor. They wanted to take him home instead and let his parents deal with the situation, so we drove to his house and knocked on the door. His father answered and they told him what had happened. The father was extremely angry. He went to the truck, lowered the gate, grabbed him by his feet and pulled him out of the truck as fast and hard as he could. The kid's back and head slammed down on the road. He dragged him to the garage, raised the garage door, threw him inside and closed the door. All the while, he was cursing and yelling, "You lie in there and sleep it off, you so and so." He told us to get the hell out. That really ticked me off. It wasn't any of my business, but I was upset about it. That was his son. We left, but I thought and thought about the boy. What if he had alcohol poisoning? He could very easily lie on that garage floor and die. I called the rescue squad and had them come to the house. I figured I had done my duty and I didn't think much more about it. The next day, I found out that the guy was in the hospital. He did have alcohol poisoning. His system had gone into shock and he was dying. If I hadn't called the rescue squad, he would have died.

24

I continued what some of my neighbors would have called my "reign of terror" in the neighborhood. It was my neighborhood and I owned it lock, stock and barrel, and nothing was done without my knowledge or consent. A lot of the adults obviously didn't like me at all. The speed limit in the area was twenty-five mph, but there were a lot of long straight roads and sometimes we would speed down them. There was one man, probably about sixty years old, who would scream at us from his porch and call the police when we sped by.

One evening, three or four of us were walking down the road near his house. He was retired and made picnic tables as a hobby and to earn some extra money. He had three different kinds in his front yard with "for sale" signs on them. As we walked by his house, I said to the others, "You know what? Couldn't we use some picnic tables?" Of course, they agreed. We went into his yard and I picked up one of the tables and put it on my back. Two of the others did the same thing. We walked down the road with them and gave them away to people. I'm sure that the man knew who had taken his tables, though there was no way to prove it. He built some more and put them out in the yard, but this time he chained them to the ground. It was like a dare to come and get them. One night we went back to his house and took those tables as well, chains and all. He never put anymore out. Naturally, he hated us even more. It was childish, stupid behavior, the kind that didn't tend to endear me to adults.

One night, it got even more dangerous. I was out by myself, coming home late, drunk. I was going seventy mph in a twenty-five mph zone. It was one or two in the morning. I took my eyes off the road for just a second. When I looked again, I was heading for a parked car. There was nothing I could do. I plowed into the back of the car. I didn't even have time to hit the brakes. The only thing I remember is the sound. I wasn't wearing a seatbelt-I never did in those days. The next thing I remember was getting out of the car. I didn't have a scratch on me. Both cars were totaled. My front end and the other car's back end were gone. The noise of the crash must have waked up the car's owner. I saw someone looking out the window of the house and thought that I'd better get out of there. Amazingly, my car started and I screeched the three blocks home, water and steam flying everywhere. The hood was completely gone. It was a mess. The engine was not in its proper place. I don't know how I was able to drive it at all. I rolled up in front of my house, cut it off and went inside to bed.

About two hours later, the light in my bedroom came on and I woke up, still half drunk and found two policemen standing in my room. I could hear my mother and father in the living room. One of the police-men said, "Get up son and get your clothes on."

I said, "What are you doing in my bedroom?"

"Is that your car out front?" I said that it was. "What happened tonight?" he asked me.

I said, "Not a thing."

"Your car is totaled."

"What? It is?"

"Get up and get your clothes on. You're under arrest."

"I'll get up as soon as you get out of the room so I can get my clothes on," I replied.

"We're not leaving the room. Get up and get your clothes on!" This went back and forth for a couple of minutes and then my father walked into the room. "Get your ass out of bed now!" he said.

"Yes sir," I said and I got up, put my clothes on and went down to the station with the officers where they arrested me for drunk driving, speeding, reckless driving and hit and run. My parents followed and bailed me out.

My mother had some connections and knew one of the most suc-cessful lawyers in town who was also one of the biggest crooks. She retained him to defend me. I went to his office and he told me right away that he was doing this for my mother, not for me. I didn't care why he was doing it, just as long as he did it. I started to tell him what happened, but he put up his hand and stopped me. "Let me put it this way," he said. "You want to keep your license and you don't want to go to jail. Is that correct?" Of course, I agreed that it was. He said that was all he needed to know and I didn't see him again until we went to court.

In court, they read the charges against me, the lawyer said a few words and the judge looked down and said, "Well, drunk driving, we can't really prove that because he wasn't driving so I'm going to dismiss that. Speeding, no one was there. We don't know how fast he was going. I'm going to dismiss the speeding. The reckless driving, well, we're going to have to do something about that. I'm going to drop the charge to improper driving. I'm going to suspend your license for sixty days and I'm going to suspend those sixty days of suspension. Ten days in jail. Did you spend any time in jail?"

My lawyer told him that I had been arrested and taken in. The judge continued, "Well, I'll suspend that with time served."

I walked out of that courtroom unscathed, with my license, and that was a terrible thing. It was another time that I got away with something, beating the system, and it didn't discourage me from doing the things that I was doing. I had always been able to get out of things in some way. This was just further evidence that the system was corrupt. I knew that I should never have been allowed to drive again, but because the judge and the lawyer were fishing buddies, I got off. It was well-known that if you had the cash, you had it made with this lawyer and this judge.

I went out and bought another car. I hadn't finished paying for the one that was wrecked and in fact, I was also still paying for the one that I had wrecked before that. At one point, I was paying for three cars and didn't even have one. It was costing me a lot of money, but that didn't make me more careful.

The third car I was paying for was totaled at Sandbridge. There was a hairpin curve and we used to see how fast we could take the turn. In the car, there would be the driver, of course, and a passenger to check the speedometer to make sure the guy was honest. We would start out at forty to forty-five mph. It was pretty hard to go around that curve at fifty and that was pretty much the top speed. Going at that speed meant taking a big risk. On each side of the road was a ditch and a swamp.

Of course, I had to win. Several people had made it at fifty, so I thought, gee, I'm going to have to make it at sixty mph. That was the number that I had in my mind. Darlene wanted to ride with me. I didn't want her to. She tried to talk me out of doing this stupid crazy thing. I wouldn't listen, so she said that she was going with me, and I finally agreed. We took off and were building up speed. I was heading into the curve at sixty mph and Darlene panicked. She didn't think we were going to make it. She grabbed the steering wheel and turned it just before we entered the curve. The car went sideways and we slid across the road, hit the ditch and flipped several times into the swamp. Darlene was thrown into me and I grabbed her and held onto her as we rolled over and over.

We stopped and I released her. She was okay except for being angry and scared to death. I had a few scratches and knots on my head. The swamp was mushy and soft, so that helped. Again, the car was totaled. Once again, I walked away unhurt and ignored the warning that the life I was leading was dangerous. The difference now was that I was including others in my recklessness. My life seemed to be a machine in perpetual motion. The more reckless I became, the more people looked up to me and the more encouraged I was to find new and more dangerous activities.

Relationships in the gang were getting more and more strained. There was a lot of animosity and resentment that Darlene and I were spending more time away from the rest of the group. I don't know why they felt that way. Maybe it seemed that by separating ourselves, we were indicating that we were too good to be with them. They told us that they didn't like it. I replied that I was the boss and if there was something they wanted to do about that, they should just let me know and we would talk about it. Of course, talking was not what I had in mind.

Not too long after that, I was driving down the road alone with my window open, probably singing along to the radio. The passenger side window was up. Suddenly, I heard a loud pop and before I could even react, I felt something pass right in front of my face. I looked to my right and there was a hole in the window. Someone had shot at me and the bullet had gone by my head and through the other window. I swear that I could feel the wind from the bullet, that's how close it was. It was about nose-high where it hit the window. Another inch back and it would have hit me in the temple. I stopped and went back, but I couldn't find anybody or anything, and I still don't know who shot at me. It may have been a member of my own gang. Once again, I had narrowly escaped death.

I began to vary my schedule. I made sure that I didn't fall into a set pattern of coming and going. It was just like in Hawaii; I was constantly watching over my shoulder. That old fear was back once again. I began to think of myself as Wild Bill Hickok who always sat with his back against the wall so that no one could sneak up behind him. I was always checking my side and rearview mirrors, always looking around and under the car. It became natural to live like that.

Things continued to fall apart in the gang. They became more adamant about Darlene and me spending more time with them. They began not to listen to me, to plan and do things on their own without consulting me. I was losing control and I didn't like it. One day, four of us were riding around and we stopped to get something to eat at Arby's. When I came back out with my food, a guy named Jody was sitting in the front passenger seat, where I had been sitting. I said, "In the back, in the back."

He said, "No, you've been in the front. I'm going to ride in the front. You get in the back."

He couldn't tell me to do that. Three or four months earlier, no one would have dreamed of sitting in my seat. If that's where I had been, that where I was going to be when I came back. I said, "Get out of my seat. Get in the back!"

"No, man, I'm not getting out. You get in the back. I rode back there long enough."

I knew what this was. It was a power play. Two other guys were sitting there watching this. I was losing face. I knew that I was losing control over these people and that they didn't respect me as much as they once had, so I couldn't let this go.

"Jody, get out of the car right now. If you don't get out, I'm going to take you out."

He didn't budge. "Well, you'll have to get me out. I'm not moving."

I reached in, grabbed him, pulled him out of the car and threw him down on the asphalt of the parking lot. "Get out of here," I told him, "I don't even want to see you. Just go."

"How am I getting back home?"

"I don't care what you do."

He started walking and got about halfway down the side of the restaurant when I called out, "Whoa, wait a minute. Come on back. Come on. I'll let you sit in the front seat." I had made my point and now I could let him sit in the front, as long as it was my idea.

He was not buying it. "No, man, I'm not coming back."

"Jody, come on!"

"No!" He kept walking.

"I said for you to get back here now!" I reached into the backseat and pulled out a rifle. I leaned over the top of the car and called his name again. He turned around and saw the .22 in my hand. I said, "If you don't turn around and get back in this car right now, I'm going to shoot you."

He obviously didn't believe me. "You'll just have to shoot me because I'm not coming back." He turned around and started walking again.

"Jody, I'm serious. I will shoot you." I really thought he would come back then, but he didn't. He was nearing the corner of the building and I had to make a decision. I was thinking that this was a show of my authority and power. I had told him what I was going to do and he was calling my bluff and I felt that I had no other option but to follow through. So I shot him. I shot him in the arm. I was actually aiming for the side of the building, but I was a little off. He took off. I guess he thought I was really going to kill him then. I got in the car and the other guys said, "What are we going to do?"

I replied, "We aren't going to do anything. Come on, let's go."

They dropped me off at my parents' house sometime later. After I'd been home a while, the phone rang and my dad answered. It was Jody's father. My dad came to me and said, "Boy, are you crazy? Have you lost your mind, Charles?"

"What, what?" I asked.

"Jody's father just called me and he claims that you shot Jody."

"Yeah, but only in the arm. He's all right."

"You shot him in the arm. You could have killed him!"

"I could have killed him, but I wasn't aiming at him."

"So you accidentally shot him."

"Well, yeah."

"Then you could have accidentally killed him."

"Yeah, but I didn't."

"Charles, is something wrong with you? Why did you do that?"

"Basically because he dared me. I told him if he didn't get back in the car, I was going to do it. He called my bluff. I didn't have any other choice but to do it."

My father was speechless. He turned around and walked away and didn't speak to me for a couple of weeks. Again, as was my father's way, it wasn't what he said or did, but the lack of communication or emotion that conveyed to me what he thought of me. Because he didn't tell me how he felt, again I was left to guess and my guess was that he thought I was unstable.

I didn't see Jody for the next several days, but when I did, he was, at first, a bit standoffish, though I can't imagine why. After a couple of six-packs, he apologized and all was well with the world. Ironically, I didn't feel bad for Jody nor did I feel bad for myself. I felt bad for my father. Again, I had disappointed him.

One night, my brother-in-law and I were out hitting the bars. At one place, we were shooting pool, playing teams for a dollar a game. My brother-in-law was very, very good. We won several games and got our money, which was enough to buy beer. After we played our fourth game, we were sitting at the bar and he said, "You know what? I don't think they gave us the money for that last game." I agreed with him that they hadn't. He had probably never been in a fight in his life and wasn't going to start now, but he wanted me to go get the money. I got off my barstool and went around to the short end of the L-shaped bar where the two guys were sitting. I walked up and tapped one of them on the shoulder. I had to reach up, as he was a pretty good size boy. He turned around and I said, "I don't think you paid us for that last game. You owe us a dollar. That would be a dollar apiece."

He turned back around and continued talking. I tapped him a little harder and he turned around and said, "What?"

"I believe you owe us for that last game. You owe me a dollar."

"I don't owe you anything." He turned back around and I tapped him on the shoulder again. He looked at me and said, "What?"

"Did you pay me that dollar?"

"No, I didn't and I'm not going to pay you that dollar."

He turned around again. Well, we couldn't have this. I reached out with my left hand and I grabbed him and swung him around. He came around and caught me on the chin with a full bottle of beer, shattering the bottle. I was knocked back about two steps. Then I let loose. Fists were flying. We were pulled apart and I was told that I would have to leave. Before I left, I said, "You still owe me that dollar." We went at it again. They broke us up again and my brother-in-law and I were kicked out.

We got into the car and I realized that my mouth was bleeding. As fast as I could spit it out the window, my mouth would fill up with blood. My brother-in-law suggested that we might need to go to a doctor, but I said I was fine. Spit. Spit. I was steadily spitting blood out for probably fifteen miles. I finally stopped bleeding about five miles from home.

When we got home, I went inside and looked in the mirror. He had really messed me up. My mouth wasn't working very well. My lip and gum were busted-that's where all the blood was coming from. I knew it was going to be really sore in the morning. I cleaned myself up a little bit and then got my .22 semi-automatic rifle and drove back to the bar. I went there not to kill the guy, but to scare him. I didn't plan to use the rifle. I wanted to get him outside and beat his ass. I had only brought the rifle in case he had a bunch of buddies and I needed and equalizer. Fortunately for me, the bar was closed and everyone had gone home. I got back in the car and drove home. I have thought about that night a lot through the years. If I had gotten there before the bar closed, I could have very easily done something stupid, accidental or not and spent the rest of my life in jail. That really frightened me and from that moment on, I began to think in a slightly different way, though my wild life was not over yet.

The next morning there was blood on my pillow and could hardly move my mouth at all. I fixed some eggs, something soft, but I couldn't even chew scrambled eggs and so I had nothing to eat that day. The next day, I thought it felt a little better. It seemed that I could move it a little bit more and I could talk better. So I thought that maybe it was fractured a bit, but it would continue to get better. The third day, it was about the same. By that afternoon, I was close to passing out. I hadn't had anything to eat in three days, actually closer to four because I hadn't eaten anything the night I was drinking. I was feeling very woozy. I went to the emergency room and the doctor examined me and said he would take some x-rays. I asked if he thought it was broken. He laughed and said, "I know it's broken. I just need the x-ray to tell me in how many places."

It turned out that my jaw was broken on both sides up near my ears, and my chin was split in half. I had been like that for three days. The doctor told me that he was going to admit me to the hospital, but they couldn't operate until they got some fluid into me and built me back up.

I was very weak. They made me drink a lot and gave me an I.V. After they had pumped me full of nutrients, surgery was scheduled. The surgery took six and a half hours. They pulled back the skin, and they had to wire my jaw back together again. They had to put braces in my mouth because all of my bottom teeth were about to fall out. If this had happened years before, they would have automatically just taken all of my teeth out.

I never took a pain pill, not even after the surgery. I was in the hospital for a week. My mouth was wired shut for ten weeks. I lost forty pounds, back down to one hundred thirty-five, which was exactly what I weighed when I went into the army at seventeen. I drank a lot of milkshakes during that ten weeks. Everything had to be liquefied. I didn't drink any alcohol during that time, which was good.

25

I didn't really have friends because I didn't trust anyone. There was one of the gang members whom I thought of as the closest thing to a friend that I had. Steve was a big guy, about six-foot five. He was married. I was over at his house one day when his wife was working and he told me that he was having an affair with a girl at work. I told him that it was a stupid thing to do. We had done a lot of stupid things, but he just couldn't do this. He said that he should never have gotten married and he didn't want to be married to her anymore. He wanted me to do him a favor. "You know I will if I can because we've always stuck together. What do you want me to do?"

"I want you to take Debbie out." Debbie was his wife.

I said, "What do you mean? Take her shopping?"

"No, I want you to take her out on a date."

I thought he was crazy and told him so. I don't know why he thought that she would go out with me, or anybody for that matter. This was a scheme to ease his conscience because he was cheating on her. If he could get her to do the same, then that would make it even. I told him that there was no way I could do that. He wasn't happy and became more distant after that.

Some time later, I went over to his house and he wasn't home. I came inside and was talking to his wife, mainly talking about him. He came in pretty drunk, said a few things and then went to bed, and Debbie and I sat there and talked for a couple of hours. Steve got up and came into the living room and started accusing us of talking about him behind his back.

"Steve, man, nobody's talking about you. Nobody's planning anything behind your back." He continued to insist that he had heard us talking about him. "Sure, you came up in the conversation, but we weren't talking about you per se." He started yelling for me to get out of his house. I told him that there was no reason for him to raise his voice at me.

"It's my house," he said, "and I'm telling you to get out."

"I'm telling you not to raise your voice at me. If you want me to leave, I'll leave, but you're not going to throw me out. I don't care whose house it is. You've got to remember who you're talking to."

He got indignant and threatened again to throw me out. He went into the kitchen that was not far from the front door and Debbie told me that I'd better leave. I went to the front door and had it open when he turned around and said, "Yeah, you better get your ass out."

I slammed the door shut and said, "All right, smart guy, now you throw me out." I walked into the kitchen. Remember that this guy was over six feet tall, weighed about two hundred and sixty pounds, and was younger than I was. I had taught this guy how to fight. He had come to me a year before asking me to show him how to fight because he was big, but clumsy. I gave him pointers and taught him the main rules of fighting, which are to do as much damage to the other person as you can while having the least amount of damage done to you, and to do it as fast as you can. The longer it goes on, the more likely it is that you'll get hurt.

The best thing that I could do in this situation was to hold on to the guy. We tore up the kitchen table and chairs. We knocked over the refrigerator. Appliances went everywhere. We ended up on the floor. I held on long enough to whip him and then he got up and left. Instead of him throwing me out of his house, I had, in effect, thrown him out.

This incident hurt me a great deal. That was the end of our friendship and I never talked to or saw Steve or Debbie again. Steve was the closest thing that I had to a friend who I could depend on and trust, and he betrayed me like the rest.

◆   ◆   ◆

I was looking ahead to 1975 and Darlene and I were making our wedding plans. Another member of our gang got married and his wife wouldn't let him have anything to do with any of us. Another one took over his father's business and moved on. Two others became alcoholics and one became a drug addict. The rest just kind of disappeared. By 1975, the gang was pretty much finished and we didn't want to see or talk to each other. Even if we ran into each other once in a while, we barely even gave any recognition that we knew each other. It happened rather quickly and I attributed it to the fact that we were growing up. We finally realized that we couldn't go on living as we had been.

One Saturday morning, I got a phone call at work from one of Darlene's relatives. Darlene's mother was an alcoholic and had peptic ulcers. On Friday night, she called the doctor at home and told him she was hurting. He actually told her to take two aspirin and come see him on Monday. Even I knew that you didn't prescribe aspirin to someone with peptic ulcers. I don't know whether she took them or not. When Darlene got up that Saturday morning, her mother wasn't up, which wasn't unusual. By ten, her father had gone to work and her mother still wasn't up. Darlene went up to her mother's room and found her dead.

After her mother's death, Darlene and I became even closer. She was the youngest child in her family and the only one still living at home. Her father was an alcoholic and couldn't handle himself after his wife died. He was of no support to Darlene. She and I spent more and more time together and I think that it was during that time that we really began to understand each other.

We began to talk about setting a wedding date. We decided it would be in the spring of 1975, just a few short months away. I felt like a terrible two-year period of my life was coming to an end, not only for me, but for my parents, who I put through hell, and of course for Darlene, who had just lost her mother.

Darlene and I told my mother that we were getting married and had set a date. I had brought home only a few girls over the years and my mother hadn't liked any of them. She had seemed to like Darlene, but she didn't like the idea of us getting married. I think that she objected more to Darlene's family than to Darlene herself. In my mother's eyes, her family wasn't good enough. She told me that if I married her, I'd be marrying her family also. We had a big disagreement about it and she was very concerned.

Darlene turned eighteen in May and we got married in June. She bought a new dress and I bought a new suit and we got the license and got married by a justice of the peace. My mother was very helpful. She helped us find a place to rent that we could afford, a nice little house. Our honeymoon consisted of spending three days at the beach.

We stayed at a Ramada Inn about fifteen miles from the beach because it was cheaper. It was actually only about two miles from where we were going to live. It wasn't much of a honeymoon trip, but I was twenty-three and my wife was eighteen. She was the first person I had been with. We didn't leave the room for three days and nights.

◆   ◆   ◆

I had pretty much settled into being a meat cutter and it seemed like it would be my life's work. The only other thing that interested me was being a singer and a songwriter, but I thought that was just a fantasy. I had gone to my supervisor and told him the date of my wedding and that I needed to take off the first week in June. He didn't want to let me because it was the first of the month, which was very busy because of food stamps and Navy payday. He wouldn't let me go and I told him that I wouldn't be there. He said, "Fine, if you're not here, then don't come back." And that's how we left it, so I thought that I was starting my married life with no employment. Darlene didn't have a job and we had no plans for her to work.

We cut the honeymoon to three days so that I could be back at work on Monday. I thought that I was bending a little bit by only being gone for three days and he should bend too. Monday morning, I walked right into the grocery store. I went over to the time cards and mine was there for the week. I punched in and went back to the meat department, where I put on my nice, white starched coat and apron, got my knives out and started to work. I went at it like nothing had ever happened. The assistant manager said, "Charles, I thought someone told me you quit or were fired." I said, "Well, I'm here, aren't I?"

I worked all morning and then my supervisor walked by the window. He saw me and motioned for me to come out. I did and he asked me what I was doing. I said that I was working.

"I thought I told you that if you were gone for the weekend, you shouldn't come back."

"Yeah, that's what you said."

"So you came back? Did you punch in?"

"Yeah."

"Where did you get a card?"

"It was in the rack."

"Well, go on back to work. I'll talk to you later." I went back to work and he never said another word about it. When you're good, you're good.

While I resumed my working life, Darlene started fixing up our house. My mother was very generous, but she is a person who doesn't do anything without a string attached. I didn't realize that at the time. She knew that we needed a refrigerator and she had three of them-one in the kitchen, one in the pantry and one in the garage. She told me that we didn't need to go out and buy a refrigerator. She would give us one of hers. I thanked her and told her how much I appreciated this. Then she added, "I'm going to give it to you, but now this is just between you and me-if anything should ever happen, if you get divorced or separated, I want the refrigerator back."

I was confused. "Mom, wait a minute. Are you giving me the refrigerator or are you not giving me the refrigerator?"

"Oh yes, I want you to have it. I don't want it back. I'm just saying if something should happen."

That's the way my mother was. We got the refrigerator. We set up housekeeping and were really enjoying our domestic life together.

Then Darlene was pregnant. Our honeymoon was actually not the first time that we had been to bed together. We had set the wedding date for June, but we actually slept together on Valentine's Day for the first time, and she got pregnant. We hadn't planned it, of course, but we knew that we wanted children and we were happy about it. We talked about moving the wedding date up because Darlene didn't want people to know she was pregnant before we got married and didn't want them to think that was the only reason we got married. We decided to stick with the June date. I didn't care what people thought and anyway, people who knew us knew that we had been together and engaged for a long time.

A short while later, I left my job at the grocery store and started working at a packing house where I would be paid more. I was working six days a week instead of five, but I was getting a lot more money. I had pretty much quit drinking heavily by that time. I was really getting into being a husband and father, and it felt good. It also felt good not to look over my shoulder all the time, worrying that someone was going to shoot or stab me or run over me. It felt good not having the police coming after me. Life was calm and quiet. Life was good.

I wasn't, however, a very good husband during Darlene's pregnancy. I left for work at six in the morning and I got off at five or six in the afternoon. After work, I'd stop off with a few of the guys and drink beer and shoot pool. I'd call her up and tell her where I was and that we were going to shoot a couple of games and I'd be home for dinner.

Of course, dinner was ready and she was sitting home alone waiting for me.

A game or two usually turned into four or five and lots of times instead of being home between 7 and 7:30 like I had told Darlene, it was more like 9:30. That happened several days out of every week, and although she never said anything about it, I knew it bothered her. She began to feel like a prisoner in our home. Fat. Pregnant. Ugly. Alone. Her friends had been the gang members and they were gone. There were a few people around that she talked to, but compared to what she had been used to, her pregnancy was a time of isolation. She did a lot of thinking.

Darlene came to the realization that she was eighteen years old and had a lot of living to do before she really settled down. I had no idea that she was feeling this way. For me, it was the opposite. I had already done all the other stuff and it was time for me to give it up. I was ready for the picket fence, the cat, the dog and the 2.5 children. As I was getting into the domestic life, Darlene was thinking, oh no, I'm not ready for this yet.

I was over at my parents' house one day and my mother asked when the baby was due. I told her November.

"Well, wait a minute now," she said, "You all were just married in June."

I said, "Yes."

"Well, that would only be six months before the baby is born."

"And your point is?"

"Oh nothing, nothing."

But she wasn't ready to leave it alone. She said to me, "Well, why don't you sell me the baby?"

"Pardon me?"

"When she has the baby, why don't you give the baby to me and I'll give you $1,500. You could use some money. Besides, you could have plenty of kids."

I couldn't believe what I was hearing. She wanted to buy the baby. I said no and that was the end of the discussion. When I told Darlene about it, she was, understandably, quite upset.

One Sunday afternoon in November, I was watching TV and Darlene was in the kitchen. She came in to where I was and said, "Okay, it's time." We rushed to the hospital. The doctor had told her that it was probably going to be a boy. I was in the waiting room and he told me that he had delivered nothing but boys for the last six days and he was pretty sure our child was going to be another boy.

I was in the waiting room until about 6:00 when the doctor came and got me and took me to Darlene. She was still in labor and having a hard time. All around us, we could hear the other women in labor, crying, screaming, yelling. After I had spent a few minutes with Darlene, the doctor took me into an empty room and told me to have a seat. He said that there wasn't really anything I could do right then. There was a football game on TV in the room. I watched it for a little while, but I could still hear the voices of all the women in labor and I couldn't stand it in there any longer. They wouldn't let me back in with my wife, where I wanted to be, so I went back to the waiting room and waited there all night long.

At about eight the next morning, a nurse came out and said, "Mr. Cross? Can we help you?" I told her that I was still waiting for someone to come tell me that my baby had been born. She said that the baby had come at about 8:00 last night, an hour or so after I left the room. I asked to see Darlene and the baby right away.

Darlene was sleeping and I didn't want to wake her. I went to see the baby, a little girl. I didn't mind a bit that we didn't have a boy. We had talked about names. If we had a boy, we were going to call him Christopher. We had several names in mind for a girl. It was the 1970s and we had thought of flowery, hippie names like Cinnamon, Wendy and Moon. Nobody liked those names. Darlene liked Wendy, but I already had a niece named Wendy, so we decided to call her Misty.

Misty was a beautiful baby. Before she was born, I had prayed, "God, it doesn't matter if it's a boy or a girl, just please do not let that child come out looking like me." I was still a little bit paranoid because in my opinion, all babies look pretty much alike when they're born. I know that mothers always think their own babies are beautiful, but you never know how they're going to turn out. My mother told me once, in front of a lot of people, "When Charles was born, he was the ugliest baby I had ever seen in my life." They had used forceps on me and my head was out of shape and they had bruised me and I had a black eye. I thought, man, I must have been one ugly kid for my own mother to have said that! Mainly, I didn't want Misty to inherit my red hair. Red-headed kids get called all kinds of names at school and I didn't think that people with red hair were attractive. I was relieved that she had dark brown hair and looked just like her mother.

Misty had colic the first few weeks that she was home from the hospital, but she was a very well-behaved infant and didn't cry much. For parents like Darlene and me, young people just starting out who didn't know much about raising children, she was the perfect child. I remember the three of us lying in bed, Misty sleeping between us. We talked a lot. Those were good times. I was working and making good money. We were getting ready to move to a bigger, nicer place. Everything seemed to be looking up.

My mother wanted, of course, to be around her granddaughter as much as possible and she was always trying to buy us gifts. Everything, though, was at a price. She began to give some of her motherly wisdom to Darlene. She had raised four children of her own-my two older sisters, my brother and myself-and she knew how to be a mother. Darlene ended up feeling like she was young and stupid and wasn't doing anything right in my mother's eyes. They got into clashes over little things. They never yelled at each other, but sharp words were often exchanged. Darlene told me that this was our child and she knew that we would make mistakes, but we would raise our child in our way.

Darlene started wanting to go out at night more and more. Even though we had the added responsibility and cost of a child, she wanted to get a baby-sitter and go out, every night if she could. By the time I got home from work, she'd be sitting there ready to go. At first, I went and we were doing what we had always done-drinking, riding around, going over to people's houses. I was six years older than Darlene and I was thinking that we really needed to settle down. We were a family now. I remember her telling me, "I'm eighteen and I'm not ready to settle down." I wasn't sure how to respond to that and so I just let it drop. We always got along so well and even as hard-headed and strong-willed as we both were, we never really argued. This time, however, it got to the point where I had to put my foot down and say, "We're not going out." She said that she was going whether I was or not. We talked about it and made a compromise. We couldn't always rely on my family and Misty was too small to leave with a baby-sitter, so I told her that if she wanted to go out a couple of nights a week with her girl-friends, I'd stay home with the baby.

That's what we did for a while. We would go out together on the weekends and one or two nights during the week, she would go out with her friends. I knew that she was home all day long by herself and really needed to get out. I was glad that we had worked something out.

One or two nights a week soon became three or four nights. We only had one car and it got to the point where she was at the door when I got home, told me the baby was in bed, kissed me good-bye and she was gone. Whenever I asked her what they did, she just said, "Regular stuff. Rode around, went to someone's house."

◆   ◆   ◆

I had begun to have dizzy spells. I thought that it was from the unhealthy lifestyle that I had been living, especially the excessive drinking. There were times that my heart would race and my hands would sweat. Once at work I thought I was going to die and they had to call an ambulance for me. By the time I got to the hospital, my heart had calmed down. They did an EKG, but couldn't find anything wrong. They just told me to come back if it happened again.

It got worse. I had pretty much quit drinking, but I was smoking. Once I was driving down the highway and thought I was going to pass out. I pulled into a doctor's office and went in. The receptionist asked all sorts of questions and said that they might be able to work me in. I felt like I was dying, so I left and went to the emergency room. The hospital was about five miles away and I was just praying that I would make it there. They did another EKG, but still found nothing wrong.

These episodes continued through 1975, 1976, 1977. I tried to make sense of it. Was it something that I was eating? Was it when I was active? It was worse the day after I had been drinking. I really believed that something was wrong with my heart even though I had no pain and the EKGs showed nothing. It continued to get worse. Not a week went by that I didn't feel like I was going to pass out, that I was going to die. No matter how many physicals I had, no one could tell me what was wrong. They kept telling me that I was in perfect health.

One night Darlene had taken the car and gone out and I was home alone with Misty. She was upstairs in bed and I was downstairs watching television. All of a sudden, my heart started racing. I'd guess that it was between 200 and 250 beats per minute. It seemed to get better if I got up and walked around. When I sat back down, my chest jumped and my heart was skipping beats. I tried to call my sister, but her line was busy. I tried every five minutes for an hour, but it was always busy. I kept thinking that I was going to drop dead, and Misty would be left there by herself. I didn't know what to do. Finally, after about three hours, the attack subsided and then went away.

These attacks continued to happen-at home, in the car, at work. I found myself in the ER again and the doctor there asked if I had a regular doctor. I told him that I didn't and he said that he knew an internal medicine man and was going to send me to him. He was confident that this guy could figure out what was wrong with me. That was the first positive news that I'd had in a while. I'd become afraid to travel. When Darlene had been pregnant, we had traveled a bit. We had gone to Natural Bridge, to Nags Head and to Florida. But now I was afraid to be too far away from a hospital. I knew that the "big attack" was going to come along eventually and kill me.

The doctor's name was Dr. Brown. He told me that he knew exactly what was wrong with me. My adrenaline was messed up. My body would release adrenaline at various times when it wasn't supposed to. Adrenaline is normally released when you get scared or excited, but my body would release it when I was sitting, standing, sleeping-whenever. I asked him if I should quit drinking completely and he said I could continue to drink a few beers. He also told me not to worry too much about smoking. It wasn't a big deal for him.

He gave me a prescription for Enderol and told me to take one half pill a day to keep my heartbeat from racing. I was so relieved and glad that finally somebody believed me and could help me. My parents thought I was lying about the whole thing because I didn't want to work. But finally I had found a doctor who understood.

I started taking the Enderol and I actually got worse. I began to have panic attacks and became very claustrophobic. I asked the doctor about this, but he told me to just imagine how much worse it would be now if I wasn't taking the Enderol. I thought that he must know what he was doing. After all, he was the one with the medical degree. He increased my dosage and I was taking one pill three times a day, 30 mg a day total. It still didn't seem to be helping, but I believed what he said. If I felt that bad while taking the Enderol, I couldn't imagine how bad I'd feel if I stopped taking it. I didn't let anyone know that I was still having the episodes. I'd just tell Darlene that I wasn't feeling well or was sick, but I never told her that I didn't really feel any better while taking the drug. I didn't want her to worry.

26

Darlene continued to want to go out very frequently, nearly every night and we did get into some heated conversations, but she refused to stop. One night when she had stayed home, we were sitting in the living room. I was reading the newspaper and she was reading a book. It was very quiet. Misty was asleep. All of a sudden, from behind her book, Darlene said, "Charles." Without taking the paper down from in front of my face, I answered, "Yes?" She said, "If you wanted to have a girlfriend, it would be okay with me."

I still didn't lower the paper. "What?"

"What I mean is if you wanted to go out with somebody else, I wouldn't blame you. It would be okay with me."

At first, I thought she was testing me, trying to see if I was satisfied or happy in the marriage. I told her that I was perfectly content and didn't want to go out with anybody. I was stunned by her remark and really didn't want to address it directly. About a month later, in June of 1977, I came home one night and there was a note from Darlene that said she had left me, taken Misty and gone to live with her father.

As I was driving over to her father's house, I was trying to figure out why she would have left. I was numb. I was her first love and she was mine. We had been through great times and hard times. We had laughed and cried together. We had been through the death of her mother, her high school graduation, her pregnancy and we were just beginning our life together. We were looking forward to owning our first house. I thought that going out with her girlfriends would change, that she would grow out of it or get tired of it. I understood that she needed to go out and have a good time. All of these thoughts were running through my head and I couldn't think what I had done to drive her away. How could I have done anything? I worked six days a week, sixty hours. I was home every night. I didn't know what I could possibly have done. Then I remembered the strange conversation that we had a month earlier. It suddenly hit me that she wanted me to have an affair because she had either had one or was going to have one. I couldn't make myself believe that. I couldn't handle the thought of her being with another man.

I got to her father's house and she wouldn't come outside. I kept asking her what I had done. She told me that I hadn't done anything. She just didn't want to be married. She felt too young to be married. She kept repeating that it wasn't my fault.

I said, "You are my wife! Do you plan on getting a divorce?"

"No," she answered.

"Well, come on back home and we'll talk about it, whatever it is, we'll fix it."

She said again, "I don't want to be married. Now please go and don't bother me. Leave me alone."

"What about Misty? She's my daughter."

"You can see her. You can come by. You can have her all that you want."

"What are you going to do with her at night? You're not going to leave her here at this house with your father who is a drunk. You're not going to leave her with any of your friends. You're not going to haul her around when you go out at night. You give me Misty. I'll take care of her. You go out and do what you want to do."

By that time, I was very angry. Of course, she told me that she wasn't going to give Misty to me. There wasn't anything I could do about it. I went out and got drunk, then went home and went to bed.

The next day, I couldn't wait to get off from work. I drove by her father's house, but she wasn't there. We had two cars at that time and hers was gone from his house. I was driving out of the neighborhood when I saw her car parked a few blocks away. I drove up in front of the house and from my car I looked through the picture window. There she was, sitting on the couch with my friend Jody, the one I had shot in the arm.

This went on for a couple of weeks. I would try to talk with her, but it didn't do any good. I found out that she had had an affair with him. I simply vowed that I would kill him. All of my spare time was spent tracking this man down. He knew that I wouldn't take this lightly. He knew what kind of person I was. If I shot him in the arm for taking my space in the car, what would I do to him for sleeping with my wife? Obviously, he had to be crazier than I was.

I couldn't find him. He was avoiding me. I knew that eventually I would catch up with him and I did. After a couple of weeks of constantly looking for him, I saw him walking down the street. I pulled up to him and rolled down my window. He was, of course, kind of shocked and scared to see me. I called out to him, "Jody, come on and get in. I want to talk to you."

"No, man. No, man. Charles, I don't want any trouble. I'm sorry about what happened, but I don't want to fight."

"I don't want to fight you, Jody. Darlene doesn't want to be married. She wants to be with you. Whatever she wants, that's fine. I'm not worried about it. We've been friends for a long time. There's no sense in this. If that's what she wants, fine. I've got some beer in the back seat. Let's go have some beer."

"No, I don't think so."

"Come on. Tell you what, I'll buy. I'll stop and buy you a six-pack and we'll just ride around and drink like old times. No hard feelings, man. Women are women."

I couldn't believe it, but he finally said okay. He got into the passenger seat and I opened a beer for him. We drove up to a 7-11 and I got another six-pack and we started driving out towards Sandbridge, towards the boonies. We were just riding around drinking and after a couple of hours, he began to relax. We were talking about all kinds of stuff and he was becoming more and more at ease. We went down a lonely little country road. There was nothing but woods and a ditch. I had both hands on the steering wheel and I said, "Jody, there is one thing that I would like to mention."

"Yeah, what's that?"

I made a fist and backhanded him right in the mouth. I jammed on the brakes and punched him a few more times. He got the car door open and fell out. I threw the car into park, got out, ran around to where he was and started beating him severely on the head and shoulders. He managed to get away from me, fell in the ditch, crawled out the other side and started running through the woods. I didn't chase him, but I did leave him out there. I don't know how he got back. I assume he thumbed a ride. I got my message across, but of course it didn't really help anything.

My mother, naturally, wanted her refrigerator back. She launched into her "I told you so" speech. "I told you from the beginning that she wasn't any good. I knew that you were making a big mistake. Now that poor child is going to be raised by this woman that you married. Lord knows what she is going to do."

We got into an argument. I told her that Darlene was a good mother and wouldn't let anything happen to Misty. I told her how much Darlene loved Misty. My mother and I became alienated because I was standing up for Darlene, supporting her.

Darlene and I were separated for a total of eight weeks. One evening I went over to her father's house to see Misty and just as abruptly as she left me, she told me that she wanted to come home. Without hesitation, I agreed and we packed up her and Misty's things and moved them back to our townhouse.

Over the next few weeks, I rented a house with an option to buy. We never really talked about what happened, and she didn't apologize. We just picked up where we had left off, like we hadn't missed a beat. She stopped going out with her friends. I think that she did a lot of thinking during those two months and she was growing up. I know that we should have talked about it, because the problem wasn't really solved. I didn't get angry at her, but if I let myself think about another man being intimate with her, I did get upset. I forced myself not to think about it. I loved her so much. I realized that I loved her more than the mistake that she had made. I knew that she felt badly and I didn't want to make her feel any worse. I decided that I'd keep my hurt feelings hidden and deal with them myself. She had scared me and I didn't want to lose her.

Everything was going well for us. We were planning to buy the house that we were renting. It had beautiful hardwood floors and three bedrooms. We were fixing it up and rearranging things. We had our first fireplace and a barbecue pit out back. I would get up and go to work, come back around 6:00 and Darlene would be there taking care of Misty. Our life seemed ideal.

One morning in October, I got up at 5:30 as usual. Darlene got up as well and went into the bathroom. I heard a scream. I ran in there and saw that she had a huge black eye. It looked terrible. She said that it didn't hurt and that she didn't know what had happened. It looked like someone had really punched her. She could see okay, but it was purple, blue, green and yellow and it went around her whole eye and extended down to her cheekbone. I thought that a blood vessel must have burst, but I didn't want to take any chances, so we took Misty and went to the emergency room.

In the ER, they asked her how it had happened. She told them that she didn't know, that she had just woken up that way. The nurse gave me a look like she knew that I had something to do with it. The doctor came in and said that there wasn't much he could do. It seemed to be a blood vessel, but he wanted her to get checked out by an eye doctor.

We went to the office of the doctor he had told us to see, but they refused to work her in. We went back home and finally found someone who would see her, but he could find nothing wrong. He told us that these things sometimes happened and that it might take several weeks for it to go away. We were reassured and went home.

A week later, I came home from work and Darlene was sitting on the couch. She told me that she couldn't stand up. We got into the car and went back to the ER They ran some tests and the doctor came in and told us that he had made an appointment for Darlene with another doctor for the following morning.

"Why?" I said, "What's wrong?"

"Your wife has leukemia."

"What?"

"I believe your wife has leukemia."

I had heard of leukemia, but I didn't know what it was. He explained that it was cancer of the blood. He couldn't really answer any more of our questions, but we were seeing a specialist the next day.

We drove home in silence. We ate dinner. She had long brown hair down to the middle of her back, and I laid down on the couch with her and brushed her hair. I told her how much I loved her and how everything was going to be okay. I told her that medicine was wonderful and that they could probably cure her easily. We fell asleep on the couch. The next morning, we got up and went to see the specialist.

He examined her and he had the results of the lab work that had been done the previous day. He told us, "There are three kinds of leukemia. The worst is what we call acute leukemia and that is the kind that you have. Usually, only children get this kind of leukemia. It's very rare for an adult to get it. It's even more rare for an adult female to get it. It's the worst kind that you can possibly have."

He admitted her to the hospital for more tests and to begin treatment. I asked him if she had had this disease for a long time without knowing. He said that it can come upon a person very quickly. She may not have even had it a month ago.

In the hospital, she was given platelets and blood. She got chemotherapy. She went downhill very fast and was in the hospital for a month. My mother and sister took care of Misty while I was working and I would go to the hospital after work. It seemed like she was getting worse every day. Her hair fell out because of the chemotherapy, and I had to go shopping for a wig.

She had a lot of visitors. Everyone was just stunned that this was happening to her. At night, I would sit in the room with her, but I found it very hard to be in the room with her when other people were there. I began to try to find out when people would be there and I wouldn't go if someone else was there. I would wait until they had left and then I would go into the room. I just wanted to be with her alone.

After a month, we had some good news. Her leukemia went into remission, she got much better, and got to go home. We threw a party and had a cookout. We had rib-eyes and shrimp and lobster and had a wonderful time. She was feeling great and was able to eat again. We knew that we were going to beat the cancer.

The next week, I came home from work and Darlene was lying on the couch. She said, "Charles, I have to go to the hospital." The leukemia had returned and she was admitted. Her body had taken one month of deterioration and only had one week of rejuvenation. The doctor told me that if she didn't go into remission and stay in remission for a lengthy time, time enough for her body to build itself back up, she wouldn't make it.

I had switched jobs just prior to all of this and the policy was that you had to work ninety days before getting insurance. I was three weeks away from getting insurance. I told the doctors that I'd pay them every week. At work, they were very kind and took up a collection for me. It was $100. Every bit helped. The medication that she took when she was at home was extremely expensive.

I had been working forty hours a week at this job and the manager let me cut back to half time so that I could spend more time with Darlene. I needed to be there with her. Then a new general manager was hired and he called me into his office.

"Charles, I heard about your wife and I understand she has leukemia."

"Yes sir."

"I'm sorry to hear that. I understand that you can't work your full schedule."

"She's probably going to die. That's what they are telling me and I have to be with her as much as I can. But I have to work as well."

"I'm sorry about that, but I have a business to run here and you either work your schedule or you don't work at all."

Fire flew into me. I was so angry that when I tried to talk, all I could do was stutter. I couldn't get out a complete sentence. I was trying to restrain myself because I knew that if I let my anger go, I would severely hurt this man and would probably end up in jail.

He looked at me and said, "What's wrong with you? Are you on drugs or something?"

I looked at him and took a deep breath and said, "Let me tell you something. I only have one wife. I can get another job. I hope you die and go to hell." Then I turned around and walked out.

I had a little bit of money saved up and I got a part-time job very close to home in another grocery store. They knew my situation. I spent my time at the hospital. After six more weeks in the hospital, Darlene's leukemia was in remission again. They let her go home and we had another party.

This time her remission lasted ten days. She woke me up in the middle of the night and I had to take her to the hospital. Everyday, she got worse. She was beginning to lose function on the right side of her face. Her right eye wouldn't open or shut all the way. She was beginning to have a great deal of weakness in her arms. Her chemotherapy treatments continued, but the doctor told me that if she didn't stay in remission for at least a couple of months, she wouldn't make it very long. She got to go home again, but it was only six days before she had to be admitted again.

Throughout all of this, rumors had begun that I didn't care about Darlene. These rumors were coming from my family and her family and they were based on their observation that I never went to see her. They assumed that I never went because I was never there when anyone else was there. If someone came into the room, I would leave. I just wanted to be alone with her and resented other people coming to see her.

She couldn't walk anymore. Her legs were about as big around as her arms had been. She had lost a tremendous amount of weight, and she didn't even look like the same person. In less than six months, I had watched the only person I had ever really loved eaten away day by day by the cancer, and there was nothing I could do about it. I had never been in a situation where I felt completely helpless.

The doctor came to me and said that someone needed to tell Darlene that she was going to die. I couldn't do it. I couldn't walk into her room and tell her that. I asked him if he would do it and he did.

I went into the room after he had gone. We never talked about her dying. We always talked as if she was going to get well. We both knew that she was going to die, but we would never say it.

On Misty's second birthday, Darlene was in the hospital and Misty wasn't allowed to go up to her mother's room. We put Darlene in a wheelchair and brought her down to the lobby and we had a birthday party. Darlene's brother and my mother and a few other people were there. Darlene still had the remnants of her black eye and she had an I.V. pole. She looked like hell. Misty opened her presents and then Darlene wanted to hold her. I picked Misty up and put her in Darlene's lap and Misty started screaming and crying. She was afraid of Darlene-the I.V., the wheelchair, how she looked. I saw the hurt in Darlene's eyes, and my heart broke. But I think that she understood.

The leukemia never went back into remission. One day I went into the hospital and Darlene was sitting up and she was just glowing. She looked like she had just come back from Florida with a great tan. She had a bow in her hair and a big smile on her face. I even took pictures of her. But I knew that this was a bad sign. After that day, she got much worse.

Darlene was in the hospital through Thanksgiving and Christmas, through January, February and March. She spent all but three weeks of six months in the hospital. It was the middle of April and she was going to turn twenty-one in May. The pain had gotten really bad. She didn't recognize me or anyone else. I would turn her over in the bed and rub her back and arms and wherever she was hurting. It seemed to help.

The pain was so bad that they had given her enough morphine to "twilight" her. She just stared with one eye half-closed and the other open looking at the wall. Her eye didn't move. Her breathing was quick and shallow. She was nothing but a skeleton. I couldn't stay in the room. I went home and closed all the curtains and blinds, turned off all the lights and waited. At seven, the phone rang and a nurse said, "Mr. Cross, your wife has expired."

"She what?" I asked. For a moment I wasn't sure if she had meant she died or what. Expired?

"She has expired."

I hung up and then I called the families and they drove me to the hospital. I went into her room and shut the door and begged her to come back. I told her all the things that I should have told her before she died, but couldn't. I remembered the last words she had ever spoken to me: "Promise me that you will not let Misty forget me."

In that room that night I made a promise to myself that if I ever loved anyone else, I would tell her while I could. It hurt so much and I wanted her back if only for five minutes so that I could tell her things that I should have said. I wanted to tell her that it was okay, that I wasn't angry at her and that I still loved her just as much as the day I saw her on the basketball court six years earlier, but it was too late.

The doctor came in and said that he knew it was a hard time for me, but that they wanted my permission to use her body to see what they could find out about the rare form of leukemia that she had. I said no. No more needles. No more chemotherapy. No more bone marrow biopsies. No more spinal taps. No more pills. No more poking and prodding. I just wanted them to leave her alone.

I left the room and my family and her family went in. I got into a taxi and went home to be with my daughter.

The next day I had to go to the funeral home and choose a casket. It was a very strange feeling to pick out a casket for my wife, for someone I loved. The plans were made and she was to be buried right beside her mother. She died the last week of April 1978, three weeks before her twenty-first birthday. I buried her in the dress that she was married in. Her funeral was one of the largest that I have attended, even to this day. I didn't realize that we knew so many people. The procession went on for miles. The church was packed. After the funeral, we went back to our house, and there was food everywhere. The last thing that I wanted to do was be with a lot of people. I just wanted to be alone.

Misty didn't attend the funeral. She was only two and a half, and I didn't want to take her, so my mother volunteered to keep her. She hadn't gone to our wedding and I found out later that she wasn't planning to go to the funeral anyway.

At the house, one of Darlene's aunts asked me, "Well, what are you going to do with Misty now?"

I looked at her and said, "What? What do you mean, what am I going to do with her?"

"Who are you going to give her to?"

"What makes you think that I'm going to give her to somebody? I'm going to raise her."

She could see that her question had upset me and she walked away. I went over to my mother's house. By the time I got home, everyone had left. Over the next two or three days, I lived at the house and Misty stayed with my mother. I stayed at the house in the dark and thought about everything. I felt guilty because in a way I felt free, that is, I had the freedom to change, to start my life over. I had no choice but to start over and to do a better job, but I had the added responsibility of being a single parent. What was I going to do with a two and a half year old girl? I knew I was going to raise her, but how?

27

I was thousands of dollars in debt and had no job. I didn't know if I was even going to be able to keep the house. I didn't know anything at that point. What was I going to do with my life? I had a chance to start over, in a way, so what was I going to do with it? What did I want to do?

I decided that I would go back into the medical field and I went to Virginia Beach General Hospital and applied for a job as an LPN. I would require some training to bring me up to date, but I got the job.

One of the blessings, in a way, was that Misty was not really old enough to remember her mother. As far as I knew, she had no memories of her and didn't seem to miss her. It was a blessing because I didn't have to explain where her mother was and deal with her pain and anxiety. What wasn't a blessing was that she wasn't able to know from her own memories how much her mother loved her and what a special person she was.

I hired a baby-sitter and started to work. I went to the doctors and told them my financial situation and asked them to please bear with me. I planned to pay them. They told me to forget about the money. That was really a wonderful gesture and it meant a lot to me. I went to the hospital and explained my situation. I owed them $10,000. They had me sign a paper and the state paid my bill. The only bill that I ended up having to pay was $4,000 for the funeral.

I found myself sitting on the couch a lot and watching television. One night when Misty was asleep, something funny happened on a show and I called out, "Darlene, come here, look at this." A second later, I realized that she wasn't there. That happened several times. I would go into a room expecting to see her.

I hardly slept at all during the next couple of months. Sometimes Misty would stay with one of my sisters because I was working shifts and I would get up in the middle of the night, get dressed and drive to the cemetery. There were times when I just went to her grave and laid down on the grass and cried and talked to her. At dawn, I would get in my car, go home and get ready for work. I rode by the cemetery every-day on my way to work and on the way home. It was only about a half a mile from the house and no matter where I went, I had to drive by it.

I continued to hear the rumors that I didn't really care about Dar-lene because I wasn't at the hospital when other people were there to see me. I was hurt that people would say these things. No one knew that I went to the cemetery, just like no one knew all the hours I had spent in Darlene's hospital room. I was angry because of what people were saying, but at the same time, I knew that I had been with Darlene and I knew how much I loved her.

After two months working at the hospital, I quit and went back to cutting meat. I moved and refused to tell anyone where I lived. Misty was too young to tell anyone where I worked or where we lived. I was slipping deeper and deeper into depression, but I didn't realize it. I needed to talk to someone, but there was no one. I couldn't go to my parents. I tried to talk to a couple of preachers, but I felt like that even though they listened to me, they wanted me to just hurry up. I went to a support group for widowers, but the youngest person there besides me was probably sixty-five. I only went there once.

When I got off from work, I would pick up Misty and we would go home and play. We would eat dinner together, I'd give her a bath, play some more and then I'd put her to bed. When she was in bed, I'd get out my guitar and write songs and drink all night, seven days a week.

My mother became very possessive. Four weeks after Darlene died, she called me on the phone and said, "Charles, you don't plan on ever getting married again, do you?"

"What are you talking about?"

"Well, do you plan on getting married again?"

"Mom, Darlene just died. No, I have no plans to get married again. I haven't thought about it. What is this all about?"

"Well, you know I'm just concerned about Misty. You know, her having a stepmother. I just don't think that's good. I had a stepmother and you know I told you how she was. I just don't want Misty to go through that."

"I don't want to talk about this," I said. "I don't believe what I'm hearing. If I ever decide to get married again, I'll get married again." That was the end of that conversation. She got mad and hung up.

My mother was baby-sitting Misty pretty much on a regular basis. On weekends, she spent the night with my mother because I would go out alone or stay home alone. Mostly, I hung around at the beach or at my apartment with my guitar. I thought that my mother was doing me a favor, but, as usual, she had ulterior motives.

Some of my friends had found out where I lived and they would come over just about every weekend and tried to get me to go out with them. I refused. I would stay in my apartment, play my guitar, write songs and drink beer. I didn't realize it at the time, but it was therapeutic. I hated to go to sleep, which is one reason that I drank. If I was drinking, I would go right to sleep instead of lying there thinking.

Just about every night, I dreamed-sometimes wonderful dreams about things that Darlene and I had done. But it was bad when I woke up because she wasn't there. On rare occasions, I had bad dreams. In one of the worst nightmares I ever had in my life, I was driving down a two-lane road with trees on each side. There was a big trash bag by the side of the road. I went by it and then went by it a second time. The second time, I looked at it and thought that I saw something moving. I stopped the car and backed up. I opened the trash bag and Darlene was in the bag, all cut into pieces. I woke up screaming and sweating, my heart pounding. I never had this dream again, thank God, but for a long time I felt guilty. Guilty that I had had such a terrible dream and guilty that maybe there was something I should have or could have done but didn't. Her death and this dream would haunt me for many more years.

One weekend my friends came by with their girlfriends and they had brought another young lady with them. I think my friends brought her because they were always in couples and I was left out. The girl's name was Pat Dunbar. She was successful, intelligent and very pretty, but I didn't really give her a second look. I finally agreed to go out with them for an hour or two.

We went to some clubs and were drinking and talking, and I began to talk with Pat. She was very funny and very nice. I was twenty-six and she was nineteen. The night went well and after two or three hours, they dropped me at home.

Somehow my mother found out that I had gone out with some of my friends that weekend and that I had, as she put it, "gone out with this girl." Well, I hadn't really gone out with the girl. My mother found Pat's phone number and called her at work. She was very rude to her and said, "His wife's body isn't even cold yet and you're trying to move in and take her place." The following week, Pat called me, apologizing, and shared with me what my mother had said. She said that she had gone out as a favor to some of her girlfriends. I told her not to worry about it. I didn't think that she was after me or any such thing. I, in turn, apologized for my mother's behavior. I was really embarrassed. I never expected to see her again and didn't really want to.

I confronted my mother about what she had done. She wasn't at all sorry about it. As she ranted and raved, I found out the reason for her concern. She didn't want me to get married again. She saw any woman coming into my life as a potential threat. She thought that it was her responsibility to protect Misty from the world, and during this conversation, she told me that she had prayed that something would happen to Darlene. She didn't think Darlene was a fit mother, and she wanted something to happen to Darlene so that I would have to rely on her to help raise Misty.

I was flabbergasted. When I could speak, I told her that first of all, she wasn't raising my daughter. Second, I didn't care what she had prayed-God had not allowed Darlene to die because she had prayed for that. I stormed out of the house with my daughter.

Too many people had found out where I lived, so I decided that I needed to relocate. I moved to a brand new apartment complex. Simply being in a new place felt a little bit better. In each building in the complex, the apartments downstairs were numbered 100, 101, 102 and so on, and the apartments upstairs were numbered 200, 201, 202 and so on. Each building had a different number, for example, my building was 2335, apartment 102. There were six buildings. If someone wasn't familiar with the complex, it was easy to confuse one building with another. In fact, I had had someone come to my apartment looking for a guy named John who was in apartment 102, but it turned out that he was in another building. Another time, I had nearly beaten up a kid that I thought was trying to break in. I hadn't locked the door, but the chain was on and he had reached inside trying to unhook it. His own apartment was actually 102, but in another building.

One weekend, I was at home and Misty was spending the weekend with my mother. It was about midnight and I was lying on the couch. All the lights were off, and I was watching a movie on TV. Suddenly, there was pounding on my door. I got up and the pounding started again and I heard voices outside. I thought that maybe some of my friends were there and that they were probably drunk. I started walking to the door when someone kicked it in. In came four men. They were definitely not there collecting for the heart fund.

I turned immediately and ran down the hallway and into the bedroom. I dove through the curtain, the blind, the window and the screen. When I jumped out, I landed on something sharp with my bare foot, probably a sharp stump, and it went through my foot. I knocked on apartment doors, trying to find someone to let me in. Finally, I found someone at home and I called the police. My foot was bleeding all over the place.

The police came and checked out my apartment, but found nothing. The neighbors had called an ambulance and the paramedics were working on my foot. The policemen said that the guys hadn't torn up anything or stolen anything, which led them to believe that they were looking for me. Now, I had made a few enemies over the past years, but I was beyond that now. I told the police that I didn't have an enemy in the world and didn't know who would be after me. I told them about the other two times that people had come to my apartment by mistake, but I don't think that I convinced them that was the case.

I decided that I needed to get out of that apartment complex, but I had to stay there until I found another place to live. One night I heard a commotion outside and saw the police at another building where they were taking two women and two babies out of an apartment. The women were arrested. They were selling drugs and had apparently ripped somebody off. They were in apartment 102. I'm sure that the guys who came to my apartment were instead looking for those two women. If my daughter had been in the apartment, she and I would surely have been hurt because I would not have been able to leave the way I did.

I decided that I would never again live in an apartment and so I rented a house. I continued to withdraw. Music became my therapy. I adopted a part of a Simon and Garfunkel song as my philosophy of life. "I am a rock, I am an island. A rock feels no pain and an island never cries." This was what I was becoming.

I began to question what life was all about, my role, the purpose, the meaning. I suppose that everyone asks those questions in some way during their lives. Why am I here? I could find no purpose and I felt that something had always been missing from my life. I was always determined not to have a nine to five job like my father. I didn't want to be locked into that traditionalism, yet I found myself a young man in my twenties, father of a three and a half year old, doing just that. I had always felt that no matter what I was doing, it was temporary because there was something I was supposed to do, achieve, be in life and I didn't know what it was.

I spent a lot of time with Misty. In fact, she was my salvation. She needed me. I remember going to the beach in the winter, all bundled up, the skies overcast, the waves crashing into the beach, the wind blowing off the water. The waves were gray and foamy and seemed more violent and chaotic than the waves in summer. I was standing on the beach looking out into the water and I thought that this would be a fitting place to die. How easy it would have been to walk out into the ocean until the bottom left me and then swim as far as I could until eventually the ocean overtook me. I envisioned myself doing that, but there was something that said no. I couldn't ever leave Misty like that.

I loved to be with my little girl, to spend time with her, to take her places like the beach and the zoo. There were occasions when being the single father of a girl presented some problems. We were in the mall one time when Misty said, "Daddy, I have to go to the bathroom." I asked her if she could hold it until we got home, but that's not a concept that a three year old can easily accept. I froze in front of the restroom doors. Which one should I take her in? Misty was squirming and had her legs crossed and was bobbing up and down. Fortunately, behind me there was a woman who had overheard us and she offered to take Misty into the restroom. I was so relieved and thanked her several times. From that time on, whenever we went somewhere, I tried to make sure that she didn't have to go to the bathroom before we got there.

One summer day, we went to Lake Smith. Misty was barefooted and I took off my shoes and socks as well and rolled up my pant legs. We walked through the grass and into the water a bit. My little daredevil wanted to get all the way in the water and we had a good time playing and trying to keep her out. I had brought along a bag of torn up pieces of bread to feed the ducks. It was a beautiful afternoon and we started throwing the bread out and sure enough, along came the little ducks, little white ones with yellow beaks. Misty was having a great time watching them eat. More ducks came along and there were some speckled ones and some black ones, all shapes and sizes. Misty was laughing and throwing the bread. Pretty soon, another duck, or maybe a goose, twice as big as any of the others, showed up. He had some kind of red protrusion on the top of his beak and something red hanging from the bottom as well. I had never seen anything like him before. Most of the other ducks took off and we were almost out of bread. He was hogging all the bread and whenever we threw any out, he made an ungodly sound. The others would freeze and he would go over and eat the bread. He was coming closer and closer to us. Pretty soon, we were out of bread and I said, "That's it. We have to go." We started walking towards the car. I glanced back to see the goose from hell coming after us. He started making that awful noise again. Then he started running. He could have really done some damage to a child's legs! We started walking faster and he started flapping his wings and coming after us. I grabbed Misty up in my arms and starting running, the goose still flapping and running after us. I got to the car, opened the door and put Misty in. She was laughing the whole time. She found the whole thing incredibly funny. I closed the door and this thing started grabbing and pecking at my legs. Remember that my pant legs were rolled up. He was drawing blood on my ankles and calves. I kicked him away, ran around to my side of the car and got in. Misty was still laughing. This was all great entertainment to her. I was thinking, can I not go anywhere without running into trouble? A lot of my problems in my life had been of my own doing, but this one certainly wasn't.

28

In my search to find my purpose in life, I began to remember my childhood. My father had been in the navy and was gone six to eight months out of every year. When he was at home, he was a deacon in a little church, Glen Rock Tabernacle. My parents were very close to the minister and his wife, and my mother could call on them when my father was away. It seemed like we were in church all the time-Sunday morning, Sunday evening, Wednesday night and pretty much any other time that the church was open. I knew about God. I learned about Jesus Christ in Sunday school, and I learned about salvation. I remember going forward at the age of nine with tears in my eyes. I went up to the altar and kneeled and accepted Jesus Christ as my Lord and Savior. I was very sincere and knew what I was doing.

I don't remember much about what I learned in Sunday school after that, but I did learn a lot in the worship service and from the sermon. Preachers fascinated me. After church on almost every Sunday morning, while my parents were fixing Sunday lunch, I would go up to the bedroom that I shared with my brother and emulate the preacher. The space between our beds was the aisle. I would get out my Bible and my hymnal and stand in the middle of the aisle and pretend that the choir was on either side of me, with the congregation in front. I would actually preach the sermon that the preacher had done that morning. I would sing the same songs. Unfortunately, on Sunday nights, I would lie in bed and listen to my mother in the kitchen drinking coffee and talking about the various people in the church, complaining about them, calling them hypocrites.

Others certainly would have said that our family was very religious, very strict. My father would not allow playing cards in the house because they were of the devil. Playing cards were for gambling and gambling was a sin. I would go buy them anyway and play War and Go Fish, games like that. Eventually my father would see them and throw them away. I couldn't understand why the cards were a sin if I wasn't gambling with them. Women in our church were not supposed to wear make-up or jewelry, except for a wedding ring. They couldn't wear shorts, pedal pushers or culottes. My parents never went to a movie. I was fascinated by movies, but I couldn't go to any until I was much older. We couldn't work on Sunday, which meant that we couldn't do anything on Sunday. It was a very strict, very conservative upbringing.

The point is that I knew who Jesus Christ was. As I was looking at my life, I began slowly to turn toward God for the answers. Why am I here? What is the point of all this? Why did you take the life of the only person that I loved besides my daughter, maybe the only person who ever loved me? I couldn't reconcile those things. I was struggling. I hadn't been to church probably in about ten years, but I secretly began to go again. I would go to one church on a Sunday night and the next time I would go to a different church. I never told anyone that I was going, and I don't think I ever attended any church more than once. I was searching for the answers and had come to the conclusion that God was the only place where I was going to find the reason that my wife had been taken away.

I had no doubt that there was an all-powerful, all-knowing, omnipresent God because that's what I had been taught and I truly believed it. I hadn't followed God or his ways, obviously, since I was a child. I was never angry at God because I knew the verses from growing up in the church. The Lord gives and the Lord takes. I didn't understand it, but I knew that's what the Bible said, therefore, it must be true. I didn't get angry, but I did want to know why. I began to search. It was, in a sense, my journey back.

At the same time I was exploring my spiritual side, I was becoming dissatisfied with my job. I was at the top of the pay scale at the grocery store and I felt that there wasn't any point in staying there any longer if

I couldn't advance. There was nothing to strive for. I decided to try something else. In the paper I saw that they were advertising for fast-food managers and I thought I could do that.

My first managing job was at Wendy's. In those days, the uniform was a blue and white striped shirt and a blue and white floppy hat. I thought it looked ridiculous, but the money wasn't bad for managers. I wanted to be an area manager, even a regional manager. My sights were set on the top, as far as I could go, but of course, before I could climb the corporate ladder, I had to go through training, which meant flipping burgers. I actually enjoyed that. I liked making the fries and putting the burgers together, and I loved to work the grill. I was impressed with Wendy's quality control, especially after some of the things I'd witnessed in the grocery business. When they brought ground beef in from the truck, the first thing they did was open up a box and stick a thermometer in it. If it wasn't a certain temperature, they didn't accept it. I thought that was great.

I was working sixty hours a week, getting trainee pay. After two months, the routine was getting old. I thought that I was doing a bad job because they were always on me, just like in basic training, always telling me what I was doing wrong, what I wasn't doing fast enough. One morning, I walked into the office and quit. The manager accepted my resignation and said, "Really hate to see you go, Cross, because you were probably the best person that I've ever trained. I really had high hopes for you." I walked outside and started thinking that maybe I should go back in there and tell him that I'd changed my mind, but I didn't.

So what was I going to do? I needed a job. I knew a guy who was in the exterminating business. He was an inspector for a pest control company. I thought that "Inspector" sounded like a nice title to have, so I got an interview and got into training as a Pest Control Inspector. I got a plastic sign to stick on the side of my car and a hard hat that had the name of the company on it.

They took me out and showed me how to crawl under people's houses to inspect them. Rule #1: Never crawl under anyone's house without finding anything. Never. If you couldn't find termites or other insects, you could always find moisture. At the very least you could sell them plastic to put under the house. That was the cheapest thing. We got fifteen percent of everything that we sold. When we crawled under the house, we always took a hammer, a flashlight and a screwdriver. If you didn't find anything, you could at least bang on the floorboards, which told the homeowner that there was someone down there doing something important.

The inspection was "free," but of course if you took your time to crawl under there, as I said, you were going to find something. There were a variety of things that you could sell. For example, I went out once with the supervisor to an elderly lady's house. She must have been about seventy-five or eighty years old. He told her that she had termites and that she needed vents in her house. By the time he was finished, he had convinced her that in another year the termites would be so bad that she might actually fall through the floor. He told her that the vents she had were not working properly and that she needed new ones. You could sell the vents for as little as ten dollars or as much as eighty. He told her that she would need twelve vents at eighty dollars apiece and she didn't question the price. He had her scared to death. She actually had to go to the bank and cash in some bonds that her husband had left her in order to pay for everything. Now, I don't know whether or not she really needed the vents, but, given her financial situation, he could have charged her a lot less. But then, of course, his commission would have been a lot less too. He also sold her a bunch of other stuff that he said she needed and her bill was in the thousands of dollars. He even had her sign a contract for them to come back and inspect the house every year for the next five years. She paid for this contract in advance, of course. This was a regular business practice and I felt terrible about it. I said, "I can't do this to people." It bothered me immensely. I had seen the paychecks of the inspectors and they were making good money. They were very competitive with each other and the company gave bonuses for the most contracts, the most this, the most that. I wanted to make money, but I couldn't do what they were doing.

I finished my training and I was out on my own. I had big doubts about the whole venture, but I wanted to see if I could do the job honestly. I knocked on my first door and asked the lady if she would like a free inspection, no obligation. She agreed. I started walking around the house. I came back to the front door. I walked around the house a second time and then walked back the opposite way. I got back to the front door and I was scratching my head, thinking, "What's going on here?" I rang the doorbell again. When she came to the door, I said, "Ma'am, where is your crawl space? I can't seem to locate it." I hated to ask the question because I felt stupid, but sometimes you could get to it from inside. She looked at me and said, "Crawl space? My house is on a slab." I looked at her and she looked at me. "Thank you," I said. I turned around, walked back to my car, ripped the sign off the door, took off my hat, threw them in the trunk and got in the car. I said to myself, "This isn't for me." I took it as a sign that this was the wrong career path for me to follow. That woman is probably still telling the story.

My next job was with a construction company that was laying drainage pipes in the middle of the road with a backhoe. I found out that women really do hang out of their car windows and whistle and cat call at the bare-chested construction workers. I even saw some guys getting dates! But I was still searching for something, and this job wasn't it either.

I went back to cutting meat. I almost cut my finger off with a twelve-inch knife. I stabbed myself in the abdomen. I dropped a twenty-five pound frozen turkey on my finger from a height of three feet. Yeah, it was much safer than a construction job!

The worst thing was that I stuck a pork bone in my finger and my hand got infected. The infection got into my blood and affected the joints of my fingers. By the time I went to bed that night, it had gone into my wrist and elbow and every joint was inflamed. I was in a lot of pain, but I didn't see any red marks going up my arm and didn't know what I had done. I thought that maybe I had sprained my arm or something. I went to bed, and woke up at about 3:30 with pain in my shoulder. Reluctantly, I got up and decided to go to the hospital. They gave me a couple of shots and took some x-rays. Finally, they told me that if I had waited any longer, I probably would have died. The infection would have gone into my neck and chest and would have reached my heart. I would have been dead by morning. Amazingly, with treatment, the whole infection was gone in two or three days. I had, however, contracted double pneumonia and had another kind of infection as well. I felt terrible. I didn't want Misty to be around me because I didn't want her to get sick. I took some time off from work and she was staying with my mother. I kept getting worse. I just laid around the house and got weaker every day. I couldn't eat. By the third day, everything that I tried to eat would come right back up. The only things that I could keep down were juice and other drinks. Then it got to the point where I couldn't even keep a glass of water down. I continued to just lie on the couch, assuming that the fever would break and it would be over. After a week, my mother was telling me that I needed to go to the doctor. I gave myself until Monday to feel better and then I would go. By then, I felt too bad to go anywhere. My lips were cracked and were beginning to swell. I spent almost two weeks like that and then a friend of mine came over and when he saw the condition I was in, he called an ambulance.

In the hospital, they stuck all kinds of needles in me. I had dehydrated to the point of being pretty delirious. Over the next couple of days, I got twenty-four shots in my hips. It was lucky that my friend called the ambulance when he did. The doctor told me later that another twenty-four hours would have been too late. Officially, I was diagnosed with a common virus and double pneumonia.

After that, I began to be even more isolated, if that was possible. I just wanted some peace. I started going camping a lot, sometimes with friends, but more often just by myself. I would take a pup tent, a sleeping bag and food and head out into the wilderness. I never stayed at campsites. I wanted to get away from people. I'd go up into the mountains and spend a weekend or several days at a time by myself.

One afternoon as I was hiking out of the woods I found a path, and decided to follow it back to my car. I stopped at a big tree to relieve myself and I heard a noise. It was a rustling, like a bird walking in leaves or a squirrel rummaging around in the underbrush. It sounded pretty far away and I didn't think too much about it, so I continued walking on the trail. I realized that the sound was getting closer and I stopped and turned around because it was too loud to be a bird or a squirrel. I thought that it could be a larger animal, or even a person. I listened closely and looked around, but I couldn't see anything. It was still getting louder. I started walking faster and then I started jogging. It seemed like it continued to get louder, or maybe it was just my imagination. I stopped again and turned around, but still didn't see anything. I was in a rather dense part of the forest. I didn't think that it was a human being making the noise but I was getting a little scared. I started walking again and the sound grew closer. At that point, I started to run as hard as I could. I came out of the forest into an open field and by then I was really frightened. I was out in the open with no trees to climb and no protection. In the woods, there seemed to be a little protection, real or imaginary. I didn't even bother to look back. I kept running. I made it through the field and to the car. A couple of days later, I stopped at the ranger station just to mention what had happened. The ranger told me that the trail wasn't really used by people. Two nights earlier, they had shot a bear that came out of the woods and was trying to break into the ranger station. I can only assume that what I had heard was a bear.

I thought, well, I can't even go camping by myself without something chasing me. I like bears. I think they are fascinating, but I didn't relish the thought of being mauled by one.

I had a great deal of time to think. Calm solitude was an enormous contrast to my volatile world and I longed to have this tranquillity in my life all the time. I realized that I needed change. Who could possibly help me find peace? The answer was not to be found in this world. Based on my early upbringing, I thought that it might be time to give God a try.

I hadn't been close to Him at all and I needed that, but I wasn't sure how to go about it. I knew that going to church and having a personal relationship with God were two different things. I didn't know how to have a personal relationship with God, but I did know how to go to church. I thought that someone there could help me and show me the way. I continued to go to church off and on, but I never really learned anything. It didn't seem to get me any closer. Then I thought I'd try Sunday school, but that didn't work either.

I finally decided that I'd have to start reading and studying the Bible on my own and I began to pray on my own. I asked God questions and talked to Him and He began to answer me and to reveal to me bits and pieces at a time. I came to realize that Darlene's death was something that had to be. Since she didn't live, I have no idea what the future would have been, but I believe that the future would have been much worse for the three of us had she lived. Hers was the first death that I had experienced and it brought me face to face with my own mortality for the first time. I had survived numerous brushes with death, but the first time that she encountered death, death won. Also for the first time, a human being existed who depended on me for survival. No matter what I had undertaken in life up to this point, everything had seemed temporary. My daughter was permanent. I believed that life had a purpose and I had to find that purpose for myself.

One Monday evening my life took a dramatic turn. My priorities changed from partying, staying out of jail and staying alive, to raising a child, settling down, having a steady income and planning for the future. Little did I know how hard that would be.

Finding peace where my mother was concerned was another story. She was keeping Misty while I was at work and sometimes on the weekends. Little by little, I was giving control to her, but I didn't realize I was doing this. Every time I dropped Misty off, she would scream and cry and call, "Daddy, Daddy, Daddy." It broke my heart, and when I got into the car and drove away, I would cry. Every time. But I had to go to work. There were times when I left her that I didn't have to, times when I was trying to work on myself and work through all my anger and pain. Yet it still broke my heart.

I was still searching. I was back to cutting meat because I didn't know what else to try. I met a man from New York who had been a clothing wholesaler, but had moved to Virginia to open a butcher shop. He didn't want to have a grocery store, just a butcher shop where people could buy quality meat, different cuts that weren't prepackaged. It seemed like his timing was wrong. Butcher shops were being phased out as grocery stores became more specialized. He had no knowledge of the grocery business, let alone the meat business. We talked about it and he asked me if I would set it up and run it for him. I thought this was great. Later we talked about a partnership where he would handle the administrative end and I would be hands-on in the butcher shop. It was a wonderful possibility.

I would get off from my other job and go in and help pick out the things that needed to be bought-coolers and cases and knives and grinders and slicers and such. We talked about which suppliers to deal with, how to promote the place, what the set-up would be, and all the other details. One day I walked in and he said, "Charles, I would like to talk to you a minute." We went into his office. He said, "I called you over the weekend and I couldn't get you, but I had your mother's number. You said that if I couldn't get you at home, I could possibly get a message to you that way. I called and your mother answered."

"Yeah?" I said, not knowing where this was going.

"Well, I'm kind of concerned about you."

"Why? What?"

"Do you have a problem with drinking?"

"No, I don't have a problem," I joked. "I can get all I want." He didn't laugh.

"Wait a minute, I'm just joking. What's the matter?" In fact, I rarely drank at that point in time. I didn't get drunk anymore.

He said, "Well, I called and asked for you and your mother said you weren't there and I asked if she would have you call me when she saw you. She said, 'I certainly will if he is able to.' I asked, 'What do you mean if he is able to?' and she said, 'Well, I'll give him the message and if he is able to call you when he gets in, if he's in any shape to call you, I'll tell him to call you.' What did your mother mean by that? I took it to mean that maybe you were out getting drunk all the time."

"No sir," I answered, "In fact, I don't drink much at all now."

"You don't have a problem?"

"No."

"Well, why would your mother say that?"

"I honestly don't know why my mother would say that."

He said, "I can't take a chance on you running this business. I've got a lot of money invested here. We're talking about being partners. If you've got a problem with alcohol, if you're a drunk or something, I can't do that."

"I'm telling you, I don't have a problem with drinking. I don't drink. Have you had a problem with me thus far?"

"Well, no. But we don't know each other that well. So you're kind of calling your mother a liar."

"I'm not calling my mother a liar. I'm saying..." Then I stopped.

"Well, why would your mother say that?"

"I don't know, but I'll find out."

"I've thought about it. I'm just afraid to do this with you. I'm sorry, but we are just not going to be able to work together."

I was furious. I went to my mother's house and asked, "Did I get a phone call? Did someone leave a message for me?"

She said, "Oh yeah, someone left a message."

"And what did you tell him?"

"Well, I told him that you weren't here, but I'd take a message."

"Is that all you said? Did you not tell that person that I was some kind of drunk?"

"I never said any such thing."

"But what you said was if he is physically able when he gets in, if he is in any shape to, he'll call you."

She didn't deny saying that, but she said that she meant if I was able, as in, if I wasn't in a hurry. She was trying to get around it. I realized then that there was meanness there. I didn't say anything else to her. I left the house and as I thought about it in the coming days, I realized what she was doing. She was trying to keep me down. I was depending on her to help with Misty and she had me where she wanted me. She didn't want me to better myself, because that might interrupt things. She had the perfect scenario the way things were and she didn't want it to change. I would discover in the future just how true this was.

A friend of mine, Pat Dunbar (the one whom my mother accused of trying to take Darlene's place before her body was cold), was a Girl Scout leader and she asked if I would go camping with them. They had a rule that when they went out, they had to have at least one man with them. It seems very chauvinistic now, but this was 1979 and that was the rule. They also had to have someone who knew first aid and I fit that requirement as well, so I agreed to help out. I fixed up an aid bag much like the one I had in the army and took it with me. I was kind of excited about the trip. The girls were six to eight years old, which turned out to be the perfect age group. When they got a couple of years older, they would know everything and if they were a couple of years younger, their attention span would have been much shorter. I showed them how to build a fire, helped them put up their tents, and taught them how to make pancakes and fry bacon for breakfast. I showed them how to wash their dishes in the riverbed with the sand, how to identify poison oak and poison ivy. I really enjoyed being with them. They would come to me and ask questions. I felt like a mother hen. I went out with them several times.

Pat and I dated from time to time. There would be times when we saw each other quite a bit for a month or two and then there would be a month or two when I didn't see her at all simply because I didn't want to. She fell in love with me and wanted to marry me. We talked about her feelings and I told her that I liked her a lot, but I could never love anybody again. That was it. I didn't want to take the chance. I was still having dreams about Darlene, even though they were becoming less frequent. It had been almost two years since her death, but still every place I went, every thing I did reminded me of her. Pat was a wonderful friend and I thought she deserved someone better than me. But she stuck by me. Whenever I needed someone to talk to, even if it was one in the morning, I could call her. She would get dressed and come outside and we'd get in the car and go riding around and talk. She never pressured me. or made any demands. She was just there for me. She wanted to help and listen. I didn't realize that she was falling in love with me. It must have been very difficult for her to listen to me talk about how much I loved Darlene. She was always there and I guess that I took advantage of that. Months might go by when I didn't call her and then I would just show up. She was always there.

I began to get involved in other things. I was very interested in ecology, the environment, saving the planet and the animals (except for the one bear that chased me-I was glad he was dead). I joined Greenpeace. I was on their flagship, the *Rainbow Warrior*. I got to go on the *Calypso*, Jacques Cousteau's boat. I visited Rhode Island, New York, the mountains and valleys of Virginia, North Carolina, and the beaches all up and down the East Coast. I wanted to go to Australia. At the time, they were giving away one-hundred-acre plots of land if you would sign a contract to raise sheep for the government for seven years. After that time, the land would belong to you. I actually talked this over with a couple of guys and we were considering it. I didn't go, mainly because of Misty.

I continued to play and write music. In a sense, music was my salvation and my therapy. I don't know if I could have survived without the music. At times I got together with friends who also played and sang. A couple of them used to sing for the New Virginians, a vocal group at the University of Virginia. We would go down to the beach, light a campfire and sit around and sing our own songs and other people's. My songs, of course, had a tendency to be pessimistic, rather dark to say the least. I tried to write upbeat songs, but that's not where I was- not what was inside of me.

I hadn't been with another woman in nearly two years and had no desire to be. I could have been with Pat if I'd wanted to. It was something that I never really thought of, but it did come out in a song that I wrote in 1979 that went something like this:

> May I lay in your arms tonight lady
> May I feel your warm heart close to mine
> Will you whisper those words oh so softly
> May I lay in your arms tonight
> May I lay in your arms tonight lady
> Can I tell her I love her to you?
> I know I have no hold to hold on you
> I promise I will do you no wrong.

It seemed that no matter who I was with, whose arms I might be in, I would be thinking of Darlene. I was still depressed and still wanted to be alone, but I hadn't been able to achieve that, to get away from society, from people. It would have been much easier if I hadn't had Misty, but then again, it was Misty, along with the music, that kept me sane. I longed for a place to be by myself and I wrote these words:

> Lord, give me a home in the mountains
> Lord, give me a home way up above

Lord, give me a home where there
is no doubt
And the wind blows free all day
Lord, give me a home in the mountains
I want a home that none can see
Lord, give me a home where there
is no doubt
And a cool wind blows free all day
You know I have traveled each and every
road the hard way
I have traveled them all alone
Every time I stop to take a look around me
It seems I get farther from my home
Lord, give me a home in the mountains
I want a home that none can see
Lord, give me a home where there
is no doubt
And the water tastes like wine.

I never found such a place.

The situation with my mother deteriorated even further. I found out that she would get Misty up at two or three in the morning and sit her on the couch and talk to her. She was telling her how bad I was. She was doing everything she could to turn Misty away from me. When I confronted her with this, she told me that she believed she was here to protect Misty. "From whom?" I asked.

"From the world."

"Well, first off, you can't protect her from the world. Second, that's none of your business. I am her father. If there is any protecting that needs to be done, I'll do it."

We got into an argument and I said, "I just can't let her stay here at night anymore. I'll have to find somewhere else."

Misty was four years old. I had a birthday party for her in November of 1979 and ordered a cake with a big clown on it. I invited some of my friends and my family for the party, but my mother refused to come. In fact, she planned another birthday party at her house. She was angry because I was having the party at my house and not hers. I kept dismissing the things that she was doing as if they were not important. I didn't realize just how far she would go to take control of my daughter.

I had a job with a new grocery chain that had moved into the area. When they opened a new store, my job was to go in and set everything up, so there was a lot of organizing and ordering that I enjoyed. Misty and I continued to do a lot of things together. We went to the zoo, the parks, the amusement park, all sorts of places, but the nights were still very bad for me. I still went to the cemetery, though not several times a week anymore. Two or three times a month, I would find myself sitting at the graveside. I knew she wasn't there, but it seemed like the closest I could be to her.

One night in the spring of 1980, I went out with my brother-in-law and some friends to a club and shot some pool. They were all pretty drunk and I was watching how they were acting. I couldn't believe that I used to act the same way, but I'm sure I was just as obnoxious as they were.

There were three ladies sitting at a table and my friends were trying to help me out. Poor Charles, it's been two years since his wife died and he needs to get out and meet some women. They kept telling me that I needed to find someone. They wanted me to go over and ask one of the ladies to dance-something I never did. I was afraid of being turned down. They kept badgering me and they dared me and double dared me and finally I agreed to do it just to get them to shut up. I walked over the women, who looked like they had just come from an office. They were all in their twenties. I chose the one who I thought was the best looking and I said, "Hi, my name is Charles. Would you care to dance?" I was just ready to pivot and go back to my seat when she said, "Sure." Damn. I made sure that it was a slow dance. It wasn't that I wanted to hold this strange woman close, but my perception of me fast-dancing was a chicken with its head cut off. A slow dance is pretty hard to mess up. We finished the dance and I thanked her and took her back to her seat.

I said to my friends, "There, are you happy now?" I was sitting there sipping a beer and I looked over and saw her looking at me. I glanced over a bit later and she was looking at me again. The guys noticed this and of course they were teasing me. They wanted me to get her phone number. I said no, but I did think about it. So the next slow dance, I asked her to dance again and she said yes. After the dance, I asked her name. She told me it was Terry. We danced two dances in a row. I was getting brave. They were calling last call for alcohol and I said, "Terry, I'd like to have your phone number." She said okay and wrote it down on a piece of paper, folded it up and put it in my pocket.

The next morning, I got up and found this piece of paper on my desk. I opened it and there were two phone numbers. I figured that the second one must be her work number. I thought, she's awfully anxious if she is giving me two numbers and that's not good, no matter how good looking she is. After several days, I got the nerve to call the first number. It was disconnected. I wadded up the paper and threw it away. It was an old trick, sure you can have my number, and then you give him the wrong number to get rid of him. Then as I thought about it, I thought, well, why would she give me two wrong numbers? I got the paper out of the trash and the next day I called the second number. It was a doctor's office. I asked if anyone named Terry worked there and she got on the phone. The first number had been disconnected because she was moving. I asked her out and she accepted.

Terry was about the same height as Darlene, five-foot four and a hundred and twenty pounds. That's where the similarities ended. Darlene had very long straight hair down to the middle of her back and was not at all buxom. Terry had short wavy hair and she was very large-breasted. Both had very strong personalities. Terry was the same age as I was, but she was classier, very high maintenance, divorced and had two children, a boy about Misty's age and a girl a few years older.

She worked for a group of orthopedic surgeons who loved to party. They ranged in age from mid-thirties to seventy. The primary qualifications for being hired in their office were looks and friendliness. We were invited to a lot of their get-togethers and basically, everyone just got drunk. I had given up most of my drinking and smoking. Terry told me that she drank "socially" and sometimes she did get drunk at these functions. The doctors would all try to see who they could get into bed that night. None of the doctors had been able to get Terry into bed and that was one reason that she wanted me there with her, for protection. She wasn't sure what might happen if she got too drunk one night, and she knew that I wouldn't let them do anything to her. After a while, they didn't want me there anymore. Since I was usually the only sober one at the parties and I wasn't joining in the "fun," they viewed me as a threat to the way they treated their female employees, as well as their patients. One thing that really bothered me about these parties is that sometimes the doctors would be half-drunk or hungover, and they would actually operate on people the next day! Sometimes they would let interns do it and they wouldn't even be there. The patient never knew the difference. The surgeon would bill the patient for the operation and get the money even though he never even showed up.

The chief surgeon had made it plain through Terry and another physician that I was not to be at another function, which I took, as usual, as a challenge. I continued to show up at their private parties and one of the doctors, in a drunken stupor, later revealed to me that the chief surgeon had checked into the possibility of hiring someone to do me bodily harm.

29

I was getting tired of working for other people. I was twenty-seven and I sat down over the next few weeks and planned out my life through age sixty. I went into business for myself as an independent food broker. That's just a fancy name for food salesman. I was working for a company that not only sold retail, but also sold wholesale to restaurants. I thought, why am I working for these people? I got hooked up with a warehouse that handled lunchmeat, beef, whole boxes of cattle, things of that nature. If it was damaged in any way or if they had an overstock, they would sell it to people at a price per pound, but I had to buy it all. I had to throw a lot of it away, but some of it was good. I was able to get an unwritten contract. I would buy all this meat for twenty-five cents a pound, and I rented space in a butcher shop where I could use their tools and storage. In exchange, I gave them ten percent of my profits. I cut some steaks, some filet mignon and wrapped them in bacon. They were eight ounces apiece. I wrapped them up fresh, put them in a box, nice and neat. There were twelve to a box, two layers of six each. I did New York strips, Delmonicos, sirloins. I made up a bunch of these boxes, about ten or twelve, which was quite a bit of money, put them in an ice chest in the back seat of my car and went out on the highway. I decided to try to sell them at a car lot. The first place I went, they were standing around doing nothing. I described the steaks as top quality, never frozen, always fresh, which they were. They wanted them, but I didn't think about the fact that they were car salesmen and they weren't going to pay sticker price for my steaks. They tried to get me to lower the price and I did. I let them cut me back to the cost of a box of steaks. I sold every box of steaks there. I didn't make a single penny in profit, but I didn't lose anything either.

I thought that I was onto something here. The next week, I made up fifteen boxes and went to another car lot. I jacked the price up and let them cut the price, but I still made money. It turned out that car lots were gold mines. The owners of a couple of the lots would buy from me. When the owner buys from you, all of the salesmen have to buy from you as well because they want to impress the boss. The other gold mine was beauty salons. I'd walk in with my box of steaks, pull off the lid and go into my speech, telling them that this was corn-fed beef that had never been frozen. I pointed out that they were individually wrapped. You could just slip them into the freezer and they were 100% guaranteed. They would buy everything I had. I went into office buildings next. That was a little harder, but it still worked.

I never advertised. I only went out once a week and every week I would pick up new people, just from word of mouth. It got to the point where people would call me at home. They would say it was an emergency, they were having people over, could I get them something? For me to take a box of steaks, I'd have to drive fifteen miles to the place, cut the steaks, drive back to where I lived and then drive another five to eight miles. By the time I did all that, I didn't make anything off that box of steaks, but I made a customer happy.

Near Christmas, I got a huge amount of hams from the warehouse. I had to take them, but I thought I'd have them for the next ten years. I had about three-hundred hams weighing fourteen to twenty-five pounds apiece. There was a real estate company that I had sold steaks to and the guy was telling me what he wanted to do for his employees for Christmas. I suggested that he give them hams. I told him that I'd sell him hams at sixty cents a pound. The cheapest I had found them was sixty-nine cents and of course, I had only paid a quarter a pound. He wanted about one hundred hams and he wanted me to cut them in half and box them up. I told him that I'd have to charge him seventy cents a pound for that, and he agreed. He wanted me to wrap them in Christmas paper, but that's where I drew the line and so he had his secretaries do that.

This gave me a great idea. I put an ad in the paper that said if you don't know what to give someone for a gift, why not give them a box of steaks? I would deliver them gift-wrapped right to the door. I did that for birthdays, Christmas, Thanksgiving-just about any holiday. I had to rent a U-Haul trailer to carry them in.

I was now doing this full time. I expanded to pork chops and other pork products, lunchmeat and bacon. I sold cases of lunchmeat. I branched out into seafood and then into produce. Now people had all this food that they had bought from me, where were they going to store it? I started selling freezers to put it in, and I started selling to restaurants. I supplied all the ground beef to several taco restaurants.

I was making money and raising Misty and dating Terry, but I would still come home at night and sit around and play my guitar, still lonely and depressed. The business kept my mind occupied during the day, but there was still something missing in my life.

I thought a lot about Misty. She had completed kindergarten and was going into first grade. I thought she needed a mother. We'd been on our own for about three-and-a-half years. I'd always thought that if a child had to be without one parent, it would be better to be without the father. Maybe it was just the feeling of my own inadequacies, but that was what I believed. I thought that a woman, a mother, would be more well-rounded, especially with a daughter. Terry had two kids and they needed a father. They were nice kids. Terry and I got along great. Maybe this could work.

The future was looking better to me than it ever had in my life, but there was still something wrong. It was like a piece of the puzzle was missing-not the last piece, but the piece that you need to put two sections together. So I kind of asked Terry to marry me. I said, "If I asked you to marry me someday, what would you say?" She said she would and I said I'd get back to her. I thought about that for a long time, but in the end, I thought it must have been meant to be. I never thought I would marry again, but this seemed to be a perfect scenario. Terry was a beautiful woman and our children got along great and it would solve all our problems.

So after a year-and-a-half of being together, we got married in the summer of 1982 and moved into a new house. She quit her job to stay home with the kids. Everything seemed the way it was supposed to be, the way I remembered it on "Leave it to Beaver" or "Father Knows Best." I had a wife who didn't have to work, a nice house in an upscale neighborhood, a nice business, three kids-what more could I want?

My mother was not happy about our marriage and said so. She knew that she'd be keeping Misty less. Terry and my mother did not get along. Terry kept trying to warn me, in a sense, about my mother, but I thought it was just the friction between mother-in-law and daughter-in-law. I was caught in the middle. I tried to keep everyone happy. I essentially just agreed with both of them and hoped that everything would work out. It didn't happen. My mother's attitude grew increasingly hostile, and she continued to tell Misty negative things about Terry and me. If Misty stayed with her over the weekend and we picked her up on Sunday, she would go into her room, shut the door and sit on the floor for hours in the dark without saying a word. It didn't matter what we did, she wouldn't speak. Usually by Wednesday, she'd be back to normal, just a wonderful little six-year-old running around. Then the weekend would roll around again and she'd spend it with my mother and come back on Sunday the same way. It was very frustrating for Terry and me. I couldn't figure out what my mother could possibly be saying to her, but knowing how my mother was, I'm sure she was still trying to undermine me. Misty finally told me that my mother would wake her up at two or three in the morning, sit her down on the couch and talk to her about how bad step-mothers were and about her home-life in general. I put my foot down and told my mother that I couldn't put up with this any more. Of course, she denied doing or saying anything that would make Misty act like that. I told her that if she wanted to see Misty, she would have to come to our house.

To my mother, that was the equivalent of a declaration of war. I think that she made up her mind to do anything she could to get Misty. She wanted Misty to live with her. She tried to talk Misty into telling me that she wanted to go live with her grandmother. Misty was six years old in the first grade and she was not doing well in school. I think it had a lot to do with what was going on in the family. They tested her for a learning disability, but couldn't find any. The teacher wrote me a letter saying that Misty was going to be held back in the first grade, and I went to pieces. My daughter was not going to fail, especially first grade. Part of the problem was the kindergarten that she had attended. I had allowed my mother to choose it because she was the one who would pick her up while I was at work. I found out later that it wasn't really a kindergarten. It was just a day care, a baby-sitting service. Misty was probably one of the oldest ones there and she didn't learn what other kids were learning in kindergarten, so she was behind from the very beginning.

I went to the school and talked to the teacher. I told her that Misty would not be held back. I knew that she could catch up. It might be difficult, but I knew that if I worked with her, she would get to where she needed to be. The teacher allowed her to be promoted to the second grade.

I remember working with Misty one night. She brought some papers home and they were just terrible. I was sitting down with her and helping her do her writing. She wasn't writing on the lines of the paper. I told her, "Misty, your words have to be on the line."

"They are on the line," she said.

"No, they are not on the line. Let's sit down and do this." We sat down at the table and I told her to write something. She was writing and I said, "No, stop right there. Write on the line."

"It is on the line."

"No," I said, "It's not on the line. Do you see the line?"

"Yes."

"All right, then write that word on the line." She wrote it and it wasn't on the line. I said, "Misty, that's not on the line."

She said, "Yes, it is."

"Do you see the line?"

"Yes."

"Write that word on the line."

She wrote it again and it wasn't on the line. We went around and around. I did something that I have only done once in my life to a child. I have never done this to any child before or since. I was frustrated and said, "Are you that stupid that you can't write on the line?" It was one of those times when the words came out of my mouth and I tried to grab them back, but it was too late. The hurt that those words inflicted on my daughter couldn't be undone. She was frustrated and crying, and I was at my wit's end. I said, "Fine. Forget it. Go to bed." That was the end of that. I apologized to her the next day and told her that I didn't mean it.

It wasn't too much after that that Misty was sitting in the back of the classroom misbehaving and talking too much. The teacher moved her to the front and her behavior improved. She was bored in the back because she couldn't see the chalkboard. She didn't have anything else to do. When she was moved to the front, she could see what was going on and she did much better. The teacher suggested that we have her eyes tested. I took her to an eye doctor and it turned out that she saw double. That was why she couldn't write on the line. When she looked at the paper, she saw double lines and she was writing on the line that she was seeing, but that wasn't there. Her vision had apparently been this way since birth. Her eye muscles were weak and he needed to do surgery to shorten the muscles behind her eyeballs.

Having my daughter's eyes operated on bothered me. I couldn't stand for her to go through that. I thought there had to be a better way. I went for a second opinion and the second doctor told me that she wouldn't try surgery then. In fact, the doctor had the same problem and had been able to correct it with eye exercises. We started doing the exercises with Misty and her vision got much better, and fortunately, didn't have to have the surgery.

My mother was becoming more and more of a problem. She would call me and we would end up shouting at each other. We found out that she had hired a private detective to follow Terry and dig into her past to see if she could find any dirt on her. Terry told me that she thought someone had been following her. I thought at first that it was her imagination, but she persisted. I mentioned it to my mother and she got quiet all of a sudden. It dawned on me then that maybe she had something to do with it. I asked her about it, but of course, she denied it.

I had been allowing Misty to go to my mother's house to see her if someone else was there also. I wouldn't allow her to be alone with Misty. This didn't sit too well with my mother, obviously. In a fit of rage, she told me about hiring the detective and that she had also hired a lawyer and she was going to give me one last chance to straighten up and let Misty come live with her. If I didn't agree, she was going to take me to court and then she would ruin me and my marriage. I told her that as far as I was concerned, she would never see Misty again. That was it. No more contact.

Soon after that, we got a letter saying that we had been subpoenaed to court. I couldn't believe it. I couldn't believe that my mother was actually taking me to court to fight for custody of my daughter.

We went to court. We had to wait in a small hallway for the judge- my mother, my father and me. My father was an interesting character. He had made up his mind years before that he couldn't control anything that my mother wanted to do. He had fought for years in the marriage and I guess he had just given up. He had his work and his hobbies and he really just wanted to be left alone. He was only in court because the judge had ordered him to be there.

Finally, we went in to the judge's office. We hadn't said a word to each other. The judge was looking over the papers and he said, "Mrs. Cross, you are suing your son. You're bringing your son to court to try to take his daughter from him. I have never in my life seen anything like this, a mother taking her son to court to get his daughter. I think that before we do anything else here, we need some counseling."

He ordered that we go to a social worker, a licensed counselor. My father had to go as well and who did he blame? He blamed me. The first time we went was the only time that we all went together. The counselor was asking some questions and then she said to my mother, "From reviewing the questionnaire that you answered for me and from talking to you, I believe that first of all there are some concerns, some problems that you might have from your childhood. I think that we need to deal with those issues privately."

My mother exploded. "I'm not the one who needs help! You're the one who needs help!" She got up and walked out. My father followed her. The counselor looked at me and I shrugged and said, "I told you so."

Terry was very angry with me. This was not what she had planned when she married me. She didn't expect my mother to be like this. I told her that I had no idea that my mother would do something like this and I wouldn't have gotten into a marriage if I had known this was going to happen, which was not completely true. My mother had trouble with Misty's mother and I knew that there would be trouble if I got married again, but I was not going to stay single simply because of the possibility of her causing trouble. I should have solved the problems with my mother much earlier. There was a tremendous strain on our marriage, trying to bring our two families together. A blended family is a very difficult situation at any time, but adding my mother to the mix made the situation horrendous.

Misty was having a hard time understanding why she couldn't see her grandmother. She loved her and she was really the only mother that she had known. I knew that it was important to her, but I didn't see how I could allow her to be with her grandmother under the circumstances.

We had to go back to court again and this time I was surprised to see not only my mother, but both of my sisters and a friend of my mother's. My father wasn't there, so I thought that maybe they were there for moral support. I said hello, but no one returned my greeting. We sat in the hallway for about twenty minutes in an eerie kind of silence. Finally, we were escorted into the judge's chambers and we all sat at a big table. The judge said, "The counseling didn't work. We tried it and you refused to go back, so let me hear the rest of the petition before I make my final decision."

My mother had really pulled out all the stops. My oldest sister talked about what a bad father I was and what a bad person I was. She said that I had said terrible things to my mother and that I wouldn't let Misty go over there just for spite. My sister had actually said to me in a previous conversation that if she were me, she would take Misty and move as far away from our mother as possible. She told me that she wished she had left with her own daughter. She had obviously told me this in confidence and I would have never shared it with anyone, but she sat in the judge's chambers and lied, saying what my mother wanted her to say. I had not planned to accuse anyone of anything. I was simply going to answer the questions that the judge asked me. But my sister went on and on and I finally looked at her and said, "Did you not tell me two weeks ago that I should take Misty and move away from our mother and that you wished you had done the same thing?" She looked me square in the eye and said, "I never said any such thing. You are a liar."

I could understand her siding with our mother over me. I could try to understand her being on her side. I could even understand her repeating things that my mother said as truth, whether she knew them to be true or not. But I could not for the life of me understand how this sister could look me in the eye and call me a liar when she knew the truth.

My youngest sister sat there with her head down and never said a word. We had always been close, but obviously not as close as I thought. Her problem was that she did believe my mother. She refused to believe that my mother was capable of doing these things to my daughter-like hiring a detective to follow my wife or spreading rumors and lies. I didn't blame her. No one wants to believe that their mother is capable of such things against one of her own children. I didn't want my sister to necessarily take my side. What I wanted was for my sisters and brother to stay out of it. It wasn't their business. But just by being there with my mother, my younger sister showed that she was against me.

My mother had her say and nothing that she said surprised me. Then she turned to her friend and said, "My friend here, Mrs. Williams, has something to say." I had no idea what this woman could possibly add to the proceedings.

"Before his wife died," she began, "I saw them in the middle of the street. I saw him beating his wife and this was about a year before she died."

My mother knew, of course, that I had a temper and I assume that she thought that this outrageous lie would make me so angry that I would explode in front of the judge and she could show him that I was indeed a crazy man with no business raising a daughter. I was stunned. What the woman said was a complete fabrication. There's no way in the world that I would hit a woman. I never have, never would, never will. And if I had, Darlene would probably have beaten me up. I was surprised at the control I had in the face of this lie. I just sat there and shook my head and said to the judge, "Your honor, that's just a complete lie and I don't know what to tell you except that it's not true. This woman is a friend of my mother's who is only saying what she wants her to say. That's the best I can tell you."

That was pretty much it. The judge ruled in my favor. The lawyer and the private detective presented no evidence and there was no reason why my daughter should be taken from me. I was ashamed and embarrassed to even be involved in this custody battle with my own mother. She was very angry. On the way out, she threatened to get me, whatever that was supposed to mean, but I thought that would be the end of it.

30

Terry and I had been talking about moving. She was into English riding and had been getting involved in the business side, the working side of the horses, not just entering the shows, but actually working at the stables learning the business. She was gaining knowledge and expertise and wanted to get into the business for herself. There were already several stables and farms nearby, and it was pretty competitive. In order for her to get into the business, we would have to move somewhere else. We talked about going down to Mississippi and starting a business there. The idea was tempting, but I wasn't ready for it yet. This was my home. I'd lived here all my life except for the time that I was in the army. As bad as things were, I wasn't ready to leave.

I was also reluctant because my business was growing, booming, in fact. I was getting ready to hire other people. Terry told me that I could open up the same kind of business in Mississippi. She had picked Mississippi because there really wasn't any English riding there. Everything was quarter horses and cowboys. We would be in on the ground floor in the horse business. I started putting out feelers for selling my business and found a couple of interested buyers very quickly. Terry started finding out about the horse layout in Mississippi and started looking for a house and some land there.

Things were moving faster than I wanted them to until one night when I went over to my mother's house. I had decided that my mother would not have contact with either Misty or me. I had tried earlier to talk to my father about the situation. I went over to my parents' house one day when my mother wasn't home and his only response to the situation was, "Well, you know what kind of a woman she is. She's always been that way." So I knew that I wouldn't get any help from my father. He just wanted to stay out of her way himself. I had come to the conclusion that I wasn't going to have anything to do with my mother for the rest of her life. My marriage had been hell because of this, my daughter was not emotionally well because of it, and I looked like the bad guy because I was keeping Misty from seeing her grandmother. Misty, of course, was too young to understand why she couldn't see her grandmother. I never talked badly about my mother to her, but I couldn't let Misty continue to be influenced by my mother.

I still had some things at my parents' house and so one night I went over there to get them. I dreaded this visit because I didn't want to see my mother. I knocked on the door and when she opened it, I went in. I told her that I'd come to get some of my things and she told me to go ahead and get them. I got my leather fringed coat and a jean jacket and a few things like that. I told her that I wanted my picture album from Hawaii and the 1907 silver dollar of mine that she had and a few other things.

"Those belong to me," she said, "You're not getting those. You gave me that silver dollar. I don't know where that picture album is and even if I did, I wouldn't give it to you."

She was building up to hysteria and I said, "Fine, fine, it's not that important."

It was interesting that she had hated Darlene and had told me that she prayed that she would die, and yet she had turned much of her house into a shrine of sorts. I brought up what she had told me and she said, "No, I never said that. I prayed that something would happen to your marriage. I didn't want her to die."

"You told me the word 'die'. You said you prayed that she would die." She maintained complete denial that she had ever said such a thing.

There were pictures of Darlene and little things everywhere that had belonged to her. She had a bedroom set up for Misty and she wouldn't let anybody touch anything in there, even though many of the things Misty had outgrown. I reached over and picked up a picture of Darlene's high school prom. When I picked it up, my mother went ballistic. She grabbed it out of my hand and starting screaming and swearing, "This is mine! You can't have it! Darlene gave this to me!"

I said, "This picture doesn't belong to you. You didn't like her. You hated her. You wanted her dead and now look at this. You've turned this place into some kind of shrine because you feel guilty. Those pictures belong to Misty and me."

We were yelling at each other, and where was my father? He was out in the workshop, working on his wood projects. My mother was really losing it, going berserk. She was so angry that she could hardly contain herself. She said, "If you don't get out of here, I'm calling the police."

"Fine, call the police, but this is my property and I'm taking it."

She walked back a few feet into the kitchen and picked up the receiver of the wall phone. She threatened again to call the police and I told her to go ahead. She replaced the received and started ranting and raving again and told me to get out. I told her that I'd get out as soon as I got all of my stuff. She went berserk again. Then she said something that just stunned me. She was about four feet from me and she looked me straight in the eye and said, "I'll fix you. I should have killed you when I had the chance."

I could not believe what I had just heard. She took off through the living room, down the hall and into my father's bedroom. I was standing in the living room holding my two coats and thinking that I must have misunderstood what she said. Then I wondered where she had gone. I thought that she must have gone to call the police, but there wasn't a phone in my father's bedroom. She had been standing right beside a phone. She'd said, "I'll fix you" and then she went into the bedroom where there was no phone. She didn't turn any light on in the bedroom. All of this was going through my mind in the span of about three seconds. The next thought was, what's in my father's bedroom? The gun cabinet is in my father's bedroom. I thought that couldn't be it. She was my mother. She wasn't going to kill me. Then I thought about the number of people who die violently in their own homes. I decided that the smart thing do was leave. I went out through the kitchen and garage to my father's workshop out back. I had my stuff in my hand and I said to him, "Did you not hear Mom in there? She's lost it. I'm telling you. Something is wrong with that woman. I'm getting my stuff and I'm not coming back here again."

My father just looked at me and didn't say a word. I thought of all the times in the past when I had needed his support and he wasn't there. I knew that I wouldn't get any help from him. Maybe he thought it was best that I leave forever. I was rocking his boat, after all, disturbing his serenity. He had separated himself from my mother. They slept in different rooms, had separate lives and never went anywhere together. He didn't want to be involved in our dispute. I walked out of the workshop and down the side of the house, which was in total darkness. I walked to the driveway and about the time I reached my car, I heard my mother call my name. I turned around and looked at the front door, but she wasn't there. I glanced over at the corner of the house where I had just been and she came around the side of house in darkness. She didn't come past the corner of the house. She stood in the dark. Then I saw it. There was a gun in her hand. My mother was going to shoot me. I ran to the car and got behind it on the driver's side. I stayed low, opened the door and threw my stuff in. I got in myself, staying low, started the car and took off.

I was in complete disbelief. I played it in my head over and over again. It couldn't have been a gun. It had to have been something else. But the more I went over it in my mind, the more convinced I was that it was a gun and that my mother was going to shoot me.

I never told anyone what happened that night. This is the first time I've ever said it. I thought, could I really be such a horrible person that I drove my own mother to want to kill me?

For everyone's sake, it was time to leave. I accepted an offer to sell my business. We spoke to a realtor in Mississippi who sent us pictures of homes. We made a preliminary agreement to buy a house before we even saw it. Terry and I were going to take our family and start our lives again in Mississippi.

PART IV

31

We had called movers to move all our stuff from Virginia to Mississippi, but they wanted $4,000, and I knew that I could move our things cheaper than that. I decided that we would move ourselves, so we got rid of a lot of things and sold one of our cars, reasoning that we could buy another one in Mississippi. I rented the largest U-Haul truck they had and we loaded it full, but there was still a lot of stuff that wouldn't fit. For example, we had a California king waterbed, hand-carved with stained glass, beautiful, but massive, and we gave it away. We gave away our living room furniture. There were still a lot of things we wanted to take with us, so I rented a trailer to pull behind the truck. We got the trailer loaded and there were still things that wouldn't fit. I thought that maybe I didn't pack it right, so I unloaded the truck and repacked it, unloaded the trailer and repacked it, and it still wouldn't fit. We decided that we'd just have to buy whatever we wanted when we got there. It was nice to have enough money to be able to leave things behind, knowing that we could replace them.

Terry drove the car with two kids and I drove the truck with one kid. We took off at 3 a.m. I never told anyone I was leaving, and it would be many weeks before my family knew that I had left the state, but they didn't know where I had gone. I didn't speak to anyone in my family for the next three years. The last thing I did before I left Virginia was go to the cemetery and say good-bye. I felt guilty, but I knew I had to let go. I never planned to come back to the state of Virginia. I said to Darlene, "I hope you understand. I hope you approve. I'm not trying to replace you. I think Misty needs a mother."

I had never been away from the beach except for the time that I spent in the army in Georgia, and I didn't know what I was going to do without the water. The nearest beach to us in Mississippi was over two hundred miles away, and I didn't know how that would affect me. The beach was my place of solitude, a spiritual place, and I could go there in any season and the water was always there, the waves were always there. It was a friend and part of who I was. I was leaving part of myself, the place where I was born and grew up. I was leaving all of my memories, and even though many of them were not good memories, they were still mine. There were a lot of memories that were good. Racing with my car trying to impress the girls from the Shoney's restaurant. Surfing and trying to impress the tourist girls from Pennsylvania and New York. Going to dances and hanging out.

I had to give up my dream of being a singer and a songwriter because of my daughter. I couldn't drag her to New York or Memphis to pursue that career. I couldn't live that kind of life with a child. I was happy to give it up for her. I was thirty years old, a milestone. I wasn't in my twenties anymore, and I was ready for some peace and quiet. Earlier in my life, I never wanted a nine to five job like my father had, the same routine, day after day, year after year. In twenty years, my father never missed a day of work. After all I'd been through, I started thinking that's exactly what I wanted. I wanted to raise these kids and love my wife. I wanted to have things and give them things. I wanted to grow old and watch my children grow up and have grandchildren. That sounded good to me.

It took us a day and a half to drive to Mississippi. Our house was beautiful, a very long one-story brick ranch house with a huge family room, about the size of a three-car garage. There was a fireplace that we could walk into and dining room was surrounded by glass on three sides and had French doors. There was a brick patio with built-in gas torches. The house was on a hill and there was a barn. A creek ran through the back of the property, and we had twenty acres of pasture and more than three acres of lawn. There was a gazebo in the front and a multitude of trees, pecan trees, petaga trees and pear trees. A place like that in Virginia would have cost at least $200,000-$250,000 in 1982, maybe more. The man who had built the house was divorced and wanted to sell and so we moved in with an option to purchase at a later date for $108,000. The house had been on the market for two or three years and he had cut the price a lot. The market was flat because the oil industry had taken a dive and a lot of people were out of work.

The house was out of town, out in the country and there were only a couple of houses within a mile of us-the perfect place for me. It fit right into my plans of what I wanted by the time I was a certain age. In fact, it looked like I was going to be ahead of schedule. I was pretty excited about that.

We thought that we would take two or three months to get settled in, get organized and get to know our new home. The place had been empty for some time, so there was a lot to do. The town closest to us was three or four miles down the road, a town of about 2,000 people with one stoplight, one grocery store, a couple of restaurants, and a couple of feed stores. It was just what I had dreamed of. Everybody was friendly, even though they could tell that we weren't from around there. Everybody waved, whether they knew us or not.

We went into the feed store and introduced ourselves. I noticed that people were looking at me kind of funny and I couldn't figure out why. Then I saw myself in a mirror and realized that all of the people there were dressed in jeans, flannel shirts, bandannas, boots, cowboy hats and the like. I was wearing a white oxford shirt with a button-down collar, slacks, and loafers. I looked like an Easterner who had gone out west in the 1840s. I realized that I'd have to change my image if I wanted to fit in. Nevertheless, people were friendly to us and asked where we were from and where we were living. Our house was forever to be known as "Billy Gunther's house," as he was the original owner. I don't think it would have mattered if we had lived there for the next fifty years, it would still be Billy Gunther's place.

I started thinking about starting my own business in addition to the horse business, and so I traveled around looking for opportunities. The business that I had in Virginia wouldn't work because the homes were too far apart. Also, it was a different culture. Many of the people lived on farms and raised their own cows, chickens and pigs for meat. There were also quite a few people who ate deer, squirrel and rabbit. A fresh bacon-wrapped filet mignon probably wouldn't go over too well. Then I thought about sausage. Italian sausage was really big and I knew enough about it to open a sausage shop.

We purchased our first horse. We went out to a huge farm and the owner sent one of her hired hands out to find the horse that was for sale. It had been out in the pasture for the better part of the year, and she hadn't seen it. While we were waiting, she told us about it. It was a red quarter horse whose father was a world champion barrel racer with all kinds of trophies. About the time I asked how much she wanted for the animal, the man brought the horse up and it was limping badly. The hoof was all infected. She didn't know what was causing the infection and said that she'd have to get the vet to check it out.

I asked again how much she wanted for the horse and she told me that she had originally wanted $10,000, but now she was willing to take a great deal less. She wanted to find out what was wrong with him. I asked how much she wanted for him right then. I was thinking that I'd take a chance. I didn't know what was wrong with its leg. It could have been crippled for life or it could have something very simple wrong with it. She thought for a while and said that she would let me have it for $3,000. I countered with $2,000 and we finally agreed on $2,500. I wrote her a check and we loaded up the horse. We found out that the horse had just stepped on something sharp out in the pasture and within a couple of weeks, the horse was perfectly fine. We got a wonderful deal. This was the horse that we were going to use to create our dream: a registered horse with a good blood line.

I came to the conclusion that I would have to postpone starting my business in order to get the horse business off the ground. We bought another twenty acres of land about twenty miles from our house. We bought not only the land, but also the mineral rights, as there were stories that lots of oil was out there. The land also had a lot of good timber and a small house on the property that was about a hundred years old. It was a good place to train horses. We bought a pick-up truck and began to purchase horses. We got a business loan from the bank and things were really rolling along.

One day in the fall of 1982, I was traveling down Highway 98, a very dangerous two-lane road. The speed limit was fifty-five, but log trucks and cement trucks and tractor trailers zipped up and down the road at much faster speeds. I was in my brand new 1982 Ford Thunderbird. There was a car in front of me and the car in front of him stopped to make a left turn. I glanced in my rearview mirror and saw a very large asphalt truck coming toward me. It seemed like he was coming awfully fast, but I didn't think much about it. Certainly he saw the car, saw that I was stopped. I glanced in the mirror again and he was still coming. The car made the turn and the one in front of me took off and I realized that the truck was not going to stop. By the time I hit the gas, the asphalt truck hit the rear end of my car and went up over it, crushing the roof, flattening my car. I managed to lie down in the front seat, and the car rolled over into a ditch. I was partially conscious. I knew only that when I moved, I had terrible pain in my back.

I laid there for close to an hour, but it seemed much longer to me. The rescue workers had to cut me out of the car, and I was taken in the ambulance to the ER. It was amazing that I survived the accident at all. The first thing I wanted to do after I got home was see the car. It was impossible to tell what kind of car it was. The back was totally gone and the front was torn off. It was as flat as a pancake. Looking at the car, I thought to myself that I had managed a narrow escape from death once more.

The truck driver had a suspended license, and I sued the company. They paid my hospital bills, bought me a new car and gave me $10,000. I just felt fortunate that I hadn't been killed. Maybe fortunate isn't the right word. How many times can one person be fortunate? I had stopped believing in luck much earlier. No one's luck could be this good. As I look back now, these incidents scare me and I know that someone must have been continually watching over me in order to snatch me from death's door so many times.

32

The horse business was doing well. At first, we were not allowed to enter some horse shows because we weren't riding western, but they couldn't legally keep us out. Terry began to board, train horses and riders, and show horses. That's where the money was. If you showed a horse and he won a lot of trophies, you could put him out for stud and that made the stables worth a lot. It took time to build the stables up, but we worked very hard at doing so.

We had been in Mississippi for about a year and it seemed that everything we touched turned to gold. I was making a lot of money. I had met a man from Hattiesburg who owned some grocery stores and his business was terrible. He wanted me to help him out. He turned his stores over to me and I had free rein to reorganize and do whatever I needed to do in order to make the stores profitable. I was traveling five or six days a week to Hattiesburg, which was about a hundred and sixty miles round trip.

I had also purchased a taco and snowcone stand. People in that area didn't go to restaurants after church on Sunday; they lined up at snowcone places. In the fall and winter, we sold Mexican food. There were no fast food restaurants at all in our area. I had wanted to open a Taco Bell, but they wanted $100,000 up front and I didn't want to risk that much money. I heard about the taco and snowcone business for sale and I bought it. It was very profitable. In 1983, I cleared $26,000 to $30,000 just in the summer months.

Financially, we were doing great. I was way ahead of the time table that I had set up for myself. We had a house, cars, horses, dogs, cats, trailers, a boat, land. We ended up being the President and Vice-President of the Southwestern Horse Association. Whatever we wanted, we could get. I saw a truck for sale and I stopped and just bought it. I sold the timber off of our twenty acres to Georgia Pacific for triple the money that I had paid for the land. I made an agreement with Shell Oil to come in and do some surveys and drill for oil. They drilled day and night for two months, but never found any oil. I'm still convinced that there is oil there, but they didn't want to invest any more time and money looking for it. They were paying me one hundred dollars a day to drill. I talked to a couple of independent oil drillers, but they wanted $100,000 to come out and drill for a certain amount of time. I thought there was oil there, but I wasn't that convinced.

One day we drove over to look at the campus of a small college that wasn't too far away. A young woman that we had met at horse shows had gone there and we just wanted to see it. We were looking at the grounds, and out back, near the woods, we saw a cage with a cement foundation and an anchor fence. The fence was probably about ten feet high and the cage was about twenty feet by twenty feet. In the cage was a bear. He was right out in the sun with no protection. It was nothing in Mississippi for the temperature to be 100 degrees every day in the summer with 100% humidity. We went closer and saw that his water supply consisted of green slimy water filling a hole in the cement foundation. On the fence, there appeared to be dried food, as if the food had just been thrown through the fence and some of it had stuck there. The bear's fur was patchy where much of it had fallen out, and he was not very responsive. He had a hard time walking. It was a pitiful sight.

I couldn't stand the thought of this bear being treated in such a poor manner and I contacted the college about him. It turned out that he was their mascot. I visited him several more times and saw that they were feeding him scraps left over from the cafeteria. At the end of the day, a man would come out with a pot of leftovers and throw it all through the fence. The bear had to get what he could off the cement. The water was stagnant.

I went to see the dean of the college and asked if they ever took him out of the cage. He hadn't been taken out in at least five years. I told him about the terrible conditions the bear had to endure, but he brushed me off.

I left his office and called the nearest Greenpeace office, which was in Florida. I was still a member. I explained the situation and they agreed with me that something had to be done. I contacted the state and local governments to find out what kind of regulations existed for housing wild animals. I had to go all the way to federal guidelines. I read all the information that I received and then I went back to see the dean.

I walked into his office and told him that I was still upset about the treatment of this animal. I told him about the laws stating that the bear must have running water and a shelter. He had to have a tree and things to keep him occupied. He had to have a certain kind of food, not slop from the kitchen. He had to have a vet inspection every so often. The cage had to be a certain size. He had to be let out to get exercise.

The dean seemed irritated with me and with the whole situation and tried to brush me off again. To him, it was just a bear and no big deal. I asked why they didn't just give him to a zoo, since they didn't take him to games anymore. He said that it was their bear and they were going to keep him and they didn't plan to change anything.

At that point, I pulled out my Greenpeace card and laid it on his desk. I said, "Have you ever heard of Greenpeace?" He said that he had. "Well, sir, do you want me to get the television and the newspaper, to get Greenpeace up here from Florida? Do you want this to be a big deal?"

Apparently, he knew Greenpeace's reputation for very actively trying to save animals and he relented and asked what he could do. I gave him a copy of the guidelines and told him that I'd be back in a week.

A week later, I returned and the dean told me that they could give the bear some better food and put up some sort of shelter, but they couldn't do everything else that was required.

"No, sir," I said, "This is not a bargain. All of the things on paper are federal guidelines. You are breaking the law. I will not only call Greenpeace, I will call the government as well. Every one of these things needs to be done."

He realized then that he had no choice. They got the vet to come in and examine the bear and it turned out that he had a condition that was making his hair fall out. The vet began to take care of him. Every few days, I took the bear a jar of honey and fed him through the fence. After a couple of months, he had a brand new home three times the size of his original cage, with running water, and he was getting the right kind of food.

Word got around about what I had done and I became known as "the bear man." I would hear people whispering when I went into a place, "There's the bear man." When I met someone new, I would introduce myself and the person would say, "Charles Cross, Charles Cross, oh yeah, you're the bear man." At first it was kind of embarrassing and I didn't know whether people thought of this as a good thing or a bad thing, but eventually I got used to it and was happy that I had made the bear's life a lot easier.

33

One of the promises that I had made to myself was that I would start going to church, so while we were starting our business, we were also looking for a church. We did find one and we went sporadically, probably once or twice a month. Once the business was more established and we were doing so well, I began to go more regularly. It was a Southern Baptist church with a congregation of nearly three hundred.

Terry would go with me once in a while, but she was not a very spiritual person. Her goal was to achieve, to succeed and to have as much stuff as she possibly could get. There were a lot of things about church that she didn't like. She wasn't saved. Of course, at that time, I couldn't have cared less. I didn't ask God about marrying her and didn't care whether God agreed or not.

My job with the grocery store in Hattiesburg ended and I was glad. I was tired of driving all that distance. About forty miles from us, just over the Louisiana line, was another grocery chain that was losing money. The owners had heard about me and hired me to help. I took care of the frozen food, meat, produce and deli, and in just a few months, I was able to increase sales in my departments fivefold.

I was traveling to Louisiana five days a week and doing horse shows on the weekends. At night there were meetings about horse shows. I built fences and enclosures. I learned how to give the horses their shots. The only thing I didn't learn how to do was shoe the horses. I had seen too many people get kicked and I didn't want any part of that.

Everything seemed to be great. We were busy. The kids were doing well in school. We had every material thing that we wanted. We took trips and we spent a lot of money.

During the second year that we were there, Terry began to sleep in our bed less and less. She spent more time on the couch, watching television, and she would fall asleep there. This happened three, four or five nights a week. I didn't think much about it. I knew that she was tired and we were both so busy.

I started going to the horse shows less frequently because I was beginning to feel overwhelmed with all that I had to do. Preparing for a horse show begins weeks in advance. There is the grooming and training, packing and unpacking, a lot of work. I was becoming more involved in the church and I didn't have the time or energy to do it all. Sometimes the shows were in different states and we had to be gone overnight. I couldn't afford to be away that much.

We had become friends with another couple who raised horses, Kenny and Debbie Grimes. They went to the same shows we did. Eventually, just the kids and Terry and Kenny would go to the shows. That way, they could just take one truck and one trailer and it made a lot more sense. Debbie would stay at home. Kenny was a good friend and I was glad that Terry had someone to go to the shows with.

One day I was driving in town and I saw Debbie walking down the sidewalk. She flagged me down and I stopped. She got into the front seat and she looked upset. I said, "Are you all right? What's wrong?"

"You don't know?"

"Know what?"

The first thing I thought was that Kenny had been in an accident, that maybe he'd fallen off of a horse and gotten kicked. I asked her, "Is he okay? Is it a horse injury?

She replied, "You really don't know, do you?" She reached into her purse and pulled out a package. "Terry and Kenny are having an affair."

I laughed at her. "No, no. You're wrong, Debbie. Why are you saying that?"

"It's true."

"No, it's not. I know my wife. I trust her. She wouldn't do something like that."

"Well, she is."

"You're wrong. I don't know where your suspicions are coming from, but I'm telling you that you're wrong. Do you have proof?"

She opened up the package and pulled out some photographs. She had been suspicious for some time and had hired a detective. I saw photos of one of our trucks hidden underneath a bridge and Kenny and Terry getting into his truck. I saw pictures of them at horse shows, acting in ways they shouldn't have been. I saw pictures of them sitting in a truck, kissing. I saw them coming out of a hotel. I still refused to believe it. I told her that there had to be another answer, a rational explanation. She got upset and got out of the car. She said, "It's going to hit the fan because I'm going to take him for everything he's got." She slammed the door and left.

I went home and Terry wasn't there. I drove to the other land, which was about twenty miles away, running everything through my brain. I wasn't angry, I was scared. I didn't really know why or of what- I was expecting Terry to be able to explain the pictures.

When I arrived, she was there with one of the horses right by the driveway, surprised to see me. I didn't get out of the car. She came up to the window, holding the reins. I rolled down the window and we had about thirty seconds of small talk. Then I said, "I just saw Debbie. She gave me some disturbing news. She has this idea that you and Kenny are having an affair."

"Well, that's ridiculous. Where did she get an idea like that?"

"All I'm telling you is that's what she told me. She said she could prove it." I didn't tell her about the pictures.

Terry asked, "Do you believe her?"

"No, I don't believe her. But should I? Is it true? If it's true, then tell me. I need to know."

"No, it's not true."

"Okay. Where would she get an idea like that?"

"You know how she is."

"No, I don't. She must have gotten this idea from somewhere. There's nothing going on?"

Silence.

"Terry, I'm asking you again, are you having an affair with Kenny Grimes?"

Again, silence.

"Please tell me."

I suppose that she thought that by her silence I would know the answer without her saying it. I was hoping that she would give me a reason. At that moment, I didn't care if it was a lie. I would have accepted a lie. I was hoping that she had a reason, an excuse, a way out, something that I could hang onto, something to convince me that this couldn't be happening. I asked her again.

"Yes, it's true."

I felt like my heart stopped. In a split second there was anger, then it went away. My body was weak. "Why? How could you do this? Why?"

"It's not what you think."

"You slept with the man."

"Yes and no."

"What do you mean, 'yes and no?'"

"I did sleep with him, but nothing happened. We didn't do anything."

I said, "You're a slut. You're a whore. I'm going to kill him and that's it."

I threw the car into reverse, spun out of the driveway and took off down the road. My whole life had been jerked out from underneath me. It was gone. It wasn't a gradual thing. All of a sudden, I had no life. I felt that I had no present and no future. I had nothing. I couldn't believe it. I was speeding down the two-lane road at about sixty-five miles an hour. At a crossroads, I noticed a vehicle on the road to my right. He had a stop sign. I continued my speed and right before I got to the intersection, he decided to try to make it across. When he saw that he couldn't make it, he panicked and jammed on the brakes. If he had kept going, I probably would have been all right, but he stopped right in the middle of the intersection and I had no place to go. The only thought that I had was to turn the car sideways to slam into him on the passenger side instead of hitting him head on.

The next thing I remember was seeing my Green Bay Packers hat on the back seat. For some reason, I had reached to put my hat on and it wasn't there. I turned to look for it and saw it. I didn't have to reach very far to pick it up because the front seat was pretty much in the back seat. I picked the hat up and it was full of blood. I realized that something must be wrong. Then I saw that the windshield wasn't there and knew that my head must have gone through it. I reached up to my head and to my mouth and there was blood everywhere.

My left arm was still on the steering wheel. I had such a grip on it that the steering column was actually snapped in half. That's the only reason that my chest didn't go into the steering wheel. I hadn't been wearing a seat belt. I had a great deal of pain in my left arm. The next thing that I thought was that I had to get out. I had to walk. I opened the door as far as it would open and fell out of the car. I crawled across the road into the grass by the ditch and I kept thinking to myself that I had to get up. I forced myself to stand.

I knew that my arm was broken. My mouth was full of blood. It felt like my teeth were knocked out. My head was bleeding. People started stopping. Someone made me sit down by the side of the road. My pastor came along on his way to the church. I recognized him, but I couldn't hear what he or anyone else was saying. I was in a daze.

An ambulance had been called and it took about twenty minutes for it to get there. They bandaged my head and face. I asked the pastor to call Terry and tell her what had happened and to have her pick up Misty from school.

When I got to the hospital, I found out that my arm wasn't broken. It was blue and black and yellow from my wrist to my shoulder. It had absorbed the impact of the crash and had saved me. My teeth were loose again, as they had been when my jaw was broken back in the 70s, but they weren't knocked out. There was a hole in my lip and a gash in my head, but other than that, I was doing pretty well. The driver of the other vehicle had sustained absolutely no injuries because he was driving a full-size pick-up truck that was built like a rock-the kind built in the sixties made with metal, not plastic.

I was lying in the ER waiting to get some stitches. I really wanted Terry to be there. Even with what had just happened before the accident, I wanted her there. After about three hours, they were ready to release me and that's when Terry came in. She asked me what had happened and how I was. I found out that she knew about the wreck and where I was more than two hours before she got to the hospital, and she had been only twenty minutes away. She had been there for about forty-five seconds when she said, "Well, I have to go."

I said, "You can't just go. You have to pick Misty up at 6:30."

"Well, I can't."

"What do you mean, you can't? Where are you going? I'm lying here half dead and you're talking about going somewhere. You have to pick up Misty."

"Okay, okay, I will."

"I'm going to need a ride home. Are you coming back?"

"Yeah, I'll go pick up Misty and I'll take her to the baby-sitter's. I'll be back in about an hour."

About thirty minutes after she left, the hospital released me. I was pushed into the lobby in a wheelchair to wait for Terry. Another hour passed. I called, but there was no one at home. I wasn't sure if Misty got picked up. I could hardly walk. I was afraid to call a cab, in case I missed them. I waited another hour. Every so often the nurse would ask me if someone was coming for me. I told her that my wife was supposed to come. I waited in the lobby for a total of three hours before Terry returned.

When we got in the car, I said, "Where have you been? You said you'd be back in an hour and I waited three hours in the lobby for you. Where's Misty?"

"Misty is at the baby-sitter's. She's fine. I picked her up on time. Everything is fine."

"Well, where in the world have you been?"

"Well, Charles, I had horses I had to get in. They had to be fed. I can't just leave them out there unfed. I got back as soon as I could."

I said, "Okay, okay, okay. Let's just get home."

I spent the next several days just lying around. Over the following weeks, we talked about the affair that she had with Kenny. She was able to convince me that they had slept together, but hadn't done anything. It was an overnight trip and they stayed in the same room, but they were watching television and sitting or lying on the floor and they fell asleep. I believed it because I was trying to find something to hang onto. I think that she realized I was searching for any excuse, no matter how flimsy. She told me that there was nothing going on and it wasn't what I thought. She started talking about how paranoid Debbie was and placed the blame on her. I wanted to believe her. I told her that we would just put this behind us and forget about it. I wanted to continue with our lives the way they had been.

34

As I slowly recovered, I got more involved with the church. I felt what I thought was a call from God. It was as if the Lord was telling me, "You know, Charles, you've tried everything else. You've done all sorts of things. You've tried to find peace and contentment and happiness. You've tried to find your place. You've tried to fill that place that is in you that is empty and I'm telling you now that it's time for you to come home. I am what is missing in your life."

I had been reading my Bible every night for several months and I was really getting into it. I really felt that the Lord was speaking to me through His word. One Sunday night, I was in church and I don't even remember what the preacher was saying because I was wrestling with the Lord. I knew that He wanted me to go forward during the invitation and give my life to Him. Though I was saved at an early age, I wasn't sure that I was really saved, and I never really lived for Him. I felt that this was what the Lord wanted me to do. When the invitation was given, I held onto my seat and I refused to get up. As soon as the service was over, I practically ran out the back door. I got into the car and took off for home.

As I was driving home, I was scared to death because I knew what the Lord wanted me to do and I refused to do it. It was as if He was sitting right beside me, talking to me. On the way home, I said, "Lord, if you will spare my life until next Sunday, I'll be the first one at the altar."

I was very careful that week. I was afraid that something would happen to me and I wouldn't be able to make it back. I couldn't wait to get back to church that Sunday and at the invitation, I was the first one there. I knelt down and cried and said, "Lord, there's not much here, but from this day forward, I turn my life over to You. You do with it what you see fit."

I had some ideas in my mind about what I could do and how the Lord might use me. Up to that point, I had served myself. I had my life planned out and I was way ahead of schedule. I was going to retire at age fifty and live it up and be financially secure. I would have everything that a person could want. I was still in my thirties and I had accomplished everything that I wanted to accomplish up to age forty. I knew that I could help the church financially. I could cut the grass and drive the church bus and do things like that. Those are the ways that I thought I could best serve the Lord, but I had no idea what He had in store for me.

As it happened, both our pianist and our choir director left our church at about the same time. There were several people in the congregation who could play the piano, so that wasn't a problem. One Sunday morning, the minister asked if there was anybody who wanted to volunteer to be the choir director. They wanted to hire someone inside the church if there was someone who felt the call from God or wanted to do it. They weren't looking for a professional musician, just someone to lead the choir. I had written some songs and played the guitar, but for me, getting up in front of people was a no-no. But I felt that the Lord really wanted me to do this. Again, it was like He was sitting next to me telling me to do this job. Of course, I argued with Him and for the next two weeks and thought about it every day, but I didn't do anything about it. The idea didn't go away. It kept getting stronger and stronger. Finally, I approached the pastor and told him that I'd like to put my name in for choir director, but there were two stipulations. First, if anyone else volunteered, my name would be taken out. Second, when they found someone more qualified, they would replace me with that person.

I was sure that someone else in the church would volunteer and then I wouldn't have to do it. See, Lord, I'll put my name in because that's what You want me to do, but it's not my fault if they find somebody more qualified. I could get the guilt to go away by doing what the Lord wanted me to do and yet I wouldn't have to take the job.

A couple of weeks later, the pastor called and said that the music committee would like to interview me for the position of choir director. No one else had volunteered.

The next day I went to the church to meet with the pastor and the seven members of the committee. The pastor was sitting back in his chair behind a big mahogany desk in a suit that didn't quite button. The committee members were sitting in chairs lined up against a wall. They told me to sit on the other side of the office. It felt like being in front of a firing squad.

They started by asking me questions about music. I told them that I could read music a little bit and that I had written songs. I hadn't sung in the church choir. They asked me why I had volunteered and I told them that I believed that it was what the Lord wanted me to do. After about a half an hour, they thanked me and told me that they would let me know. I left thinking that I had blown it. I had no qualifications and I figured that they would keep searching for someone else.

The next day the pastor called me at home and told me that I had the job. I was very excited and very scared though not as surprised as I thought I'd be.

When I told Terry that I had accepted the job of music director, she said, "What do you mean you accepted it? You didn't talk this over with me. Why didn't you tell me about it or anything?"

"It's not that big a deal. You don't go most of the time anyway. I didn't think you cared if I did it or not. I really didn't think that I'd get the job. But they gave it to me. I can turn it down."

"Well, did you?"

"No, I accepted it."

She said, "I won't go to that church again."

"What do you mean? Why? What's wrong?"

"You're not going to embarrass me."

"What do you mean, embarrass you?"

"You're going to get up there and embarrass yourself. If you want to embarrass yourself, you go right ahead in front of all those people. But you're not going to embarrass me."

"You don't think I can do it?"

"Hell, no, you can't do it."

I said, "Whoa. Actually, I think I can do it. Not because of me, but I think that by the grace of God, He will enable me and give me the ability to do it because I believe that's what He wants me to do."

She just kind of sneered and said, "Well, don't count on me supporting you. Don't count on me to be there on Sunday mornings."

"Fine, you're not there most of the time anyway."

The first night of choir practice, I was scared to death. I had rehearsed in my mind all week what I was going to do and how I was going to do it. I knew enough to start out with something very simple. We were just going to do some basic hymns and let me get comfortable before we tried to do anything more complicated. Everybody can sing hymns. Then I thought, no, that's not right. If I'm going to do it, I should do it right. It should be something special.

The first song that I taught the choir to do was "Morning Has Broken" by Cat Stevens. It was in the hymnal. They had never sung anything like it before. There were about twenty-five people in the choir and the average age was probably fifty to fifty-five. They were used to singing hymns and not doing much else. This was something really modern to them.

On Wednesday night, we had a Bible study and prayer time and then we had choir practice from eight until nine. Usually, everyone except the choir members left, but on that first practice night, there were about twenty people sitting in the church. I figured that they were there to see how the new guy was doing. That made me even more nervous. I could feel holes being drilled into my back by twenty pairs of eyeballs. We made it through the practice, however, with little trouble.

The first Sunday, I practically begged Terry to come. I was so nervous. I told her that it would look bad if she wasn't there and besides that, I really thought it would be nice to have her there. She told me that I had done this on my own and she wasn't going to let me embarrass her.

Everything went very well. People were very encouraging. After church, many of them came up to me and told me how well I'd done. Some said that it seemed as if I'd been doing this for years. As I played it over in my mind, I realized that not only had it gone well, it had been perfect. Nobody missed a note. Everybody was on time. Everything ended on time. I was sweating bullets, but everything was perfect.

That was the last time that it was perfect. But I knew that if it hadn't been, I would have quit. If I had messed up or something had happened, I wouldn't have had the courage to try again. I knew that I could do it. I wasn't great at it, but I could do enough to get by until they found someone else.

I really got into being the music director. I loved planning the songs and was really excited about the work. When Terry found out that I wasn't embarrassing myself, she started coming to church once in a while. She never said that she was wrong or that she was proud of me, but she did come occasionally.

The horse business was still growing and I was still driving back and forth to Louisiana five or six days a week. At night I'd work on the music and, of course, on Sundays and Wednesdays, I'd work with the choir. We had family time and we were able to get away once in a while.

Terry had pretty much taken over the horse business. She made all the purchases and everything was in her name, and that was fine with me because I had enough on my plate. Our relationship seemed to be going well. Kenny and Debbie had reconciled and I had been able to talk myself into believing that Debbie had just overreacted and that the pictures were taken out of context.

I was feeling that the Lord was leading me to do something other than the music. I felt that He wanted me to preach, to deliver a sermon. I had been working on that and thinking about it for several months. I approached our pastor and said, "I believe that the Lord wants me to preach."

"Is that so?" he asked.

"Yes. Now wait a minute. I'm not saying that I'm supposed to be a pastor or a minister or whatever. I believe that He wants me to preach this one sermon and that's it. Just one. That's all. I could never be a pastor. I don't have time for the backbiting, preaching about gossip and money. I just believe that God wants me to preach this one sermon."

"Okay. When would you like to do it?"

"I guess as soon as possible."

"Do you want a Sunday night or a Sunday morning?"

With my personality, I would logically choose a Sunday night, when only a few people would be there-the fewer the better. I opened my mouth to say Sunday night and I said, "Sunday morning." It was like someone else had said it.

The pastor said, "Sunday morning?"

"Yep, if I'm going to do it, it might as well be with as many people here as possible." Who was talking here? This was not Charles. I wasn't doing this.

"Let me check the calendar and I'll get back to you and give you a date."

I was going to deliver a sermon.

35

Thanksgiving Day, 1983, I went to Louisiana for a few hours, and when I returned home, I could tell that something wasn't right. I said hello to the kids and they were silent. I walked into the back bedroom and I saw suitcases.

"What's going on?" The first thing I thought was that Terry was going on a trip to a horse show in another state.

"I'm leaving."

"Where are you going?"

"I'm leaving you."

"What do you mean? For what?" I felt weak.

"I can't take it anymore."

"You can't take what anymore?"

"When we got married, did you not say that I was number one in your life?"

"Yes. You still are."

"No, I'm not. God is."

"Well, yes, but He's not physically here."

"You're not the same man that I married."

"That's true. I'm not quite the same man that you married. In fact, I'm a whole lot better than I was."

"Well, that's a matter of opinion. I want back the man that I married."

"I'm the same man. This is just a little more improved. What's really bothering you?"

"If I can't be number one in your life, I'm not going to be in your life. Who do you pick? If it were another woman, I could fight her. I could understand. If it were a job or something else, but you picked God. How can I compare? How can I fight God?"

"Who said you're fighting God?"

"The bottom line is that you choose. Either I'm first in your life or God is."

"I'm not making a choice like that. You're not forcing me to make some kind of silly decision like that."

"Fine. I'm out of here."

"Where are you going?"

"I'm going to live in the other house. I'm out."

I got angry and we argued. She yelled and screamed. I yelled and screamed. The kids got scared and started crying. She left with her kids.

Misty and I didn't have a Thanksgiving meal. The next day, the house felt so empty. The furniture and everything was still in it, but we were missing three people. That night, there was a knock at the door. I opened it and there was my lawyer. I invited him in and asked him what he was doing there.

"Well," he said, "I'm wondering why you haven't been answering my mail or returning my phone calls."

"Probably because you haven't mailed me or phoned me. I don't know what you're talking about."

"I have mailed you three letters."

"I haven't gotten any of them."

In our town, there weren't any mail carriers. Everyone had a post office box and you had to go there to pick up your mail. Terry was the one who always checked the mail. She would go through the mail and put the bills on my desk and I would write the checks and she would mail the payments. I never questioned any bills. We had a system going and it seemed to be working fine. I told him that Terry checked the mail and then asked what the letters were about.

"The first letter was about the mortgage on your two homes. You were two months behind on your house payments."

"That's not right. That's not true. I sit down every month and pay the bills. I know I've paid them."

"I wrote you three times and didn't get a response. The bank contacted me again and said that they couldn't get in touch with you. They have called and sent letters. Finally, they sent me a letter that said you are four months behind on your mortgage payments and they're going to foreclose on your homes."

"That can't be. I'm telling you." I explained our bill paying system to him.

"I believe you paid the bill. You wrote out the check. Did you mail it?"

"No, Terry mails it when she picks up the mail."

"Obviously, she didn't mail them."

"But the money is not in the bank."

"She must be taking the money out of the bank for the exact amount of the checks. Where is she?"

I told him that she had left and was living in the other house. I said that I could get the money to catch up the payments.

"It's too late. The last letter said that they have started foreclosure proceedings."

"Oh no. I'll call them and I'll wire the money."

"It's too late."

"It can't be too late."

"It is."

I was upset and I went to find Terry. We had it out. I asked what she had been doing with all the money and she told me that she had been saving it because she knew that she was going to leave. I asked if she was still seeing Kenny Grimes and she said that she was.

"So you've been lying the whole time?"

"Yes, pretty much."

"Now tell me again what you've been doing with the money."

"I've been spending a lot of it. We drive a long way to get out of this area so that we can be alone and so no one will know."

Terry hadn't been doing much work in the daytime. Kenny would come over every day after I had gone to work and the kids were already at the baby-sitter's or daycare. They had been doing this for months. She bought him a Rolex watch, a bracelet and a ring. She had a whole new wardrobe that she had hidden from me.

I found a man who was willing to buy the house I was living in. The bank foreclosed on the other one. Of course, I started getting the mail. I got a water bill that was just astronomical. I went to the water department and it turned out that the bill hadn't been paid for months and they were ready to turn the water off. I paid the bill and then decided that I'd better check on a few other bills as well. I went to the phone company. The phone bill hadn't been paid. Nothing had been paid. Not one bill. I went to all the places where we owed money and paid all the bills. Everywhere I went, I got strange looks. I finally realized why. I was the only one in town who didn't know what was going on. I think that the whole population of 2,000 knew, except for me.

Misty and I rented a house in town, a big old house with three floors that was built in the 1800s. It was Christmas and I didn't feel much like having a tree that year. That's the only year that I didn't have one. Misty was nine years old. I bought her some gifts, but it didn't feel like Christmas.

I was not eating and was losing weight. I went from sorrow to anger about a million times a day. One day I got a phone call from Terry and she asked me to meet her for lunch. I thought that she had finally come to her senses and that she was going to come crawling back to me.

I met her for lunch and after making conversation about the weather and asking how the kids were, she said, "I was wondering if you were going to do anything for the kids for Christmas."

"No. I wasn't planning to."

"You're not going to buy the kids anything for Christmas?"

I said, "Why don't you buy them something for Christmas?"

"We're still married and you're their father."

"No, actually, I'm not their father. You wouldn't let me adopt them and you're not living with me. You're with Kenny Grimes, so you two go buy Christmas."

"Well, that's not his place. He's not going to buy Christmas for them."

"Then you do it."

But she kept talking and she finally convinced me. She suggested that we go shopping together. I agreed and we set up a time.

We went shopping in the mall and I was feeling hopeful that maybe with the holiday season and the warm fuzzy feelings and the family memories, maybe we could get back together and try to make our marriage work. She said that she wanted to get me something for Christmas and I wanted to do the same for her, so we agreed to shop separately for a while, then meet for dinner. She asked me if I had any money because she didn't have much cash. We had a Visa and a Mastercard that we hardly ever used. I had them in case of an emergency. There was about a $2,000 limit on each one. I always carried one with me. I gave her one of the cards and told her to put whatever she bought on that.

After the shopping, we had dinner and then as she was getting into her car, I asked for the Visa card back.

She said, "You know, these cards are mine too."

"Yeah, but no."

"Can I keep it? I'd like to have it just for emergencies. I promise I won't use it, but you know driving on theses country roads at night with the kids, something could happen. I might need it. I won't use it except in a dire emergency."

"Okay, but promise me, promise me that you won't use this card except for an emergency."

"I promise. I swear." And then she went on her way to wherever she was living. She wouldn't tell me where, but she said she wasn't living with Kenny. At that point, I shouldn't have trusted anything she told me.

In January, we were still in contact. She called one day and said that she needed to see me. She gave me a location to meet her, an intersection with a little country store that was no longer open. I would have to drive about a hundred miles to get there, but I agreed. It was a deserted place in the middle of nowhere. We were supposed to meet at noon and at two-thirty there was still no sign of her, so I drove all the way back home.

Two days later I got another phone call. She told me that something had come up before and she had no way to contact me. She apologized. I complained that I had driven for miles and wasted a day for nothing. She said that she would make it up to me and suggested that she come over to my house the next night so that we could talk. I thought, well, maybe there's something here. She asked if I would fix our favorite meal, which was filet mignon and Maine lobster. I agreed and she said she'd be there at eight.

At eight, I had the meal ready. Misty was in the bedroom watching television. I had candles lit and a bottle of wine open. Nine, ten, eleven, midnight, and she never showed up. I ate some of the meal and threw the rest away. She called a couple of days later and said that she was sorry she couldn't make it and gave some excuses. I asked why she didn't call. She said she knew that she should have, but she would make it up to me. How about Friday? Same meal, same time? I said okay.

I prepared the same meal on Friday night. About eleven, she finally showed up. The food was cold. She said that she was sorry, she got held up, this and that happened. We made small talk for about an hour and she nibbled at the food. She said that she had to go and then we got into a heavy discussion. I tried to find out where she was living and she wouldn't tell me. I finally said, "The reason you won't tell me is because you're living with Kenny Grimes."

Terry admitted that she was. We got into a shouting match and she got into her car and swore she would never come back. I was so angry. I didn't like the way the night had ended, with us yelling at each other.

A couple of weeks later, I told her that we needed to sit down and talk, and I offered to fix dinner again. Once again, I waited and waited and finally at eleven she showed up. I was really upset, but I didn't say anything. She ate a bit and after about thirty minutes, she said she had to go.

I said, "Now wait a minute. You're always leaving. I wait for hours whether it's here or out on the road. I do whatever it is that you want. I bought Christmas. I did all of this stuff and you can't show up on time and sit down and eat dinner. Just like the hospital. When I was at the hospital, you weren't there thirty seconds and you had to leave. What was so important that you had to leave?"

"I'll tell you. Kenny was out in the parking lot. He's the one who gave me a ride to the hospital."

"You mean to tell me that while I was lying in a hospital bed, the reason it took you three hours to get there was because you were out with him and then he drove you to the hospital and you couldn't stay thirty seconds because you had to get back out and go wherever you were going with him?"

"Yeah."

I called her a whore, a bitch and a slut. I told her to leave. I told her that I hoped she rotted in hell and that I never wanted to see her again. She got into the car, slammed the door, and took off.

In the meantime, we were losing everything that we had. It had been the bank president's idea to put our personal and business assets together in one account earlier in our marriage. Over the past year, Terry had been taking everything out of her name and putting it in her children's names, Kenny's name, a friend's name. Horses, land, trailers-anything that was in her name. The only things that remained were things that were in my name or in both our names. She was not making business payments and people were coming to me. I went to see another lawyer and asked him what I could do.

He said, "I can help you, but you are going to have to promise me something first. You have to promise that you are going to divorce this woman."

"Divorce her for what?"

"I'm not going to go into this and get you out of this mess and then have you stay married to her because she is just going to do it to you again. I don't care if you pay me or not. I'm not going to go through this for nothing. It's going to happen to you again. You have to get away from this woman."

"I can't do that. First off, I'm a Christian and I don't believe in divorce. Nobody in my family has ever been divorced. That's a foreign word. No way can I ever get a divorce. For whatever reason, I married her, and I've got to stay with it. I have no choice. That's the way it is."

"Well, I can't help you then."

I left his office, not knowing what to do. The bank began to seize the land to pay off what we owed. That took several months and all kinds of negotiations. The bank would set up a meeting with both of us and she wouldn't show up. I still didn't know where she was living.

One night, I took Misty to a friend's house. They had children, girls, and she was spending the weekend with them. I began thinking about going out and finding a bar, a place with dancing where I could go and get drunk. I hadn't had a drink in probably five years. I found a bar with country and western dancing, got a beer, and sat at a table and sipped it. I had drunk about half of it in thirty minutes and then I decided that I didn't want to sit inside anymore. There was a big balcony and so I went out there. It was chilly. I was still sipping the beer and after another half an hour, I thought, no, this isn't it. I didn't even finish the beer. I threw it in the trash. I got in my car and went home. That was my last attempt at drinking.

36

One day Terry came to me and said that she had made a terrible mistake and that she was sorry and wanted to come back. She wanted to know if I could forgive her and if we could just go back to the way it was. I said, "I can do that. I don't know if we can stay in this area."

"We have to. The business is here. Our life is here. Our friends are here. Everything is here."

"We can try, but I don't know if it will work out or not."

She moved back in. My friends all thought I was crazy for taking her back, but I saw only that she was sorry and wanted us to be together again. Everyone was entitled to mistakes, and she was my wife. I didn't know how I was going to be able to deal with it, but I thought it was worth a try.

I helped her move her belongings. We took one of the trailers and went to the place she had been living, which was a new house in the woods about fifty miles away. This was where she had been living with Kenny. He was at work.

When I walked into the house, it was like a flood of dizziness came over me. I was looking at the place where my wife lived with another man. I became very angry and tried to keep that under control. There were a lot of things to move, personal things as well as horse things. That kept me busy for a little while. I was actually hoping that he would come home unexpectedly. Did he know that she was leaving him? I didn't know and I never asked. On the way out for the last time, I took one of his cowboy hats from the hat rack, put it on the floor and stomped on it. Squashed it flat. Just a little message to let him know that I had been there. It was a shame. Kenny was one of the first people that I had met and gotten to know in Mississippi. He had taught me and helped me to put up various kinds of fences, introduced me to people and showed me the ropes at the horse shows.

We tried to get back to the life that we'd had before, and I was trying to act like nothing ever happened. We talked about the fact that we were bound to run into Kenny around town or at horse shows. She was afraid that I would try to kill him, and I was afraid, too, of what I might do when I saw him. Terry told me that Kenny kept two guns in his truck all the time and had a house full of guns. She was worried that if I did something to him, he would try to shoot me. I was glad she told me that, but as it turned out, I never even ran into him.

I was very apprehensive about leaving Terry alone, but I thought that I had to trust her. A week and a half went by and things seemed to be okay. We were doing the right things, going through the right motions, saying the right words. I still hadn't come to the place where I could touch her, make love with her. We didn't talk about it. We were putting on a good show.

One night I came home and we were sitting in the house when she said, "I'm leaving."

"Where are you going?"

"I'm leaving again. I'm sorry."

"You haven't left this man alone have you? You've still been chasing him since you've come back. You two have still been meeting haven't you?"

"Yes."

"Fine. But let me tell you what. Don't even think about coming back. Pack your stuff and get out."

I went out to pick Misty up and when I got back, she was gone again. So it was just the two of us once more.

◆   ◆   ◆

I was still leading the music at church. People there knew Terry and I were having problems, but no one, not even the pastor, said anything.

I was still working on the sermon that I felt the Lord wanted me to deliver. One Sunday I drove up to the church and there was Terry waiting for me in her car. We sat in her car talking and she told me that she wanted a divorce. This really upset me. Somehow I was still thinking that we could work it out, that everything would get back to the way it was. She told me that she didn't think that I would ever be able to live with her after this and she was probably right, but it was really just an excuse for her to ask for the divorce. I said, "So, divorce. That's it."

"Even if we get divorced, that doesn't mean that we won't ever get back together again. I just need freedom. I need my time."

"Are you planning to marry Kenny Grimes?"

"No, I'm not marrying anyone."

"I'm sorry, but I can't give you a divorce."

"Why not?"

"It's wrong. I can't give you a divorce."

"You can't make me live with you."

"I realize that. If you want a divorce, you'll have to get it because I'm not going to be any party to it." That made her mad. I knew that there was something else, another reason. She hadn't come all the way to the church early on a Sunday morning to tell me this, but she got angry and I never found out what else she wanted that day.

People were starting to arrive at church and they saw us in the car. It was embarrassing. Church was about to start and I invited her to come to the service, but she declined. I got out of the car and went inside. As soon as I was in the building, she floored her car in the gravel parking lot and there were rocks flying and wheels spinning for about four seconds. Rocks even hit the side of the church. I was about midway up the aisle of the church and I just kept walking. The older people were beginning to look at me. If anybody didn't know already that we were having problems, they certainly knew it then.

One night I had to go on a business trip to Hattiesburg, and Misty spent the night with a girlfriend. I was hoping to get home by 8:00, but I ran into a storm. I had never in my life seen it rain like it did that night. Most people had pulled off to the side of the road. The wind was blowing. It was summertime and the windows were fogging up, but it was impossible to roll them down. I tried the air conditioner and the heat. I was stubborn. I wasn't going to pull over to the side of the road and sit there. I stopped long enough to look at a map to see if I could find a shorter route and I found one that looked pretty good. I would have to go off the main road and get on a few country roads, but it looked like only a couple of turns.

I got off the main road and drove for probably about half an hour. It was still raining. There was nothing but woods everywhere and ditches on both sides of the road. I could barely see two feet in front of the headlights. I turned right and followed the road. I could roll my window down a bit at that point because the wind was blowing from the opposite side of the car and the rain wasn't coming in my side as much. I was going about twenty-five miles an hour, which was pretty fast considering that I couldn't see anything. The rain wasn't letting up. All of a sudden, I heard a blood-curdling scream. It sounded like more than one voice right outside my window. It frightened me so much that I froze. I didn't slow down or speed up. I didn't look. After about ten seconds I looked out the window and I couldn't see anything. There were no lights from houses, only my headlights. I was really scared. The scream had sounded like a person. I had a .22 pistol in my glove compartment, but I didn't want to stop the car and take out the keys in order to unlock it. I tried to speed up a bit and was going maybe thirty. All of a sudden, I came to the end of the road. It just ended and I had to go left or right. I had been on this road for about twenty minutes and this wasn't the right one. It wasn't on the map. I had wasted all of this time so I might as well just retrace my route and get back to the main road and just stay on it. That was the only thing I knew to do because I was completely lost.

I turned around and drove for about ten minutes when I came upon a tree that had fallen across the road. It was probably about a foot in diameter and looked pretty rotten. I thought that maybe I should just speed up and run over it, but I was afraid that I might damage something under my car. I was still thinking about the scream that I heard and trying to convince myself that it was an animal and not a human. As bad as the storm was, it would have been impossible for a person to be out there. It had to be an animal. I opened the car door to get out and move the log. As soon as I got out, I was totally drenched. My shoes were full of water. I got in front of the headlights when I was knocked to the ground by two men. I was dazed, but I jumped back up and there were four guys. I said, "Hey man, I don't want any trouble."

One of them said, "Give me your wallet."

That really angered me. I was lost, scared, in the rain out in the middle of nowhere. I thought that there had to be a house nearby, but I couldn't see anything. The next thought that went through my mind was that they were going to kill me no matter what. Why did they bother asking for the wallet? They were going to kill me and take my car. It didn't make any difference what I did. So I did the most logical thing that I could think of in that situation. I said, "Bite me."

The next thing I knew, I grabbed one of them around the neck and kicked another one in the face. I took my fist and tried to break the nose of the one that I had in a headlock. By then, all four of them were on me and they held me and beat me in the stomach, face, head and ribs. They took my wallet and went through my pockets. They continued to kick me in the stomach as they held me. I threw up. I lost my breath. I think they picked me up and I had a sensation of flying, so I assume that they threw me. I landed in the woods and my ribs hit a tree stump that was about two feet tall. I was about half conscious, in great pain. I thought that the next sound I heard would be a gunshot and that would also be the last thing that I heard.

I laid there in the mud for what seemed like minutes, but was probably only seconds. I tried to raise up. I hadn't heard a thing. I was afraid to look because I knew I was going to see one of them standing over me with a club, an ax or a gun. The next thought that went through my mind was Misty. What would happen to her? I wished that she was in Virginia. I tried to get up, but I couldn't raise up all the way. I had severe pain in my stomach. I thought that I was bleeding inside and was going to die. I looked and there was nobody there. They were gone. All of them. The car was still there and running. The car door was open and it was raining in. I knew it had to be a trick. They were going to kill me. I leaned against the stump for a few more minutes and finally crawled through the ditch and back to my car.

I checked the back seat. No one was there. I got into the car. I was still feeling sharp pains in my stomach and I thought that they must have torn something loose. Something had to be bleeding inside. I drove over the log and my suspicions about it being rotten were right. I got back to the main road and made it home by 1:00 a.m. I wasn't coughing up blood, so I decided that maybe I wasn't bleeding after all.

What scared me the most was thinking about dying and Misty being left alone with no parent to care for her. Obviously, Terry wouldn't have taken care of her. She would be totally alone.

I felt that once again the Lord had been looking out for me. I must certainly have a guardian angel, probably several, because I had worn out a few of them already.

Two days later I went back out and tried to retrace my steps to find out where I had been. I spent most of the day looking for the spot. Finally, I found it. The tree was no longer there. There were no signs of it ever having been there. There were no houses. I thought that maybe I was in the wrong place, but I drove all the way to the place where I had turned around and I recognized it. I went back the way I had that night and tried to see the clearing where they had thrown me. I stopped and looked out of my window and saw the spot. But it wasn't a tree stump that I had been leaning on, it was a tombstone. I had been in a cemetery. I never mentioned the story to anyone and I never contacted the police. I had never been a big fan of the police nor they of me and I liked to handle situations in my own way, without involving anyone else.

My friends in Louisiana were continually trying to get me to move there, but I kept putting it off. I think that I had a psychological barrier about moving to another state, even though it was only forty miles away. I still held out hope that Terry and I would have some kind of reconciliation. One of my friends who owned several businesses, including a construction company, offered to build me sort of an apartment where I could stay as long as I wanted. The plumbing was already in and they would put in a refrigerator, washer, dryer and stove. I decided to take him up on the offer.

A short while after I had moved in, Terry called me to say that she wanted to come home again. She didn't know that I had moved to Louisiana. I told her that the place where I was living wasn't big enough for all of us so I would get back to her. I talked to my friend and he said, "Charles, you are stupid. Why do you want to take this lady back? She is just going to do the same thing again."

"Look," I said, "don't give me that. I need a house and I need it quick. Do you have any homes that you haven't sold?"

He told me that he had one that was about halfway to the Mississippi state line. It had just been finished and didn't have appliances in it yet. He would let me buy it for just what it cost him to build it. It didn't have any land for the livestock, so I asked him if he knew of any I could rent to keep thirteen horses, and he agreed to let us keep them at his place without cost until we could find somewhere else. He had dozens and dozens of acres. It was quite a generous offer on his part because he couldn't stand Terry.

Terry didn't want to keep the horses at his place because she knew how he felt about her. I tried to convince her that he was being really nice and it would be the most logical thing to do, but she wouldn't agree to it. She wanted to keep the horses in Mississippi, but I didn't like that idea because it would put her too close to Kenny. I told her that I didn't want her to ever even talk to that man again. If we were going to get back together, her relationship with him had to be completely over. She told me that I had to trust her and I finally relented.

We had to go out and buy everything for the house-appliances, furniture, and so forth. It felt like a fresh start. In December, we went to a Christmas party and Terry quickly realized that most of the people there didn't care for her. She felt guilty that they knew what she had done. After about a half an hour, she wanted to leave. I wanted to stay, but I left with her.

Several nights later, she said that she had to go do something with the horses and told me what time she'd be back. I stayed at the house with the kids. I sat there thinking that I had never even seen the place where she boarded the horses. I decided that I would go take a look. I got a baby-sitter and hopped in the truck to go see it. It was about forty miles away and it was dark by the time I got there. The place looked pretty deserted. I didn't see her vehicle. I sat there for ten or fifteen minutes wondering what I should do. I figured that I must have missed her. Maybe she had already been there and was on her way home.

I started back home and the truck overheated. I was in the middle of nowhere and I didn't have any water. I would drive until the truck got really hot and then stop, turn it off and wait a few minutes. It took me twice as long to get home as it normally would have. I thought that she would be at home and wonder where I was and what I had been doing. I finally got home and she wasn't there. She didn't come home for another two hours.

She came in the house and I was sitting in the living room in the dark. "Where have you been?"

She told me that she had been with the horses.

"Well, you were there an awfully long time weren't you?"

She listed some things that she had had to do and something was wrong with one of the horses and then she had started talking to someone.

"Oh, okay. When did you leave?"

"I just left a little while ago."

"No. You didn't. I was out there."

At first she thought I was pulling her leg. I told her to ask the kids if I had been gone. Then she said that I must have just missed her.

"No, I didn't miss you. I have been back here a long time. You were with Kenny Grimes weren't you?"

"No, no I wasn't."

"Yes, you were."

"All right. Yes I was."

"Okay. When are you leaving?"

"I'm not leaving."

"You're not? Well, you can't stay here with me and still see him."

She said, "No, this time you're leaving. I've left the other times. You're leaving this time."

"I don't think so."

Of course, we ended up in a big argument. I slept on the couch. For the next two or three days, we went about our business and nothing much was said. One day I was coming home with Misty and as we drove up to the house I thought that something was different. Something wasn't right, but I couldn't put my finger on exactly what it was. When I got to the front door, I realized that there were no curtains at the windows. I opened the door and we walked in. The place was empty. There wasn't a stick of furniture. Not a fork or a spoon or a knife. Not a plate or a bowl. Everything was gone except for my clothes and Misty's.

Misty was very hurt and crying. "They took my toys."

"What?"

"They took everything. They even took my toys."

I went up into the attic. Even that stuff was gone. Obviously, she had planned this. When I left, she had movers come in and load everything up. I was really hurt, but I had to put on a brave face for Misty. I wanted to downplay the emotions that I was feeling. We went out and bought some furniture and some plates and silverware, enough to get by for a while.

Terry called me a few days later. I just couldn't believe what she had done. She said it was my fault because I didn't trust her. The fact that she was actually out with the man didn't seem to put any of the burden of blame on her, at least not in her eyes.

37

I had been in contact with my mother and sisters over the past couple of years. We hadn't made up, but I let Misty call them. We hadn't had any contact at all for the first three years, but I decided that it was important for Misty to have those relationships, so there had been calls every few months, usually on birthdays and holidays. I knew that Misty was not in a healthy environment in Louisiana. I talked to her about returning to Virginia and she wanted to go. She wanted to get out of the uncertainty in which she had been living.

I talked to my mother about having Misty come to stay with her and she was very grateful. She apologized for all the trouble that she had caused. She told me, "For the last three or four years, I have been under a tremendous amount of guilt for what I have done to you and to Misty. I hope that one day you can forgive me."

Misty was almost ten years old. I put her on an airplane, her first plane trip, and my parents met her in Virginia. I planned to return home as well, but I didn't know when. I had loose ends to take care of in Louisiana. Misty was excited about the flight and excited about going back, but she was sad that I wasn't going with her. I explained that I'd be there in a few weeks. I got on the plane with her and stayed there talking to her until they finally made me get off. As I was walking down the aisle away from her, the tears came. People were probably looking at me funny, but I couldn't hold them back any longer. Fortunately, Misty didn't see me crying.

I watched the plane take off. My heart broke because I really didn't know for sure when I would see her again. I wondered what she really thought and felt. I thought about how I had screwed things up, had ruined her life. I thought about the scars that she would have from this experience. Maybe my mother was right. Maybe I should have let her have Misty. At least she would have had a consistent, safe, normal home. I know that my mother loved her, warped though her love was. I knew that she would have anything she wanted there and that she would be protected. I felt that I hadn't done a very good job as a father.

I had forgotten all about the credit card that I had given to Terry the previous Christmas to use in emergencies. I got a phone call from the issuing bank and it seemed as if my wife had been having quite a few "emergencies". They had also, upon her request, reissued her the other card. They each had a $2,000 limit and she had charged much more than that on both and wasn't paying on either one of them. I called her and she denied that she had been using them. I highly doubted that this was true, but she continued to insist that she wouldn't do that, that she hadn't charged anything.

I called the bank and told them that there must have been a mistake, that my wife said she hadn't used the cards. The man asked if we were separated or divorced and I confirmed that we weren't together. He told me that there was no doubt that she had been using the cards and he said that he would mail me copies of all the receipts.

I got a package in the mail and discovered that Terry had charged jewelry, gasoline, clothes—both men's and women's—a trip to St. Louis, a watch. It went on and on. Since the cards were in my name, I was going to have to pay the bill. I was going to have to pay for the gifts that she bought Kenny. Obviously, I was not happy about this.

Terry called me and wanted me to meet her to talk. I agreed and when I got there, I found out that what she really wanted was to give me divorce papers. I told her that I wouldn't sign them. If she wanted the divorce, she would have to get it, but I wouldn't sign the papers.

She said, "Kenny and I have split up. We aren't together anymore. I just want to be free. I need some time. I need my space. If you love me and if you hope that there's ever a chance of us getting back together again, then you'll sign them. Just because we get divorced doesn't mean that we can't get back together at some point."

I took the papers and read them. It gave the reason for the divorce as "irreconcilable differences." I told her that if she wanted me to sign the papers, they would have to say something like desertion or adultery or mental abuse or child abuse. I had found out that she had mistreated Misty mentally and emotionally, which was one of the reasons that I sent her back to Virginia. She blamed Misty and my mother for the problems in our marriage. Since my mother wasn't around, she took her anger out on Misty. Terry believed that a lot of people thought Misty was better than her children. Terry was vindictive and vengeful towards Misty or anyone else who didn't view her children in the same light that she did. Looking back now, I know that what Terry was displaying was defensiveness for her own inadequacies in raising her children.

When I said that to her, she went on about how she had done all she could for that child and had been her mother.

"You're not much of a mother even to your own kids. The only way that you know how to show love is to throw money around. When is the last time you hugged one of your children? When is the last time that you told them that you loved them? When is the last time that you kissed them or spent some time with them? I can't recall a single time during our entire marriage that you did any of those things. I know that you love your children, but you show it only by spending money on them. You have made Misty feel like a second-class citizen. Forget it. I'm not signing any papers."

She kept talking and said, "Do you still hold out hope that we'll get back together?"

"I don't know. It would be nice if we could start over one day."

"If you have any hope for that, you'll have to sign the papers."

"Fine," I said. "I'll sign the damn papers."

I signed them, gave them to her, got into my car and drove away. That was the last time I ever saw Terry.

I had put my sermon on the back burner until I straightened out my family situation. I was driving back to my house and thinking. I no longer had a business. I no longer had my child living with me. I no longer had a wife. I no longer had a home. It was just a year earlier that I had had everything a person could want and I had lost it all. I said, "Lord, I thought that things were supposed to get better when you're a Christian. Ever since I have given myself to You, ever since I have dedicated my life to You, things have been going the opposite way. What good is it? What's the point of Christianity? What's the point of any of it? I was in better shape before You. Where's the protection? Where's the blessing? Where's the good stuff that I'm supposed to get out of all this? I don't see it."

I was almost thirty-three years old and I had nearly nothing. It was time to preach my sermon. The church knew that the marriage was over. I was never so scared in my life as when I got up to speak.

My message was centered on the footprints in the Sand poem. I talked about how short life is, as it was for Darlene, and how even if you live to be one hundred, that's short compared to eternity. My sermon also dealt with investments. I had to learn that the only investments that really pay dividends are those that pay eternal ones. That means investing in people. And the third point of my sermon was that it is not that important how long you live but what you do with the time you have. I had a whole lot of catching up to do. I've heard it said that the worst people make the best preachers. If that's true then I should be a great one.

Everything went perfectly. It was just like the first time with the choir. If it hadn't been right, I would never have gotten up there again. Of course, I wasn't planning to get back up there, but after the congregation heard me, I was encouraged to become licensed as a minister. It went that well.

A strange thing happened during the service. The church was way out in the country, off the main road. It wasn't the kind of place that you stumble across. Visitors were rare. During my sermon, I noticed a young lady come in and sit on the back row. As she came in, the swinging doors squeaked and the wooden floors creaked and everyone

WE EACH GET A TURN   273

turned around to look at the stranger. During the invitation, the woman stood up without hesitation, walked down the center aisle, knelt at the altar for several minutes and then went back to her seat. It was a shock to me. As the pastor was doing the benediction, I was thinking that I had to talk to this woman. I needed to find out why she came to the altar. I felt like I had really touched somebody's life. When the pastor said, "Amen," I lifted my head and she was gone. There was no noise from the floor or the doors. She was just gone. Afterwards, I asked just about everyone if they knew her, but no one did. Several years later, I decided that she was probably an angel. I believe that it was a confirmation and a blessing. I believe that she was an angel sent by God.

I talked to Misty several times a week on the phone. My mother had redecorated her room and bought her a stereo and all kinds of things. I think that she was trying to make up for what she had done. I still thought that Misty was better off there than in Louisiana with me. I would be joining her soon, but not as soon as I had hoped.

My father had been diagnosed with cancer and he wanted me to come home. He wanted me to live in the house with my mother after he died. I didn't feel that the Lord wanted me to leave right then.

My ministry was taking off. I had first tried prison ministry, but of course going inside a prison, even of my own volition, and hearing them lock the doors made me very uncomfortable. The first time that I went into a prison to visit the inmates, I just knew that someone was somehow going to find something illegal that I had done in the past and incarcerate me! The second opportunity that I had was singing in different churches, which led to invitations to preach. I was beginning to move beyond Louisiana and go to other states. I even thought about buying a tent and traveling from town to town doing revivals. I would have done that if it hadn't been for Misty. That would not have been a good life for a child.

I saw my life progressing and I didn't see my divorce as a step backward. I don't think that we ever really go backward. Everything that I had gone through in my life was a step forward, a progression. Some of the steps were in mud. Sometimes the steps were on ice and they were slippery. Sometimes they were on sand. Sometimes the steps were even on strong, solid ground. The circumstances weren't always great, but I learned about myself and other people. I realized more and more with each step that God was in control. There had to be somebody watching over me because I should have been dead many times over.

On the outside, I believed what I was preaching. I ministered to people and people were saved. Young and old alike told me how I affected them, changed them. I was actually able to help people, but the one person I couldn't help was myself. Despite being surrounded by people so much of the time, I was alone more and more.

At Christmas, I decided to go home to Virginia for a couple of weeks. I wasn't going back permanently. I couldn't wait to see Misty, but I was apprehensive about seeing my parents for the first time in five years. I was concerned about that, but the excitement of seeing my daughter again overshadowed my anxiety. I flew from New Orleans on Christmas Eve and my friend Pat Dunbar had offered to pick me up at the airport. We had been in contact for several months and I was under the impression that she still had strong feelings for me. I couldn't imagine loving anyone else at that point, or ever again for that matter, but I appreciated her friendship and the fact that she had always been there for me.

Pat dropped me off at my parents' house Christmas morning. They hadn't been expecting me until that afternoon and Misty was really surprised. It was wonderful. The visit was awkward for my parents and me, but they began to act as if nothing had ever happened, like I lived next door and hadn't been gone for all those years. My sisters and their families came over later in the day and it was the same. We talked, but there was something missing. Something had been destroyed. I knew that things would never be the same between us.

My father had only a year or two to live and wanted me to come back to Virginia. I told him that I would be back, but I had things to take care of in Louisiana. There were still debts from the horse business. We had set up a plan where I paid half and Terry paid half. The bank in Mississippi called me in April and told me that she hadn't been making her payments. I talked to her on the phone and she kept promising that she would fulfill her obligations, but she never did.

I finished all of my scheduled bookings for singing and preaching. By then, I was doing twice as much preaching as singing. The biggest thing that I had to do before returning to Virginia was to forgive my parents and my sisters. I had a lot of hurt and a lot of anger at them as well as at Terry and Kenny. I knew that I couldn't carry that burden with me. I couldn't go back home feeling that way and having anger and hatred toward my family. It wouldn't work. I had to get rid of those feelings. There was only one possible way I knew to do that. One night, I prayed to the Lord. I said, "Lord, You know it's time to go. I can't stay here. I don't want to go. I really have no choice. I can't leave with this anger and these feelings. I can't go back to Virginia with the anger that I have toward them. I know that it supposedly takes time to get over feelings like this, but Lord, something has to be done."

The next day, about midday, I realized that I no longer had that anger toward my family and that I was able to forgive them and not hold it against them. The hurt wasn't gone, but the anger was gone. The anger toward Terry and that man were gone. I knew that I could have stood in front of that man and instead of beating him to death, I could have witnessed to him. I knew that only God could do something like that. I asked Him and He took it away.

I talked to Terry on the phone and told her that I was leaving at the beginning of September. She said, "But you promised you'd never leave me."

"I didn't leave you. You left me. I took you back three times and you still left and you're gone now. Do you plan to marry this guy?"

There was silence and I knew what that meant. "You've already gotten married."

"Yes. I got married a couple of months ago."

"Well, I guess I really am leaving then. There's no reason to for me to stay."

"But I don't want you to go."

"As long as you weren't married, there would maybe be some kind of hope. But you've decided and you've made your choice now. It's over."

38

The first sermon that I had ever preached was about the parable called "Footprints in the Sand."

One night a man had a dream. He dreamed he was walking along the beach with the Lord. Across the sky flashed scenes from his life. For each scene, he noticed two sets of footprints in the sand: one belonging to him, and the other to the Lord.

When the last scene of his life flashed before him, he looked back at the footprints in the sand. He noticed that many times along the path of his life there was only one set of footprints. He also noticed that it happened at the very lowest and saddest times in his life. This really bothered him and he questioned the Lord about it.

"Lord, You said that once I decided to follow You, You'd walk with me all the way. But I have noticed that during the most troublesome times in my life, there is only one set of footprints. I don't understand why when I needed You most You would leave me."

The Lord replied, "My son, my precious child, I love you and would never leave you. During your times of trial and suffering, when you see only one set of footprints, it was then that I carried you."

—*Author Unknown*

I walked around the church that Saturday before my first sermon and looked at my life. I saw victory about to unfold in front of me. I saw the excitement of an unknown future. I knew that I wanted peace. I wanted quiet.

I began to realize that I hadn't gotten through all the things in my life without some major help and it certainly wasn't human help. I could look at my life in two ways. One way is that I was very lucky and fortunate to have survived everything I did. The other way to see it is that I was very unfortunate to have gone through what I did. I never looked at it the second way. I realized that there were certainly times in my life when there was only one set of footprints in the sand. I realized that there is a God. There is a higher power, a supreme being. I believe that there is a plan for every human being, but we never follow that plan as it is divinely given. Life is a spiritual journey. The end of this life is not a consummation of that journey. This life is to prepare you for life eternal. This life is not an end in itself; it is a beginning. Each step, each task, each struggle, defeat, victory, each step was a step forward and a progression of my life. Even the times that are the most trying are part of the progression. People only go backwards if they choose to look at it that way.

So on September 15, 1986, I closed yet another door in my life and decided to move on. I left everything behind except my clothes. Where would I go? I had plenty of states to choose from. My first inclination was to head for the mountains with Misty, but that would not have been fair to her. So I headed to Virginia Beach where Misty wanted to live, and that was home.

A new life lay ahead, a life of exciting uncertainty, a life of peace and joy, a life in which I knew that someone else was in control, and that someone was Jesus Christ. The empty space that had been in my heart for so long was now filled. No longer must I roam for now I had a real purpose, a higher calling. I would spend the next fifteen years in church ministry.

I have written this book to tell you that you are not alone. You are worth a great deal just because you exist. You are unique. You do not have to remain who you are and where you are in life. I want to share with you what I learned, that dreams are opportunities waiting to be fulfilled. No matter what you have done or not done, no matter what you have gone through:

You can succeed and achieve if you realize that you are not alone; alone in the spiritual and physical sense. No one succeeds without help from others. In my first business, my employer allowed me to store my product that I bought from him at a great discount in his store, which allowed me to be competitive. Even if someone means to do you harm, God can and will use it for your good. It was a terrible thing that happened to me in Mississippi, but God brought immeasurable good out of it.

You must not listen to criticism. I was told if I stood on Sunday morning and spoke I would be making a fool out of myself and my family. I was not good enough as a human being, nor was I qualified. If I had listened to that criticism, I would never had made that first step.

Dreams are opportunities waiting to be fulfilled. I had a dream not to remain where I was in life. I had a dream to make a difference in the lives of others. I had a dream to have my own business. I had a dream to have this book published. Those dreams (opportunities) have now been fulfulled.

Whatever you choose to do in life, invest in people. The returns are truly out of this world.

There will be times when you will need to be carried (I needed to be carried at times in the army, after Darlene died, after I lost everything in Mississippi, when my family turned against me, and in church.) and that's all right.

Rev. Charles A. Cross now holds a Doctorate of Religious Philosophy and is a licensed Clinical Christian Counselor-Advanced Certification. (National Christian Counselors Association)

If you would like to have Dr. Cross speak to your organization, you may contact him at:

Cross Success Seminars and Counseling Center
1-540-949-4058
1-540-847-4095
email: **spring1@ntelos.net**
Website: **www.charlescross.net**

0-595-25036-X